T0077619

Freedom of the Soul

Whispers of Wisdom from Your Inner
Being to Live a Life of Purpose

Liliana C. Vanasco

BALBOA.PRESS
A DIVISION OF HAY HOUSE

Balboa Press books may be ordered through booksellers or by contacting:

Balboa Press
A Division of Hay House
1663 Liberty Drive
Bloomington, IN 47403
www.balboapress.com.au
AU TFN: 1 800 844 925 (Toll Free inside Australia)
AU Local: 0283 107 086 (+61 2 8310 7086 from outside Australia)

ISBN: 978-1-4525-0747-7 (sc)
ISBN: 978-1-4525-0748-4 (e)

Print information available on the last page.

Balboa Press rev. date: 10/26/2020

CONTENTS

Dedication

This book is dedicated to all those who would love
to connect with their inner light, and through the power
of that connection live a purposeful and fulfilling life.

~ ~ ~#~ ~ ~

Once upon a time there was light, and the light became human,
then man forgot he was light, all-powerful light.
Now it is time to remember, and by doing so,
man will obtain the freedom he was born to seek.

~ ~ ~#~ ~ ~

INTRODUCTION

The Message Within

Before you and I begin this amazing journey together, I would like to give you a brief account of how this book came about and, by doing so, share with you a bit of my story.

This book is the result of my personal journey and of my soul seeking expression. I believe the book has been gestating since I was a child, maybe even since before I was born. Ever since I can remember, I have had a special feeling about something inside of me: a message to be shared. When I was a child, that something inside of me found expression through the stories I used to write. I loved writing and enjoyed the delightful sensation of being lost in my imaginary worlds, where everything was possible. School was a great platform for me to express what I wanted to say, and it provided me with various topics on which to do so.

Remembering all those stories, I see now that all of them shared a common theme: feelings. It amazes me to recall how I used my imagination in order to give voice to those feelings from my perspective as a child. The stories were usually about people, but I often had objects or elements of nature and animals play major roles. I never hesitated to create a dialogue between the moon and a quiet pond or to engage the last autumn leaf on a tree in conversation with a lonely bird. My stories were very much liked and celebrated by my teachers, family, and friends, but that praise was not as important or rewarding to me as the great, warm feeling that engulfed me every time I lost myself in writing.

All of my stories had a common message about a special something that lives within each of us, that we can feel but cannot see. Connecting to that something has an extraordinary effect on one's life. Many years later, I realised that everybody and everything is made of this something. The ability to talk about it, find it, connect with it, and live it is the key to well-being. This was my inner message.

The truth is that there is a message in each of us that seeks expression in infinite ways. My way has always been the written word. I love the feeling of a pen in my hand, writing ideas that did not exist before on an empty sheet of paper. I immensely enjoy writing things that are meaningful, beautiful, inspirational, or even humorous. I also love reading, and I admire and appreciate those who created what I read.

Continuing with my story, I didn't put much thought into writing once I graduated from school; it was just a hobby. I was busy living my life and had barely any time to spare. With the knowledge I have now, I also appreciate that in those early days, I was not ready to address the truth inside me. Between childhood and adulthood, I was gathering resources and skills, learning, preparing, and maturing into the person I am today so that I could deal with my inner something at the time that was right for me.

My life was going well. I had accomplished many of my dreams and goals, and I thought I had it all figured out. Little did I suspect this was not the case. After the arrival of my first child, grateful for the blessing of becoming a parent to a healthy and beautiful little person, I was learning to adjust to my new role, and I started to notice that something was shifting in me; something was beginning to stir. At first, I put it down to the stress of being a new mum and the incredible pressure inherent in that role. However, even after life in our home had settled and become normal again, the restlessness in me didn't go away.

A continuous stream of challenging questions demanded my attention. "What am I here for?" "Is this all there is to life?" "Why am I not as happy as I used to be, when I have every reason to be happy?" "What is my purpose?" All these big questions wanted answers, which I didn't have. To say that those were testing times would be an understatement. All I wanted was my normal life back, but things were not that simple anymore.

After a while, I managed to gather some energy and time to observe what was happening to me. I noticed that when I paid attention to my inner nagging and listened to that restless feeling, answers came and offered me some clarity. On the other hand, when I ignored the nagging and tried to shut it up, I felt upset and confused.

Shedding Old Skin

Don't get me wrong, my life was blessed in many ways; I had everything to be happy and grateful for. I had an amazing husband and father to my beautiful children, a loving family, good health, a great job in my field of study, a generous income, a beautiful, sunny home, great friends, money in the bank, curiosity and desire to learn new things, and above all, plenty of love. However, I was not as happy as I wanted to be.

I knew that I had too many responsibilities; I would have needed more than twenty-four hours in each day to fulfil them all. I was doing too much, and I didn't have any time left to myself. I didn't have enough time to enjoy the beautiful life I had. Most importantly, I had forgotten the magic of dreaming, which had always been a primary ingredient in my life. I needed to find a balance, but I didn't know how. I asked everyone around me for advice, but they couldn't help much; they kept on telling me that my life was normal and modern. So why was I so resistant to the idea of living a normal life?

I slowly figured out that people were giving me advice based on their own experiences. It was obvious that I wanted to have a different experience of life. I discovered that the nagging feeling inside of me could lead me to many of the answers I was looking for, but in order to find them, I would have to look to change. By the end of this stage I was certain of two things:

Liliana C. Vanasco

1. I had come to the physical plane to discover life in my own unique way and to enjoy it. I had done so for most of my life so far, and I intended to continue.
2. I could be happy to whatever extent I decided—there was no limit, regardless of external circumstances. I just had to figure out how to achieve it.

With those two pieces of knowledge in my heart, I embarked upon a journey to find the answers to all the provoking questions that were firmly set inside me. I could sense that I was at a point of no return. A change had already taken place in me. Some part of me was different; something had awakened. Even though I was the same physically, the way I saw life had changed. I remember telling my husband during that period of transition that I felt like a snake shedding its skin. The most frightening thing was the feeling that I didn't know who I would be at the end of the process. After fifteen years, the process is still unfolding.

Looking back, I see that I was searching for the freedom to contemplate and do things outside the box of my life. All of us create these boxes for ourselves based on predetermined ideas and beliefs. However, we are all expanding beings, and therefore, when we set restrictions and limits on our lives and ourselves, we fade and suffocate. Unless we pay attention to our need for expansion, expression, and experience, we adversely affect our well-being in myriad ways. It is easy to sit comfortably in the chair of our comfort zone, watching our life play on the television of our existence. However, this is not the aim of life; we are born to grow, discover, learn, experience, and awaken to our true natures, in the process becoming happy and fulfilled.

In my quest for answers, I became involved in activities and studies that were very different from my usual interests and skills: yoga, meditation, crystals, healing, angels, and spirituality. I enjoyed each of them as a breather from my routine that opened doors to other ways of thinking, feeling, and seeing life. Out of all of them, meditation was the most valuable.

What slowed me in this journey of transformation was the fact that I was working to find answers. I was trying hard to figure them out by myself because I wanted to get quickly to the end of this stage, to get it over and done with. If I felt that I was not very successful in my undertakings or that I was not moving as fast as I wanted, I would meditate more, read more, or study more. I gained some insights, and tried to put them into practice. With experience, I realised that the time it took to incorporate these insights into my life was directly linked to frustration and impatience on my part, and especially to my fear of the unknown side of change.

Opening to the Voice Within

After lots of meditation and opening myself to what I was learning, I accepted the realisation that I already knew all the answers. I had known them since I was a child, but for some reason I had forgotten them. I also realised that in order to move forward, I needed to reconnect with that knowledge and follow its guidance, which at that point was telling me it was time for me to write again.

However, I didn't do that straight away—that would have been too easy! Instead, I postponed writing for many years due to myriad excuses such as, "I don't have time," "I am not a writer," and "I'm not good at writing." Deep down, I was scared. What could I say that hadn't yet been said? And who was I to write about the purpose of life? These questions immobilised me and stopped me from taking action while also making me feel disappointed in myself and powerless. The more I tried to silence the nagging thoughts, the more inner doubts I had. The more I tried to distract myself from my feelings of uneasiness, the more distressed and unhappy I felt. It was a vicious circle. As you can imagine, I didn't like it.

One day in April, 2009, I decided to give in and put all those fears aside. I opened up to listen to the message of that something inside of me. As soon as I made this decision, I felt an overwhelming relief. Suddenly, I could clearly see and feel that I had nothing to lose and lots to gain.

My well-being improved because I was in control again. The fears and worry that to that point had been driving my life were replaced by a sense of adventure about what was to come at the end of the process. I was also full of eagerness to learn what this inner side of me had to teach me. All in all, I became a happier version of me. This new project was totally different from my daily life and anything I had done before. I made the commitment to sit every week in the peaceful place I had chosen for meditation and write whatever came from within me. I soon realised how foolish I had been all this time, thinking I'd have to come up with something to write about, when all I needed to do was just open up, trust, listen, and write.

The road was bumpy at the beginning, because I allowed my judgemental self (my ego) to criticise the message I was receiving; it was not what I had expected. I was going through another stage, shedding more skin, letting go of my ego, expectations, perfectionism, control, fears, and welcoming my true, wise self. Once I'd crossed this barrier and finally understood the process, I was happy and eager to come to write every week. I was learning so much!

The result of these writing sessions in which I opened up to the infinite wisdom inside me and listened to it with love and respect is written in the pages of this book. Despite all the ups and downs, this has been an incredible journey of growth, discoveries, wonder, and happiness. For that reason, I am sharing my learning with you. I hope it inspires you to embark on a journey of growth to your own inner something.

Each of us has a voice within that wants to speak up. I refer to mine by many names: my soul, my higher self, my inner being, my inner knowing, my spirit. I use these names interchangeably throughout the book, depending on how I am guided in any given moment. I hope this will not confuse your reading. No matter what name we use, it is always the same thing: the infinite wisdom in each of us. What name do you give your voice? You have a voice within you, and you are one with that voice.

This book is the voice within me talking to the voice within you. Even though you are reading this with your physical eyes and processing the words with your physical brain, the effects of what you read will go beyond the physical. They will plant a seed inside you that will germinate, grow, and bloom when the time is right for the unique gift within you to awaken.

I wrote this book out of love, in gratitude to the voice inside me that has guided me patiently and lovingly through this amazing experience. I want to share my message with those who are attracted to it, whether they are only embarking on their journeys of self-discovery or are already on them. I hope you enjoy learning and growing from the insights contained in this book as much as I enjoyed writing them.

If You Picked Up This Book . . .

If you picked up this book, you are in a period of change. Whether you know it or not, you are in a phase of transformation; perhaps you don't know who you are anymore, what you should be doing, what your place in the world is, what would fulfil you, what would make you happy, or what is bothering you.

If you picked up this book, it is a sign that your soul is calling out for your attention. It craves to speak and connect with you in a profound and unique way. It wants to tell you that you are ready to live your life more consciously, with more awareness, as a spirit enjoying the glorious opportunity of the human experience. If you picked up this book, it means that you are ready to move to the next step and shed some old skin.

Or maybe you didn't pick up this book; maybe the book found its way to you and picked you. Either way, all that matters is that it has reached you.

Be warned that after reading this book, you will not be the same person. Something deep inside you will have ignited; the glimmering light that has been burning in your being all this time will come alive and await your next action. What will you do about the whispers from your soul?

Life is about choice: your choice. You have the power to choose what to do. Will you choose to listen to the calling from within, to grow and expand? Or will you choose to remain dormant and blind to the immense power you possess to live the life you are meant to live?

Remember what I have learnt: we can choose how happy and fulfilled to be. Therefore, you decide whether to stay inside the box you, yourself, have created, or to get up off the chair of your comfort zone to experience a life guided by your inner light, thus reconnecting with your essence and soul. This book will provide you with the guidance and tools to achieve the latter.

I hope you choose light.
From soul to soul with love,

Liliana

PART I

About *Freedom of the Soul*

Freedom of the Soul is not a conventional book, but it is a very especial one. Therefore, before I delve fully into its content I thought fitting to include a section dedicated to the book itself.

The aim of this section is to explain and clarify some important points about the book, which will make your reading experience easier. You could, of course, skip this section, but I advise you to be patient and take the time to prepare yourself for the journey.

CHAPTER 1

The Key Elements

The writing of this book was a beautiful process that I discovered and refined over the course of the two years it took me to complete it. The insights and teachings contained within its pages are easy to follow, however, for my own peace of mind, I'd like to share with you some notes about a few key elements that appear throughout the book. These unique elements are what give the book its magic; if they are not fully understood, the reader might be robbed of the full experience of reading this book.

These specific elements are the two voices (which I mentioned earlier), the meditation, and the two metaphorical instruments.

The Two Voices

As I stated in the Introduction, this book is the result of my opening up to the inner voice within me. The process of doing so developed in a way that created the best environment for me to quiet my mind of internal chatter and allow that voice to be perceived.

I use the word "perceived" because I did not always hear my inner voice as words; it also expressed itself through images, feelings, and sounds. Some passages in the book are graphic and colourful. I am trying to show you, as clearly as I can within the limits of the language, what I saw, heard, and sensed during the writing of those passages.

Each time I conducted a writing session, I followed the same process: I sat in my most comfortable chair, put on some soft music—my favourite is the sounds of the forest and the ocean—and then I performed a self-guided meditation to quiet my mind, discontinue any mundane thoughts, and connect and interact with my inner voice.

Sometimes our conversations would take the form of questions and answers. This was usually triggered by matters affecting my life at the time or topics that I had just come across in reading or elsewhere. Other times, I just wrote down the channelled messages I was perceiving. This book ended up being a mix of contributions from my outer and inner voices.

To distinguish between the voices, my inner voice's unedited input is set in the typeface Goudy Old Style, whereas my own ideas and contributions are set in Segoe UI. The difference in fonts will initially assist you in determining which voice you are reading, but after a while you will find that you can easily recognize the difference between the two voices from their words alone. The authority, wisdom, and kindness of my inner voice are unmistakable.

The discovery of my other voice is one of the outcomes that has most struck me in this whole experience. I had not been aware of its existence before—I'm sure most people aren't. For that reason, throughout the writing of this book, I asked myself repeatedly where so much knowledge and insight came from. I know now that it came from the light within me; it is a light that every one of us has. I know, accept, embrace, and trust this truth with all my heart, and I hope that you will, too.

My contribution and that of my inner voice combine effortlessly to allow information to connect with you on two levels: the conscious and the unconscious. Although it may seem odd at first to read from these two different voices—it was odd to me, I have to say—I can assure you that you will soon appreciate the contrast, which will greatly assist you in learning how your own voices operate and how to work with them to grow and move forward. I hope that as you read this book you will get to know, accept, and trust the voice within you, which is every bit as wise and powerful as mine is. You have only to consciously let it show.

The Meditation

I have also included in this book the self-guided meditation that I used during the process of writing. Meditation served as a bridge between my conscious and unconscious minds, my outer and inner voices. I surrendered so fully to the wonderful experience of meditating that many of the insights I received took place during the meditation, before I meet with my higher self or spirit guides. It is my desire to share this practice with you, not only for your enjoyment, but also for two other reasons:

1. Much of my writings are interpretations of the feelings, images, sounds, and colours of that I experienced during these meditations. In various instances, I have included parts of these meditations in the book to introduce certain given topics or subjects. Therefore, it makes sense for me to provide you with the context of that meditation to make it easier for you to understand what you are reading.

2. I have been using meditation since long before I decided to write this book. I meditate every time I seek inner guidance or to connect with my spiritual side. I'd like to share the practice with you in case you desire to use it for the same purpose. You'll find that as you go, you will adapt the activity to your own liking, adding elements, removing others, finding your own place to meet your higher self, and most importantly, making it uniquely yours.

The Eagle and the Man

I tell a metaphorical story in Chapter Three whose message runs through the first part of the book: the story of the eagle and the man.

The purpose of this story is to encourage us to bind together pieces of its message by using our imaginations rather than logic. If you try to interpret the story with your logical mind, you will—as I did—struggle to see the wisdom behind the metaphor. However, if you let yourself fantasise, as a child would, what the story is telling and showing you, then you will reap the benefits of its message.

The man represents our human nature, our physical being. The eagle represents our spiritual, nonphysical being. At the beginning of the story, the eagle enjoys being spirit while the man struggles with his human life, unaware of his inner light. Then the man realises that something is missing within himself. He embarks on a journey to discover that something, his inner light. Finally, when he realises who he is, he is united with the eagle, his soul, and he learns to live in partnership with it, as one.

The man represents both men and women, all physical beings on this planet. Since the beginning of time, across a range of beliefs, philosophies, and cultures, the eagle has been a symbol of strength, courage, wisdom, enlightenment, and creation. The eagle also represents great power, determination, grace, intuition, connection with higher truths, and the ability to see the overall pattern of life. In our story, the eagle represents the soul, which connects the lower nature (the physical self) with the higher nature (the divine self).

I hope this information adds to your understanding of this metaphoric thread and triggers you to search for your own meanings.

The Essence of the Book

This book is the story of the soul's journey, told from the soul's perspective. Not only do the author's words fill the pages, but also the author's transcriptions of channelled thoughts.

Many of you talk about being "a spiritual being having a human experience," but do you understand what that really means? You will discover the answer in the pages of this book. You will also find answers to other important questions like these:

How is a soul born?
What is a soul's purpose?
What is the relationship of the soul to its human expression?
What is man's journey to the light?
Is there available help to guide man on that journey?
How do you live life more consciously, as a powerful soul?

There are also some insights in this book on the so controversial year 2012, and beyond. This year marks the beginning of a new era, a new consciousness called the "Era of Light."

All readers who pick up this book are, with awareness or not, already on their journeys to the light; they will find this book enlightening, refreshing, instructive, and awakening. In some of you, it will awaken the leader within, inspiring you to go further and to share your discoveries; in others, it will consciously light the flame that is the desire to initiate or continue the journey from darkness to light. Everyone, even those not on a spiritual path, will benefit from these teachings as they provide information and insights on everyday issues that are usually created by ego-driven ways of life.

This book is a gift from us—being of light, and God—to you, our physical expressions, who have forgotten your way and need a torch to bring you back on track to rediscovering who you really are. In this rediscovery, we all contribute as one to the growth of universal consciousness.

With all our love.

CHAPTER 2

Purpose and Content

The Purpose of This Book

Everything in life has a purpose, a reason to exist—this book is no exception. I discovered its purpose from the very experience of writing it, and my inner voice and I would like to share with you.

I came up with the title *Freedom of the Soul* long before I started writing the book. I chose the word "soul" because the book essentially relates to your inner being, your higher self, the non-visible part of you. I chose the word "freedom" because it also addresses your ability to liberate yourself from the restrictions and limitations that rule your life by exposing, exploring, and acknowledging that something inside you. Thus, "freedom of the soul" perfectly summarises my intention in this book to show you how to understand, connect to and unite with your soul, and ultimately acknowledge that when you free your soul, you become conscious of your light, and at that moment start living *as* "soul" in your human existence.

The purpose of this book, therefore, is simple and clear: to bring forth this truth so that you can finally accept that you are actually a spirit having a human experience, and to offer you principles for understanding, connecting with, and developing your inner nature.

We intend for you, as you read these pages, to become progressively contented with the idea of getting in touch with your soul, so that as you allow yourself to engage more in your journey of self-discovery, you will feel comfortable with the connection. Thus, you will begin to open doors through which your soul can shine into your everyday life. As you realise the infinite ways that you can be soul in this human existence, you will gradually learn to master the journey of your life and you will gradually learn to feel connected with the universal consciousness creator of everything that exists: the galaxies, your planet, including you. This divine consciousness, addressed as Source or God throughout the book, is the invisible, powerful and infinite life force that lives within you and never dies.

The Soul's Message

The messages in these pages are of profound wisdom and grace. They talk about change, strength, willpower, and freedom of the soul. Do you believe that it is possible to let your soul be free while you live your human life? You need to truly believe it to be able to allow it to happen. Next, you must live it in order to inspire others to do the same.

The purpose of this book is to guide you to find your essence, your core. Once you have achieved that, you can achieve anything. You can do it—do not doubt that.

Support yourself with both patience and appreciation for where you are at any given time. These are the best allies to help you to stay on track and not give up. If you can keep on going, despite any hesitation or fear, you will discover an amazing journey of growth. Be open to receiving your soul's message; be loving and the rewards will be unmeasurable.

> *Once upon a time there was light, and the light became human,*
> *and then man forgot he was light, all-powerful light.*
> *Now it is time to remember, and by doing so,*
> *man will obtain the freedom he was born to seek.*

I am sitting here writing these words with the intention of bringing, through the light, clarity about the essence of men and about who you are. Because that is the eternal question: who am I? You are yourself, and you are everything. I am writing these words to help you on your quest. I am pondering the best way to clearly present these messages so that you can follow them without error.

It doesn't matter which channels I use, which words you interpret, or how you choose to understand our messages—the only thing you need to do is trust in your ability to be creator of your own life. You persistently undermine yourselves as being limited, "only human." All the messages in this book are meant to help you regain trust in your divine power. Once you find your way back into that feeling of trust, you will understand and accept that everything you desire is already available to you, waiting to be taken and enjoyed.

The purpose of this book is to help you change the way you experience life by reconnecting you with your soul. When you accomplish this, life will change before your eyes.

Rejoice.

A Closer Look

This section is an overview of the book, showing you how the information is organized so you can easily access the chapters you want according to your own situation. Each part of the book focuses on a specific aspect of the journey of self-discovery.

Part I provides an overview of the book's content and prepares you for the journey. It explains key elements and information that will aid understanding and enjoyment of the book.

Part II takes you straight into the spiritual realm and gives you a strong foundation for the rest of the journey. This section explores our inner nature. It explains topics such as the birth of a soul, our vibrational being, and the steps to happiness. It also sheds light on the concepts of purpose, destiny and destination, the flow of life, and the building of a partnership with the soul.

Part III is an invaluable tool kit: the guide, the roadmap, the vehicle, the fuel, and the purpose for the journey. This part describes clearly and concisely the nine inner powers that everyone is born with, and includes practical and easy-to-apply methods of incorporating these powers into daily life.

Part IV offers new perspectives on how to deal with life issues and empower oneself. It allows you to put into practice what you have learned so far through soul-based alternative approaches to some of today's common challenges. This part explores and analyses the way we experience life, the need to slow down and simplify, sleeping problems, and the quality of the bonds we create with the surrounding world.

Part V fully opens the doors to the soul by acknowledging you as an awakened being, a teacher, leader, and student in the "Era of Light," the new era of conscious evolution. It introduces spiritual and life truths to support you in your desire to participate in the awakening process. This information will enable you to further your connection with your inner self, higher levels of consciousness, and the entire universe.

Part VI challenges you to take control of and responsibility for your life by making better choices, rather than becoming dependent on the dictations of your ego, that is, living in autopilot mode. This part of the book encourages you to celebrate your newly enhanced awareness, and motivates you to initiate change with some simple actions that will start you on the road to freedom.

In the **Appendix**, you can find information about my self-guided meditation and how to meet your spirit guides. For the reasons explained in Chapter One, I suggest you read my self-guided meditation before you dive into the text. If you are already familiar with the practice of meditation, I urge you to include my meditation in your routine, as it will enrich your experience and open new doors to the spiritual realm. If you do not meditate, do not see this as a downside, but as motivation to begin practising this wonderful activity. My meditation may be slightly advanced for a beginner, but it should entice you to begin simple meditation—eventually you will be able to perform this specific meditation.

One piece of advice based on my own experience: do the suggested exercises, even though it means stopping your reading until you notice some results. The exercises will produce changes within the fabric of your being that no amount of reading alone can achieve. If you prefer, you could first read the whole book to familiarise yourself with it, and then read it a second time (or third or fourth) and do the practices then. The real journey is the growth you will achieve by engaging in these activities.

Some Housekeeping Before You Commence

Finally, before you start, consider the following important points, which might enhance your experience of *Freedom of the Soul*:

1. *The main goal is to enjoy the journey.* Don't worry about whether you fully understand what you are reading, or even whether you believe it. Do not worry about whether you are doing the exercises correctly or getting results fast enough. Rid yourself of any expectations about how much you should achieve and instead immerse yourself completely in the journey of self-discovery. It might take you a few reads of this book and many rounds of exercises, but are you in any hurry?

   We are all at different stages of our journeys, and for that reason, we grow at different rates. Everyone processes concepts and skills differently, in unique and appropriate ways. Even if you don't see obvious results, changes are happening in your unconscious self. They will eventually be noticeable, and in time, you will discover a powerful new person, a new awakened you. Trust me.

2. *Be open to new concepts and ideas.* This book reached you because you are ready to accept its content. The more openness you show, the more you will take in, even if you are not aware of it. When you engage in something new, no matter what its nature, the more open you are to learning, accepting, and taking part in the process, the more you will gain from the whole experience. Therefore, be open and receptive to the teachings I share with you here.

Understand that being open doesn't mean forcing yourself into accepting anything that you are not entirely ready to learn. Being open means allowing the flow of new ideas to enter your mind in a relaxed manner. If you think a concept you read seems a bit farfetched, please do not disregard it; you would be closing doors instead of opening them. A better way to deal with challenging concepts would be to take one of the following approaches:

- Reflect on what you are uncertain about in order to find some clarity.
- Talk to someone who understands and/or has experience with the topic to seek clarification.
- Research the subject, engage in specialised reading, and/or pay more attention to the "now" in order to find answers.

If you cannot accept or agree with a new idea, leave it for the time being. In this way you are leaving the door ajar so it can be fully opened later, when and if you are ready to understand the concept. You will open doors when you are ready to do so, not before. You will realise that as you open your mind to new concepts, your life will open up to you in amazing ways.

I can relate my own experience on the subject of openness to learning by sharing an event that happened to me many years ago, when I had many questions about life. Someone suggested a book to me. Although it was a bit advanced for my development at the time, this person thought it would offer me some clarity. Sure enough, it was a high-level book on metaphysics. There were many concepts I didn't understand, but I still read it through to the end. Even though I didn't comprehend everything in the book, I found answers to many of my questions; that new knowledge brought me confidence and more clarity, and also showed me where to look for information that I needed to continue my search. I didn't force myself to try to understand things I found unclear or complex; I just accepted them and continued with the reading.

3. *Keep a journal.* Journal writing is a very powerful tool for healing and personal growth. Those who create the habit of writing in a journal reap immense benefit at many levels. I suggest you find yourself a nice journal. It can be a notebook of any size or loose paper, which you can then place in a binder. It really doesn't matter what you use as long as it is pleasing to you. Make a nice cover for your journal and get a pen with smoothly flowing ink to record your own insights.

   As you read this book, write anything you discover about it in your journal, including insights, changes you experience as a result of practicing the exercises or meditations, guidance from your inner voice, any successes or breakthroughs and how they affect your life, new ways you behave or interact, changes to your emotions as you progress, affirmations or empowering thoughts, goals you want to set, and quotes that grab your attention. Make the journal your best friend; use it to build a bridge to connect with your inner voice.

I started writing in my journal when I was a teenager and needed to express things that I was not comfortable talking with anyone else, not even my mother. These were mostly dreams about how I wanted life to be and my feelings about them. It was about the usual teen stuff: boys I liked, my friendships, my studies, and my body image, of course. My journal was a great friend, always ready to listen to me, never criticizing or judging me.

I stopped writing when I started university. During that time, I was clear about what I wanted, and life was giving it to me. I had a great job and I was learning a lot. I had an awesome boyfriend who later became my husband. I was going out and enjoying good friendships and family relationships. My life was flowing and I was flowing with it. I now understand that I didn't feel like writing in my journal then because I was so tuned into my inner being and had such clarity and purpose that there was no reason to express anything in a journal.

Many years passed before I again felt the need to write in my journal. When that inner nagging started to bother me, when I had lost sight of who I was and where I was going, when I was trying to find answers to questions about every aspect of my life, I knew what I needed to do. I reached for my faithful friend: my journal.

Many of the examples and insights in this book come from the pages of my journal. By telling you about my experiences, I hope to encourage you to start your own journal. Even if your life is flowing right now, not in transition, take time to write a few entries now and then. For example, you might write about the abundance in your life and the gratitude you feel for it. Many teachers and authors recommend and practice journal writing. I hope you follow our lead and discover the faithful and unbiased friend a journal can be.

4.   *This is just another starting point.* The journey of life has many legs, many beginnings and ends, many bends and detours; this book might be another starting point in your journey.

The concepts included in here are only a small set of things to know about personal growth. If I had written about everything I wanted to, this book would have been too big to comfortably pick up. Even if I were to write many books, I'd never be able to address all there is to learn and discover.

Recognize that as you increase your awareness and grow by applying what you learn, you will be guided to engage in other activities to continue your progress. The path of growth never ends; change and transformation are constant elements in our lives up until the day we depart our physical existences. So do not despair about how much you've done or have yet to do. Any step you take, big or small, helps you to evolve into spirit having a human experience of life, and guides you to lead the life you were meant to live.

Now, take a deep breath and enjoy the beginning of this new journey.

PART II

Look Inside: Here I am

You Are a Divine Expression of Soul

Who am I? The answer to this question is the reason this book exists. Who do you think you are? Have you ever before thought about it? Have you tried to figure out the answer without asking anyone for guidance? Or have you done what most people do and accepted whatever you were told?

From a very early age, you learn to use a variety of labels to help identify yourselves in relation to your life situations, other people, and your environments. For example, you say, "I am a man/woman/child" and "I am young/old, successful/a failure, strong/weak, worthy/unworthy, artistic/untalented, loved/lonely" and so forth. The list of labels is endless. As your life progresses and your life situations change, you continue to pin labels to your already extensive collection in order to describe who you are. Some of those labels are temporary—"I am a student" or "I am single"—but some other labels are never lost. They stay with you, even if they no longer have any relevance to your current situations. Examples of these labels are "No one loves me," "I am not a smart person," and "I cannot control my spending."

If you understand that labels are just an aid, a point of reference to make your life easier, you won't be too attached to them, and as a result, you will feel freer. Most of the time, though, you grab tight to your labels because you believe that they are true; to support that reality, you end up becoming your labels. Thus, it is easy to see how you can come to equate who you are with the pack of labels you identify yourself with. "I am this and I am that"; "I have this and I have that"; "I am not this"; "I cannot have that." These labels are called the ego.

The ego is an instrument that serves you. It functions in this physical plane and allows you to interact with the various aspects of your life. Therefore, the ego is necessary. However, when you give the ego excessive control over your life, it stops being useful and deprives you of the ability to be who you really are—not the labels, but the true you, a divine expression of the soul. You are more than the labels you surround yourself with. You are more than the ego that controls you. You are a divine, eternal being, a powerful, loving soul living in a perfect physical vessel.

This is a universal truth that man persistently tries to ignore. For what reason? You may ask. It is because the mere thought that you are a powerful entity and constant creator of your life is something most cannot accept. It is easier to use the labels, to accept the ego, and to live the life you have been handed, having little or no control over it, than to take responsibility and assume your role as powerful creator. By ignoring this truth, you provide yourself with reason to blame everything and everyone but yourself for your disappointments, dissatisfaction, shortcomings, pain, and failures.

No matter where you are positioned in the ladder of life, whether you are on the sunny side or the dark one, no one is immune to life's intricacies. Everyone at some point will encounter pain, heartache, disillusion, struggle, doubt, fear, worry, failure, and death. Each person handles these setbacks in different ways, with different attitudes, as a result of different forms of thinking. The degree to which you consider yourself the creator of your own life can make a huge difference in the quality of your experience of life; this attitude transforms a journey of disappointment, failure, and stagnation into one of discovery, challenge, and growth.

Only when you acknowledge who you really are and accept your power and the role you play in the scheme of things does life become a journey to be enjoyed and appreciated, on which every experience is another step in the road to fulfilment of your purpose.

You Have a Purpose

This raises another question. What is your purpose on Earth? Why are you here?

People's ideas about life's purpose are varied and range from thinking there is no purpose at all but to just endure life, to thinking it is a very worthy task to discover and accomplish purpose, with many variations in between.

But the true answer is very simple: the purpose of this physical life is to be happy and to enjoy the abundance that surrounds you. It is available to you through an infinite array of experiences that you have the freedom to choose and create. Your purpose is to embark on the journey of life, which has an unlimited number of possible pathways, to reach the destination of pure love and joy.

Purpose is not inherently big or small, worthy or unworthy, important or insignificant. Purpose is the series of life challenges or lessons you undertake, both consciously and unconsciously, to reach your desired outcome in life. To that end, you exercise your free will; it is always within your own power to choose where you are going and who you are being.

CHAPTER 3

The Eagle and the Man

The Soaring of the Eagle: A New Birth

The sun rises on the horizon. The silence is infinite across the high mountain peaks. The eagle perches on top of a mountain, quietly waiting for the first rays to appear; these first rays of light bring the source of being into existence.

Once sunlight paints the sky yellow, the eagle spreads its wings and soars up into the empty firmament at the speed of light, with only one intention: to immerse itself in the light that brings life into existence every single day.

Each day is a new birth. Each day, the eagle rises into its source to be re-energised and reconnected with it. Then it comes back to the mountains and flies with outstretched wings through Earth's skies on the flight of freedom.

The Man: The Journey Begins

The green fields, covered in fragile wildflowers, move in the fresh morning breeze. The sun is rising, changing the colours of all the living things. The darkness of the night slowly disappears. The sounds of day become louder, and the music of the Earth starts playing its song of love and beauty, the song of Mother Nature. There is nothing imperfect, unnecessary, or imbalanced in the vast green fields. All exists in perfect unison, dancing the rhythm of life.

In the distance, the sound of water trickling its way down the stream adds to the melody of Nature's song. Life blooms in the fields. It is there that souls come into existence and merge, becoming the magnificence of Nature. Every expression of life transmutes into the Earth, and the Earth transmutes into energy. The essence of life remains the same; all is one, from beginning to end.

The man is lying down, resting by the stream and contemplating the blue, bright sky. His arm is outstretched. His hand reaches into the water and carelessly plays with the freshness of the pure liquid. Suddenly, he feels thirsty, and bends over the stream to quench his thirst. He drinks with pleasure as his insides are refreshed and satiated. His thirst is immense—he has never felt such thirst before—and the more he drinks, the more he wants to drink. Then he jumps into the stream and bathes himself. He feels extremely happy and satisfied, playful and carefree.

He stays in this state for a while, until he cannot drink any more water; he is completely refreshed and overflowing with happiness. It is then that he realises his senses have been enhanced in some way. He notices with new clarity the blue sky, the exuberant vegetation, the sounds of nature, the clear water of the stream, the exquisite smells in the air of the fresh breeze and the strong earth that supports him while he rests. He feels like he is in paradise, and he loves this place. His heart swells and he loves this place more and more. He becomes aware that this feeling of love comes not only from inside of him but also from outside, and all directions. He cannot explain why he feels this way, until suddenly, he has a flash of realisation: love is not inside or outside or all around—in fact, he himself is love. Moreover, he is part of everything, and everything is part of him.

The excitement of this discovery wakes him; he realises he was dreaming and now he has returned to his reality. However, something has changed inside him; he has received an extraordinary insight. He knows that what he felt was not a dream, but real and wonderful. What he felt was a reality he intends to seek now.

The day seems like night. Every day in the man's life is the same. But he knows there is a place where the day is bright, the earth smells fresh, and the water is clear as precious crystals; where peace abounds, and he doesn't need to worry or rush, and he is happy and joyous. He knows that this place exists somewhere because he has seen it and felt it. He needs only to find it. He doesn't want his days to be like nights any longer. He is determined to find that magical place, and thus, his journey to the light begins.

CHAPTER 4

Who Am I?

In the man's journey to the light, the light has different meanings, which are interconnected and necessary to one another. The light can refer to

- *Clarity, illumination*: the knowing within you that guides you and calls you towards who you are. The clarity of your inner wisdom allows you to believe, even when you cannot rely on your physical senses. Belief triggers the shedding of the veils impairing your vision, so you can finally see the truth. In this context, you are on the journey to clarity.
- *Destiny, purpose*: the ultimate purpose of your human existence is happiness and growth. There are infinite pathways available to you for achieving that purpose. Light in this context refers to these pathways you will travel in your life as you journey towards your destiny.
- *Soul, essence*: the whole reality of you, your inner voice, and your divine and powerful eternal being. Light refers to the journey to your soul.

By embarking on the journey to the light, not only will the man gain clarity about his essence, he will also learn to trust and follow his inner knowing. In the process he will discover, step by step, how to realise his purpose.

People want to remember what they came here to do as physical beings. The first step to achieving that goal is to find and understand who they really are. Most people go about their lives not knowing what or who they are. They lose themselves on the infinite pathways of their own journeys, reaching no specific end. They lose track of what they are supposed to be doing and where they are meant to be going because they are oblivious to their inner guidance and their divine grace.

You will not know what to do or where to go until you discover your essence, accept your true nature, and find your place in the scheme of life. This knowledge will bring joy and peace to your heart. It will bring you what is rightfully yours: freedom.

The knowledge that gives you this sense of direction and empowerment comes from clarity; it comes from the light within you. This light lies at the centre of your heart and is the source of your being. No one can consider himself alive if that light is not beaming inside his heart. If you can find the light within you, you will find your power and your purpose. However, in order to do that, you will have to go back to the beginning. You have to return to the darkness.

The Birth of the Soul

You, as true essence, are part of the infinite wisdom that creates universes. You exist as spirit in a state of pure perfection, pure love, and total peace and harmony. However, you constantly seek to experience more and you want to expand; your desire to explore and grow is never-ending. Time after time, part of you chooses to emerge from the state of pure bliss to give birth to the human expression of you, and so fulfil your desires.

The birth of a soul into human expression has been explained in many ways; people have tried to express, within the limitations of language, what they saw or understood about the soul's birthing process. All the stories have one thing in common: they say that when a soul is born, it is a joyous event, not only on the human realm but also on the nonphysical one.

When a soul's yearning to experience joy; to grow and to interact with others, the environment, and the world; to contribute to the expansion of the universe is so intense, it produces a staggering explosion of energy that culminates in the manifestation of a new human life. This newborn life knows its power, its knowledge, its purpose, and most importantly, its connection to the source of life.

What is the process that gives a soul birth into human life like? Imagine a void like an immense cavern in the depths of the Earth, full of silence and peace. There is not much light in this place, only emptiness and darkness. Spirit lives in this void, enjoying eternity until it desires to experience something else. The power of that desire is what triggers the creation of a new physical life.

Imagine now that the intensity of this creation causes millions of passages or tunnels to emerge from the void, going out in all directions. Each passage leads to a different life journey, a different destination or purpose. The soul that is born must choose one passage, which will determine the roadmap of its journey. Which one will it choose? The passage that is most illuminated; the one whose blinding light overshadows that of all the other passages. That is the path for the soul to take; it is attracted to that path by a magnetic force.

The soul stands now at the entrance of the passage. The brightness of the light obscures what is on the other side, but what could it be but goodness, when the light is so warm and welcoming? The soul moves forward, and immediately, a gentle force sucks it in and pulls it down the tunnel at an amazing speed. The ride is exhilarating and seems to last forever; however, eventually it slows down. The soul comes out in the unknown physical world.

The soul—now a person—is no longer ethereal. It can feel its physical form when it breathes air into its lungs for the first time, and air comes out in the form of screams when it gives its first cries. The human is scared, but knows it is powerful, and knows the purpose of its journey; that was shown to the soul during its trip down the tunnel. The human knows it can accomplish its purpose, that it can do anything it desires. But it also knows that it will come to forget all of this until it is the right time to remember again.

The soul has just been born into its new life. It is joyous and beaming with happiness because it knows the glorious journey it will walk together with its human form. This is a beautiful explanation of the birth of a soul—don't you think so?

Meditation: The Birth of Your Soul

A beautiful way to connect with your inner being and to develop a solid relationship with it is to relive the experience of your soul's birth. This is an amazing sensation that can be experienced in the quietness of meditation. By engaging in this exquisite activity, you will not only deepen your sense of wholeness from the closer connection between you and your soul, but also discover insights about your life's journey and purpose. If you have a genuine desire to be more in tune with your inner being, then this is a meditation that will reward you in many ways, and also one that you will enjoy enormously.

———————————————•

Sit or lie down in a quiet place with your eyes closed. Take a few deep breaths.

As you breathe in and out, feel yourself becoming more and more relaxed.

Your whole body feels relaxed. You feel content and relaxed all over.

If any thoughts are coming into your mind, just let them go. Acknowledge them, but don't follow them; just let them go.

Spend a few minutes breathing in and out, relaxing more and more, disconnecting from your surroundings and focusing your awareness on your inner world. As you do this, imagine yourself going deep within yourself, searching for your inner voice. You want to connect with your power, with the source of your infinite wisdom.

Keep on going within, as though you were walking down a staircase taking you to that place. Keep on going until you feel you have reached the place where you merge with your essence.

Now imagine you are floating in this dark, quiet, empty space. You are joyous, not at all scared or worried. This place feels safe and warm, and you feel nurtured and loved. You are floating in this womb, carelessly, effortlessly, taken care of—until you have a sudden urge to experience something different.

You want to create, you want to play, you want to be something more, and as suddenly as that thought occurs to you, millions of passages emerge all around you. Each passage leads to different experiences, different life stories. Which passage are you attracted to this time around? Which passage do you feel like walking? Look at the myriad choices—which one is calling to you? You look around and choose the one with the brightest light. As you make your decision, all other passages disappear.

Now go towards the passage entrance. You are standing on the threshold, but you cannot see anything; the light is too bright. You are feeling excited, anxious, and joyous.

You move forward and are sucked into the tunnel. You are travelling at an amazing speed. You go up and down, twirl around. This is a joyous ride and you are enjoying every part of it.

As you go along, you see flashes of your new life. What can you see? Which activities are you pursuing? What kind of people are with you? Are there any words, messages, or signs that you can make out? Do you see any cues about your purpose?

If you desire, you can control the speed at which you are travelling; you can slow the motion down to see the pictures of your new life more clearly. Take a few moments to observe what it is being shown to you. If nothing comes up, then just enjoy the experience.

Now you see bright light at the end of the tunnel. It's a different kind of light than the kind you saw before. You can also hear noises. You start to slow down.

You have a sensation of being pulled out of this warm place. You have just been born! You have just emerged into the world of the unknown. You are not ethereal anymore. You can feel your physical form; you feel yourself crying. What can you see? What are your feelings telling you? Are there any clues to tell you about yourself?

You have just been born. It is time to celebrate. You have a new life to enjoy.

You remember who you are: a divine and powerful being. You also know your purpose, and you know, with certainty, that you can achieve anything you desire. You know, without doubt, that you have the power within you to create worlds. Sense how this awareness feels. Savour that feeling, recognise it and register it in your mind so you can retrieve it any time you need to.

Spend a few minutes rejoicing in this empowerment, freedom, and unconditional love. Store the feeling in the place where your inner voice is, so you will know where to find it later.

When you are ready, slowly come out of your meditation.

Become aware of your surroundings, and feel a soft energy pulling you down towards Mother Earth as you open your eyes.

Remain in place processing your discoveries for as long as you desire.

Now is a good time to grab your journal and take note of what you have experienced. Messages, clues, visions, feelings—anything you can recall is valuable information. It might not make sense at the present, but it is nevertheless guidance you should keep for future reference.

If you did not see or receive anything during the meditation, do not feel upset. Connection with the inner being can become blocked by such factors as anxiety about what might be revealed to you, fear of seeing things that might happen or happened in the past, or just not being fully relaxed. Please, do not give up. Remember that perseverance and patience are your best allies on your journey to personal growth and self-discovery.

As you repeat this meditation, you will become progressively more comfortable with the process; you will allow yourself to be more open to whatever comes to you, and you will feel joyous about hearing your inner voice and surrender to what is within you. Soon all the barriers that previously prevented you from achieving success will dissolve. From then onward, you will receive guidance every time you wish to do so. After a while, you will discover that your inner voice doesn't speak to you exclusively through meditation, but speaks to you at all times. You just have to become aware of it.

The value of this meditation is not only that you experience the birth of your soul, but also that you claim the feeling of empowerment that comes from being who you really are. The amazing feeling that is released during the meditation is usually located in your solar plexus, although it can also be located elsewhere in the body if it resonates with you (for example, in your heart).

Make a habit of recalling this feeling as you go through your day, especially when you are swayed by life's challenges and you need a reminder that you are soul experiencing physical life, not the other way around. This feeling is your life force. Combined with the power of your intentions, it guarantees you can achieve anything you desire. Empowerment and intention combined will assist you in your journey and fulfilling your purpose.

Rejoice!

The Purpose of the Soul

When your soul manifested in human expression at the time of your birth, you knew who you were, what you were and why you were born. All that knowledge and awareness was slowly forgotten as you grew and were socialised by the world and by each of the people you interacted with. The light within became dormant, silenced by a stronger voice that directs the choices you make and the paths you follow until such time that it is ready to awaken once again.

When the time comes that the soul seeks freedom of expression, when its need to be heard cannot longer be contained, nothing will stop it from surfacing. Acknowledging and following up on the calling of your soul will lead to magnificent and rewarding experiences. On the other hand, denial and rejection of that nagging within will result in a conflicted and stressful life. The tug of war between your soul's desires and your fears produces great suffering. Trying to silence your inner calling goes against the very purpose of existence; you will be plagued with diseases not only of the body but also of the mind. No one exists in this physical plane without a purpose, and that purpose must be fulfilled to preserve the universal harmony and unity. Therefore, those who constantly avoid their purposes, who ignore the signs of discord in their lives and of unhappiness in their hearts, will likely leave their physical lives sooner than expected, as they are failing to fulfil the very reason for existence.

But embracing your purpose can be exhilarating and empowering. The very act of acknowledging that your existence is purposeful, that you are important no matter what the circumstances of your life are, and that you have all the power and resources in the universe to fulfil your mission, is joyous. It is also a fundamental step on the road to living a life of purpose.

Doesn't it feel wonderful to know, without a doubt, that you can achieve anything? You already have proof of this from people you know or maybe heard of, who overcame every adverse condition presented to them and still managed to achieve what they desired, even when it was thought to be impossible, maybe crazy. They possessed something important: they had dreams, a burning passion, a mission, a thirst for knowledge, and in many instances, a degree of obsession. These driving qualities resulted from the pulling of their inner light as it sought to fulfil the purpose of growth, happiness, and freedom. You have all that within you. You are made of the same essence as those who have achieved great, fulfilling lives.

The path is simple. Set your focus and intention on the adventure to discover your purpose. Do not focus on fear of having to carry out that purpose, which for many is yet unknown. Fear can be paralysing; it makes you feel stuck and lets you down every time. Fear can make you into your own enemy by silencing the calling of your inner voice. The more you let fear control your feelings and choices, the stronger it becomes. In this way, it becomes a force working against you and will eventually destroy you.

When you seek the light and live your purpose, you align with the universal order of things. When you accept your power and your divine origin, you agree to unite with the universal source. You become part of the whole and add to the energy of the source, and in turn, the source provides you with the energy to be a purposeful soul in a human experience.

You have a unique purpose that can be fulfilled only by you. All humans are facets of the divine source, unique expressions of its divinity. Your purpose cannot be achieved by anyone else, nor can you achieve anyone else's purpose. Your purpose is your divine mission on Earth, your soul's assignment. By manifesting your purpose, your soul grows to greater levels of consciousness, and as your soul grows, so too does the universal divine consciousness.

This is the ultimate collective purpose: *to constantly change, transform, evolve, and create, throughout eternity.*

We, higher beings of the universe, support you openly and eagerly with your journey on Earth. We are watching and waiting for your request for help and guidance. We are here for you—evolving beings, growing together and keeping the flame of life burning forever.

Don't fear your purpose; embrace it. Rejoice in the fact that you are a human being living in a perfect human body, with a mission to fulfil. Take pride in your place on the planet, in the environment you contribute to, in the relationships you forge, in all that you learn, in the experiences you have, in the energy you emanate, and in the life force you share. All that was, is, and will be your life is part of your purpose.

Embrace your purpose once and for all, because it defines who you really are, what you really are, and what you can become. Everything you need is at your disposal. Everything you need is within you, waiting to be tapped. Reach for your potential. It is our desire for you to succeed in your mission and to achieve the ultimate end of happiness, love, and life.

We, Beings of Light, love you. Be blessed.

Affirmations for the Soul

I love affirmations and I use them daily, for anything and everything. They help me direct my focus and set my intention, and they are also great tools for changing unhealthy trains of thoughts. Most of the time, I use them just to gain the feel-good sensation they provide, even when I am already in a good state of mind. For this reason, I call them "empowering thoughts."

Much has been written about affirmations, so I do not feel the need to expand on the subject here. However, I will briefly explain that an affirmation or empowering thought is a personal statement that presents a positive message or has a positive meaning. The simpler the affirmation, the better it is. For example, *"I am a powerful being living a purposeful life."*

The main rule for using empowering thoughts, whether you create them yourself or use ones already written, is that you have to feel good when you say them. You must feel strong, happy, and calm or any other feel-good sensation when you say, think, write, or even sing an affirmation. If an empowering thought doesn't make you feel better, then it is not right for you at that given time. This doesn't mean that the affirmation is wrong or that you are wrong; it just means that the specific affirmation is not providing you with what you need at that moment and perhaps you need to try a different one.

When you use an empowering thought with even the tiniest amount of trust in it, you will receive a boost of refreshing, positive energy. The sensation will make you feel optimistic, like having someone whisper in your ear that everything is all right.

The reason I am introducing empowering thoughts at this point is because I want to share with you a beautiful one that I use most days. It is particularly applicable to the topic discussed in this section. The empowering thought reads as follows, *"I am one with the divine light that created me."* This is a very simple yet powerful affirmation, don't you agree? I use it when

- I need to feel empowered and strong.
- I am overwhelmed by routine and chores.
- I need to regain perspective by feeling part of the universe and at one with God.
- I feel down or distressed because I am temporarily disconnected from my inner being.
- I need drive and an "I can do it" feeling.
- I need to feel peace and to release resistance.

I am sure there are other valid uses for it, besides the ones I have presented. I offer you this beautiful affirmation so that you can gain some power from the feelings it triggers within you. Imagine, what more can you ever need if you know from deep within that *you* are at one with the source, the creator of all? How does it feel to know this? Awesome!

Bear in mind what I said earlier. When you say this affirmation, if instead of feeling invigorated and on top of the world, you feel small, weak, or awkward, then do not force it. Keep on reading, learning, and getting to know about yourself, and in time you will be able to scream this affirmation from the top of your lungs, without fear.

Here are some other affirmations for the soul:

"I am an infinite source of love."
"I am guided and nurtured by the light within me."
"My soul grows through my life experiences."
"I am empowered when I am at one with my inner light."

CHAPTER 5

Mind, Body, and Light: Who We Truly Are

I am in one of my meditations, walking to the temple to meet my spirit guides. I am happy, as usual, enjoying the sensations that meditation brings into my being—but today I feel somewhat different. Suddenly, I realise that I have a sensation of uneasiness because I am not aware of my physical body. I cannot see or feel my body, as I usually do.

I look at myself and I am transparent, only light. A powerful, strong, white light pours out of me, through me, and all around me. I have no form. Even though I feel wonderful, I feel weird as well. I bring my attention to my surroundings and I realise that everything around me—the forest, the field of wildflowers, the temple—feels ethereal too. Nothing is solid.

My higher self is at the altar inside the temple. She feels ethereal as well. A bright, white-and-gold light emanates from her. She is radiant and warm, like a sun. I walk towards her, and as I get closer, I can feel myself becoming part of her; we are one, connected by this magical light. My higher self extends her arms towards me and I extend mine. Across the distance, we touch, forming an energetic link, a glorious, ethereal embrace. The whole experience is bizarre and wonderful at the same time.

I try to absorb what is happening and become aware that I want to experience a human hug, a physical embrace. As I think these thoughts, I start to sense physical forms. The light slowly disappears, and as I continue walking, things retake their usual shape and form.

What did you think about the light in your meditation? You've seen your true form.

It felt strange and unusual. I was filled with contradictions. On one hand, I enjoyed the powerful feeling that the light gave me of being invincible and all-knowing. On the other hand, with the same intensity, I wanted to regain my physical form so that I could again feel the world around me.

This is exactly the reason why spirit chooses from time to time to take physical form and experience life the way you do: we desire to feel, live, discover, fail, grow, and ultimately, die in order to return to the light. In your physical world, we are restricted by the limitations you impose on yourself due to your limited awareness of your true nature—still, it is worth it to experience the physical dimension.

But if, in your human life, you could become aware of and acknowledge us, your nonphysical side, we could connect and work together; then both of us would benefit. We of limitless spirit could experience the wonders of the physical world through your human existence, and you of physical form could achieve unlimited potential by connecting with your souls. This is the purpose of the journey to the light.

Those who do not realise they are made of more than just physical matter will spend most of their physical existences in darkness. However, those who choose to seek the light within will have lives of wonder and abundance from accessing the creative potential of their source of being, of the Universe. This is the purpose behind all of the souls that are born onto this planet. These souls grow through their physical experience, and this, in turn, causes nonphysical growth and evolution. It is an amazing time to be living on this planet; more people than ever are talking about light, recognising a higher consciousness, contemplating the infinite possibilities of expression, bringing the light into their lives, and freeing their souls to express themselves in all their magnificence.

We desire you to achieve your purpose and reach enlightenment, but we are not asking you to do so by rejecting your human desires, ignoring your physical needs, or giving up on life and retreating into solitude. Nor do we wish you to pass judgement on the things that you think, see, say, or do. This would go against the universal laws; everything you experience is valid, perfect, and necessary for evolution of the whole self.

What we are asking you to do is to accept your divinity. Accept that you are a physical and nonphysical being; you are mind, body, and light. When you accept this truth, you will become whole, and holy. You will know, without a shadow of a doubt, that what we are, you can be too. Who you become causes us all to evolve. We are asking you to be your human self while you experience your light, which is always burning in your heart whether or not you are aware of it. Seek and follow your light, and your life will be wonderful and fulfilling; your journey will take you to places you never imagined, you will achieve more than you ever desired, and you will rejoice in all experiences, even in the toughest circumstances.

"Light Bath" Exercise

Every day, spend a few minutes sitting in a quiet place with your eyes closed. Breathe peacefully, relax your body, and free your mind of thought.

In this meditative state, feel yourself bathed in a warm light. It is coming through your head, moving down your body, going over your arms and legs, and connecting you to Mother Earth. Feel the light growing inside your body and extending outside you, around you, above and below you. Feel yourself inside this bubble of divine light.

Do this exercise for as long as you wish, allowing the light to circulate your body. Remember to ground yourself when you come out of the meditation, otherwise you may feel disconnected from your surroundings and light-headed.

This simple yet very powerful exercise enables you to energise yourself, cleanse your aura, and recharge with positive, powerful vibrations. Most importantly, it enables you to connect with your nonphysical higher consciousness. By the power of this act, matter and light become one in you.

The more you practise this meditation, the more harmonious you will be with all that surrounds you. Your light will awaken, and in time, it will expand to your whole body, and then exceed your physical form. This will put you in a state of alertness, openness, and acceptance that will enable you to reach people, things, events, and circumstances in line with your desires. You will infuse yourself with powerful energy, becoming a magnet for what you desire as well as an instrument of love and appreciation. Of all the material benefits that you can achieve by expanding your inner light, most important is the immense gain of getting in tune with me: your soul, the light living inside you.

Seek the Light

The stronger your inner light, the stronger my presence in you.
The stronger my presence in you, the greater your power.
The greater your power, the clearer your thoughts.
The clearer your thoughts, the more purposeful your actions.
The more purposeful your actions, the sooner you enjoy your achievements.
The sooner you enjoy your achievements, the more rapid your growth.
The more rapid your growth, the greater our evolution.
The greater our evolution, the more amazing the impact on global consciousness.

You see, by seeking the light, everybody and everything wins. There is always light, even on the darkest nights. When you finally grasp this idea, you will naturally and unconsciously focus on the light in every situation, seek the light even in the darkest moments of your life, welcome light into your being, and breathe in light and seek harmony with it. In return, your soul will reward you by letting you know that even when you do not have clarity, you are heading in the direction of freedom, growth, joy, and inner peace. It is our desire for you to seek your light and manifest your desires; we will all be rewarded by this shared experience. When others see that your life unfolds in harmony, peace, grace, and joy, they will want the same.

Physical and Ethereal Bodies

You are familiar with your physical body; the one you can see, feel, feed, dress, touch, look after, love, and worship; and that some mistreat and fill with disease. Your physical body is the instrument that allows us to be on this plane; it is the home of the soul created by Source. Many people put excessive attention on their physical bodies, believing them to be representative of what they really are. These people dismiss teachings that the body is just a vessel for the light to reside in this physical plane and fulfil its purpose. People seek to perfect their physical bodies, not understanding that the body is already perfect. The human body's mechanics are a precise system; so perfect is the body that it has the creative power and ability to produce what it needs to function, dispose of the unnecessary, heal itself when out of balance, and give birth to new life. As long as humans persist in focusing on the physical body, they will miss out on discovering and enjoying the riches of the inner body. Only when they discover and rejoice in the inner world will they see their own perfection and achieve love of self.

The nonphysical body is also called the ethereal body, aura, essence, or life force. It is the eternal part of you and much larger than your physical form. It cannot be seen by the naked eye, but can be perceived by some people with high levels of awareness, such as psychics, aura readers, and those who practice meditation or similar activities that draw attention to the inside. The ethereal body can also be perceived in dreams, and by those who have had near death experiences during which they were separated from their physical bodies for a brief period of time.

To show you the relationship between the two bodies, I present you with the following visualization exercise. Imagine the shape of a person: a physical body, surrounded by the aura. Imagine the person's aura is composed of many layers; each layer overlaps another in all directions, extending into the infinite. The physical body disappears; it is a barely visible dot surrounded by layers and layers of energy. This is the simplest graphic representation of what you are. Your physical being is a small dot at the end of the immense spiritual mass of your consciousness.

Let's continue playing with these images to clarify these ideas a bit further. Let us look at things from your perspective now. Picture yourself: your own body in your real-life size. Look around you, to one side and then the other, down at your feet, up above your head, in front of and behind you. As you look in all directions, imagine again those infinite overlapping layers of your ethereal body. See those ethereal layers encapsulating your physical body as though you were the heart of an onion. The extending layers touch and connect with the layers of other beings; they interact and communicate with each other.

Now let's shift our point of reference up to a higher level, to appreciate the big picture. Imagine floating above the scene. You can now see that the layers of your ethereal body interlock with infinite other layers of other beings, forming a mesh that extends to all directions. Eventually, the layers of your own being cannot be distinguished from those of other beings. At this point, each layer becomes all of the layers, and all the layers become one, and the one becomes the all. If you zoom in close, you will find yourself, your individual aspect of the ethereal consciousness, your unique expression of Source.

CHAPTER 6

The Colours of Your Essence

Now that you understand the largest part of you is ethereal, we can expand on this concept: your ethereal body is composed of lights that vibrate at their own frequency. From the white light that is your essence, all lights in the colours of the spectrum are born. They vibrate within you, within everyone else, and within everything. These vibrations are the reason why you resonate with some people, situations, events, things, and places more than others.

Some of the aura's colours change frequently according to your current situation, while others stay constant for long periods, even your whole lifetime, depending on their significance. You can tune in more closely to your subconscious by learning about the colours of your essence, and collaborate with it by actively focusing your energy, thoughts, and guided actions. If you want to become more aware of your ethereal body and be mindful of what energy you are resonating at a given time, then it would be of great benefit for you to learn about your colours.

Everyone is capable of seeing the colours of his essence and of interpreting their meanings. You can achieve this by practicing the simple meditation described later in this section. The benefits of this meditation are greater awareness of your own vibrations and also an enhanced state of general vibration. Through enhanced awareness, you will be able to recognise that it sometimes feels unpleasant to replicate the colours of your essence in your clothing or the foods you eat, as they can be overbearing or draining on you. You will notice that in other situations, adding these colours energises and enlivens you. In the same way, you will find yourself staying away from certain situations and interactions, while being drawn to other people. This unconscious shift results from a more active knowledge of your own vibration and its enhanced state.

As your awareness increases, you can use meditation or similar techniques that quiet the mind to ask your subconscious for the best ways to cooperate with it in the process of energy work; this is a good way to gain understanding of you through your aura. Also, familiarising yourself with the colours of your essence is a great way to get in touch with your inner being; you will learn what your soul is trying to communicate to your physical being. The healthier your vibrations are, the larger and brighter your aura is; the more balanced your energy levels, the healthier your aura. You can also see evidence of the effect of your aura's field on your physical world in the activities you are involved in and the thought patterns you are attracted to. There is a direct correspondence between the colours of your aura and the activities and events in your life.

The more you practice the colours meditation, the easier it will be for you to discover the colours you resonate with. You will gradually come to own them, work with them, and effortlessly make the necessary adjustments to bring up harmony and balance to your being. There is no right or wrong way of walking through this process. Do not worry about whether the colours you are perceiving are the "real" colours or not. There is always perfection in every message you receive; therefore, what you see is perfect, even an erroneous interpretation. Trust in your feelings, your intuition, and your inner guidance, and know with certainty that the messages you receive are always sent for your own good and greatness.

A fun exercise to get you started in discovering your aura's colours is to notice what your favourite colours are. Some colours you love all your life, some you favour for short periods, and others you are indifferent to, or actively dislike. Affinity for colours (or lack thereof) is an indicator of what colours your aura vibrates with. The colours that you love link to mostly constant aspects of you, the ones that you sometimes like associate with short-lived life events, and the ones you dislike represent your shadows, the unseen part in each one of us.

Colours tell you about yourself, where you come from, and where you are going. I give you an example from my own experience. I have always liked the colour blue and its darker shades. As you will see from the list of colours and their associated meanings that comes later in this chapter, blue relates to the communication and thought, both areas I have strongly resonated with since I was a child. It was not until I started developing my interest in personal growth and my spiritual self that I became attracted to the colours purple and magenta, which relate to intuition, openness, and high levels of awareness. On the other hand, I have always felt very uneasy around red, which is the colour of power and creation. I know that I still have to work on accepting and embracing these aspects of my life in order to live in purpose.

I remember a funny incident a few years ago when I went to a Conscious Living Expo and had a picture of my aura taken. To my surprise, almost 90 per cent of my aura was the colour red, and the rest was yellow and orange hues. Red is a colour I cannot handle very well, and at the time I associated it with anger, rage, and negative feelings. I was so annoyed that I told the man running the stand that the picture he had taken was not right. He was convinced that the process he had followed was correct, and he very kindly explained it to me. Seeing that I was still unhappy, he was good enough to take not one more picture, but a third one too, at no extra cost. Needless to say, all the photos turned out the same: red.

I left the stand unsatisfied, carrying the three "incorrect" pictures of my aura. I can see now that I was reacting to my own discomfort. It was my ego's perspective that red was a bad colour. My aura's colours were showing me what was working on an unconscious level. Now I know there is no such thing as a bad colour; each one has inherent beauty and unique meaning. Looking back as I tell this story, I can laugh and feel sorry for giving that kind man a hard time. It was a lesson. I now love having the colour red in me; it pushes me to keep on going, even when I am hesitant or discouraged.

Take some time and think, which colours do you prefer? Which ones drain you, or make you feel flat? Which ones drive you crazy? Which ones do you dislike intensely? If you have a picture of your aura, rejoice in the colours it shows you. Don't fight the colours or underestimate them; instead, learn from them. As you start to recognise your colours, study their meanings and see how they apply to your life. Are those colours giving you direction? Are they highlighting a side of you that you are ignoring or not even aware of? Above all, have fun with the exercise. Like all the exercises and activities in this book, it is an opportunity for you to discover more about your inner being, the driving force of your life.

Meditation: The Colours of Your Essence

Sit or lie down in a quiet place with your eyes closed. Take a few deep breaths.

As you breathe in and out, feel yourself becoming more and more relaxed.

Your whole body feels relaxed. You feel content and relaxed all over.

If any thoughts are coming into your mind, just let them go. Acknowledge them, but don't follow them; just let them go.

Spend a few minutes breathing in and out, relaxing more and more, disconnecting from your surroundings and focusing your awareness on your inner world. As you do this, imagine yourself going back in time, before the moment of your birth, when you were still in your mother's womb. Feel yourself in that cocoon: warm, nurtured, safe, and nourished, floating in a perfect universe. You feel loved, healed and completely untroubled.

Even though you'd like to stay here, you know you have another place to reach. Keep on rolling back through the folds of time, before you were conceived, before you even decided to incarnate yourself as a human being. Go back to when you were just spirit, when you were light. What can you see? What sensations do you have?

Prompt your soul to show you the colours of your essence by picturing yourself surrounded by your aura's field. What colours do you see? Which ones are resonating in your aura? What meaning do they reveal to you? Remain in this peaceful state for as long as you desire, allowing the information to enter your consciousness.

When you are ready, gradually come back to the present time, to your current self. As you do so, become aware of your surroundings and your physical body. Gently shake your hands and feet, move your head and shoulders, and feel a soft energy pulling you towards Mother Earth as you open your eyes.

As usual, write down any messages you have received in your journal. If you feel creative and playful, you can draw the shape of your body and the aura around you; use coloured pencils to colour your aura as you saw it during the mediation. You can also add any meaning you received about your colours. This is a great activity for recording any changes over time in the colours of your essence. As you go along, you will notice correlations between the colours and the way you feel, act, and respond to situations and to people.

During the meditation, each person will see lights of different colours depending on his essence. You may see several colours, or just one—this does not mean, however, that your aura has only one colour. It means that given colour is the most predominant in your life at the time, and it emphasizes the message that your soul is trying to communicate to you. If you do not see or receive anything during the meditation, this indicates that you are somehow blocking yourself; you are resisting insight.

As I mentioned before, everyone has the capacity to see the colours of their essence and to interpret their meaning. All you need to do is bring yourself to a more open state. Some ways that you can achieve this are

- Entering deep relaxation
- Releasing any expectations you have
- Deepening your meditative state to strengthen the connection with your inner self
- Clearing your mind of thoughts of doubt
- Cleansing your chakras

Balancing of the Chakras

The *chakras* are the centres of spiritual energy in the human body. They constitute the bridge between our physical bodies and the universal energy, according to yoga philosophy. They are part of an energetic network in our bodies through which life energy flows. The chakras are spinning wheels of energy that receive life force, also known as chi or prana, transform it and transmit it through the energetic network. There are seven major chakras, which run along the spine, and many minor chakras. Aligning or cleansing the chakras creates a clear channel for the constant flow of life force, allowing the body to thrive in health and pure potential. Stress, anxiety, overwork, poor eating habits, sleep deprivation, lack of exercise, and lack of leisure time are some of the things that block the chakras, making it easy for illness to set in. Meditation and yoga assist in the realignment of the chakras, as do natural healing treatments such as *reiki* and special breathing techniques.

Here is a simple way for you to cleanse your chakras. You can include this exercise in your spiritual practice, before your meditations, or when you are guided to.

Sit comfortably upright with your eyes closed. Imagine a stream of white light above you entering your body through the top of your head, moving down along your spine, through your energy centres, and exiting you into the Earth. Imagine this continuous flow of light flowing easily through your body, clearing and unblocking your chakras. Stay in this state for a few minutes until you feel more energy and well-being inside yourself. Then take a deep breath in and imagine your chakras closing; breathe out. You can now open your eyes.

The Colours of Your Essence and their Meanings

The list below provides you with information that can assist you in interpreting the colours of your essence. You will benefit immensely from understanding the impact of the colours in your life and learning how to work with them. Our spectrum contains many more variations of colour than are compiled here; however, I have necessarily focused on the limited colours of your physical plane.

Colour	Meaning
Black	The colour of absence. It represents fear and not wanting to see deeper within. If you see a black essence, you are not really seeing; you are blind to your own light and colour. The colours of your essence are hiding behind the black void. You need to remove your resistance to allow your light to come through. To remove such blockages, do the chakra cleansing given in the previous section.
Blue	The colour of water and emotions. Blue is movement and fluctuation. It represents being in the river of life and flowing with it. Communication is the core of a blue essence. It transforms ideas from thoughts into concrete action, and provides insights into your journey and purpose. Blue indicates that the messages in you are valuable. Trust your inner voice and be assertive.

Brown	The colour of grounding and nourishment. Brown is the colour of those who set foundations and upon whose shoulders things are built. It also stands for the bridges that join ideas, things, and people together. Brown represents the smells of nature, of all entities on Earth, living and nonliving. Bring energy and momentum to your desire to connect and be connected.
Gold	The colour of richness and supremacy. Gold encompasses all the other colours, and as such, is for those who achieve extraordinary lives, attain breakthroughs, and guide others on their journeys. It indicates higher awareness and the power of knowledge.
Green	The colour of healing and softness. Green represents the smell of a fresh morning breeze or a garden in spring. It purifies all it touches, and gives life. It is the colour of air and all outdoor and environmental issues and pursuits. It represents renewal and harmony. Green may appear to be a weak colour, but it is not; even the soft touch of a hand or the healing tone of a word can have powerful, lasting effects.
Orange	The colour of vibration, joy, and life. Orange brings ideas and dreams into existence. It is the colour of creation of any kind, including sexual expression. It stands for happiness and freedom of thought. Be in tune with your creative nature.
Pink	The colour of love and tenderness. Pink is unconditional availability and joy; it means that you are open to give, and also open to receive. Pink is part of all the other colours—even though you may not see it—because love is part of everything.
Purple	The colour of wisdom, royalty, grace, and grandeur. Purple is majestic and deserving of good things. It opens the door between the physical and the nonphysical; it is the power to see beyond the constraints of the human mind.
Rainbow	Rainbow represents seeing many of the colours on this chart at once. It is the colour of playfulness, for child-like instances when innocence and total trust are needed. It reflects the inner child in you.
Red	The colour of power, aggression, and unstoppable energy, which can be used for both good and bad. Red is the colour of the driving force to build and to destroy. It represents passion and the need to be noticed and heard.

Silver	The colour that demands quickness of thought and action.
	Silver is for those who need to be guided by instinct and intuition more than by thorough analysis or understanding.
White	The colour of light and purity.
	White means that a person is close to transcendence; he doesn't have many more physical lives to live, as he has fulfilled all his purposes and can now help others without need of a physical body.
	It is the colour of an enlightened being.
Yellow	The colour of the courage to be yourself, no matter what the circumstances.
	Yellow is the colour that honours the essence of who you really are and gives you the strength to stand by it. It is the light of day shining constantly inside you, even through the night.
	Yellow is the warm feeling in your solar plexus that keeps you moving forward and makes you shine.

Refer to this list whenever you need better understanding of what the colours in your meditation are trying to convey to your conscious mind, as well as when you notice you have a marked inclination towards or distance from certain colours. Meditate on the meanings that are relevant to you and see if you can receive an expanded version that will guide you to align with your vibrations.

I'd like to share with you my experience of the colours meditation. I saw a background of darkness. Covering the black canvas was a shower of bubbles of purple light. They were various sizes, and slowly but continuously changed shape. I could feel myself being those purple shapes. The overall sensation was beautiful. I enjoyed the experience. During the meditation, I asked for clarity about what it all meant. This is what I received: "You see yourself as purple because of your psychic nature. Your essence is able to connect and channel spirit into this physical plane. The darkness you observe is the void in which all spirits reside. Beyond the void is the brightness of clear day. The light where all spirits converge and become one: God."

I hope you also experience wonderful sensations during this meditation, and that it helps you obtain greater understanding about yourself and the colours of your aura.

CHAPTER 7

We are Cells in this Universe

We are the cells of the universe. We are all part of the oneness of the universe. Let's use our imagination, one of our most powerful tools, to grasp this concept. Imagine that you are the whole universe; each one of the trillions of cells in your physical body makes up all the elements of the universe that is you. For your body to function well and be healthy, you need many different types of cells. Each of them sets its focus on fulfilling the purpose it was created for and working in harmony with all the other cells; thus, you thrive and enjoy health. Every cell has a place and a purpose in your body, and by means of a higher intelligence that coordinates them, the cells know and understand this fact; therefore, they function accordingly.

The cells in your foot might not be completely aware of the cells in your head—although they have certain awareness that there is something else besides them—but this neither hinders nor improves the performance of their jobs. The cells in your body perform their specific tasks every day, guided by an invisible force that runs and coordinates the body's functions. None of the cells feels more important than another. They function from an inner knowledge that they are all equally required for the perfect functioning of your body. Your cells have immense intelligence that makes them clever enough to know what job they are supposed to do without needing to question their existence or relevance; they fully trust in and connect with the universal force that drives them and gives them life and nourishment. Even the smallest of your cells knows it belongs to a greater consciousness that orchestrates the play. For that reason, your cells flow with the rhythm of life.

Now imagine yourself in the universe. Like cells, each one of us has a place and purpose in the unlimited universe. You are aware of the existence of other beings—people, animals, plants—but there is no need for you to compare the differences between you, nor to prove your worth. You are just as important and necessary as any other person or thing in the universe, and specifically on your planet. You are as perfect as the force that created you, and you are eternal just for being part of it. Each one of us has a place and purpose. Some might have a difficult time grasping this concept, but it is truth. Only by understanding and accepting this simple truth can you flow with life, knowing that the whole universe exists in harmonious perfection and constant evolution.

When cells are not functioning properly, perform under great strain, or come to turn against other cells, the body shows signs of illness or disease. These are physical signs of internal disharmony; the life force can no longer circulate easily due to clogs or blockages that interfere with the connection and communication of cells. Illness, discomfort, depression, and anxiety are some physical expressions of inner imbalance, that is, of your cells not being at ease with the flow of life.

This same scenario can be applied to us. When we are in harmony, when we walk in purpose, when we have direction, when we trust life, and when we seek love and peace, we are connected to the universal oneness that is guiding us, and therefore, we are flowing with life. However, when we go against the current, when we fight to be right, when we look for differences between us, when we act separately from the rest, when we need to prove our worthiness or superiority, and when we choose anything over happiness and love, we are off track. We are not fulfilling our purpose or working with the whole; we are temporarily lost.

Let's make the decision, today, to start flowing with life. Let's become consciously aware of who we are, and hold that awareness in our minds as we go throughout our days. Let's understand and acknowledge these truths:

- We are tiny cells in this infinite universe.
- We are as divine and powerful as the essence that created all.
- We each have an equally important place, purpose, and reason to exist.
- The intention of life should be to fulfil our purpose by just flowing with the current of life (there is no right or wrong way).
- Love holds everything together; by embedding love into everything we think, do, and are, we can live with purpose.
- We don't need to search for purpose because we already know what it is (just as the cells in our bodies know what they are meant to do); to get in touch with our purpose we need to become a "human being" more than a "human doing" by being more in touch with our inner being.

Let's feel joyous to be cells in this universe we share. Let's appreciate our lives and purposes, and appreciate all that surrounds us and co-exists with us. By doing so, we are contributing to the expansion of life, and working in harmony with the universal intelligence, God.

The Man and the Eagle Become One

The eagle sits on top of the mountain. The day is ending and the sky renders the last rays of light: just a few yellow patches scattered far away in the horizon. A cold mist is slowly covering the mountain peaks, but the eagle remains perched at the height of the mountain, waiting patiently for night to set in so it can freely soar into the infinite and become soul: powerful, unlimited, and eternal.

During the night, the soul breaks free from its physical boundaries and can spread its wings, wide and long, to travel to the far ends of the universe and converge with other souls. They share their learning, their experiences, and the joys that their physical lives provide them. Most importantly, in this liberated state they can be who they really are: infinite beings of light and love. At night, the soul is freed to be everything or nothing until the next day is born, and the soul must return to its human confines. Where do the souls go? They go back and forth in time; to live other lives; to heal; to gather knowledge; to spread knowledge from one place to another, from one being to another, from one soul to another. All of this happens concurrently. The same soul lives different experiences of life but has only one objective: to grow and evolve.

It's day once more, and the eagle flies in the vastness of a blue sky, among the clouds. Far below, the Earth is peaceful and beautiful in bright shades of greens, blues, and yellows. The eagle is fully engaged in its harmonious flight, its wings spread wide open, it dances with the air and fully enjoys the present moment; it is careless of the past and thoughtless of the future. From afar, it can see a narrow stream of water breaking up the scenery, and something else that grabs its attention. Slowly circling, the eagle starts to descend to the open fields, directing its flight towards the stream. As it gets closer, it can distinguish a man lying on the smooth grass by the stream, his hand playing with the clear water. Quietly, the eagle lands close by the man. It rests calmly on a low branch of a nearby tree and observes the man daydreaming.

The man is dreaming again of the land of freedom, where he is unrestricted, where he feels powerful, where he can be anything and everything he wants to be. The man doesn't want to wake up because he is bewitched by this land of dreams. He doesn't want to give up the unlimited power of freedom for the restrictive and sometimes depressing reality of his life. His fantasies give him great pleasure, making him feel whole, expansive, and well. He doesn't feel this way when he is in his real world. While lost in his visions, he is still aware of his surroundings. As such, he can sense that something has happened to alter the tranquillity of the place. This sensation wakes him from his snooze and brings him back to full awareness.

The eagle has left the tree and is now standing on the ground not far from the man. It looks attentively at him. The eagle wakes him from his slumber. Does it tell him something? Yes, it does indeed.

"It is time to wake up to life. The purpose of your physical life is to live it fully aware, being totally present. You need to wake up to life and make it like the one in your dreams. How can you accomplish that? By realising that you are the expression of the unlimited power of divine love and eternal matter, and your purpose is joy and happiness. By understanding that knowledge of the self, inner growth, and exposure to life experiences will not only bring you joy and happiness but will also give birth to new, expansive desires and dreams. Anything you can think of, you can create in your life. You need to believe in your power, and learn to command it. Your thoughts are the key to manifesting that power into physical reality. Your thoughts are creative and constantly create your experiences and your life, whether or not you like them, and whether or not you want them to. You can bring change just by focusing your thoughts on your desires. You are doing it already, in a very pleasurable manner, when you daydream, by making your thoughts into images.

"I cannot emphasise enough that by seeking and following the light, you will understand your divinity, your power, and your mission of love and happiness. Even when you see pain, death, and destruction, you will see that it is all part of the perfection of the creation of life. Suffering is only painful when you attach yourself to it and make it permanent. If you acknowledge it and then let it go, you are accepting and becoming part of the perfect process of life. Life is not meant to be a struggle. Life is meant to flow. Life is what you make of it with your thoughts. How do you know whether you are heading down the best pathway, in line with the purpose of joy and happiness? Observe how you feel. If your heart is singing, if there is always a smile on your face, if you have happy thoughts most of the time, if you feel grateful for what you have and for who you are, then you know you are walking the path of purpose. If you feel the opposite, then now, this precise moment, is the very best moment to start the change and straighten up the course of your journey.

"Find your light and start acting upon your power. You are God in the flesh. Do not feel bad or uneasy about accepting this truth. In the same manner that you accept your cells are your body because they are part of it, so must you accept that if you are part of the source, of the creative universal energy that created you, then you are that creative energy too. Accept your godlike nature and feel loved by the creator. It is not separateness that we look for, but union, wholeness, oneness. When you feel that you are less than God, that you are not powerful, that you cannot accept yourself as creator, you produce holes in the universal puzzle. Feel yourself as part of all; when you do this, you are powerful, healthy, strong, and committed. You become a manifestor of your purpose and of your life. Aim to feel good inside yourself and find the light within, to feel the source that lives in you, and then be free."

The man opens his eyes and sits up. He is astounded and shaken by what he heard in the eagle's whispers. He looks where he thought the eagle was standing, but—as he already knows—it is not there. It was there only in his dreams. As he ponders the words from his dream, he notices a light shining before him. The light is so intense that it forces him close his eyes. Squinting, he looks into the light, and in amazement, distinguishes the shape of the eagle, flying fast towards him. He knows he should feel fear, but he doesn't. He knows his instincts should make him run, but he doesn't feel an urge to go anywhere or do anything. On the contrary, he feels safe and trusting.

He remains sitting, trying to look at this blinding light from between his fingers, which cover his face. Then an impulse makes him remove his hand and openly face the light. His eyes are closed, but he knows that he doesn't need to see. He feels an amazing pull of energy in all directions, as though his body is growing, expanding. Suddenly, he feels a punch to his chest as the eagle flies straight into him to become part of his expression of life. The blinding light reduces to a small, glowing ball of light, making its way into his chest and filling him with awe. The light is now within him, he does not need to seek it any longer. They have found each other. He needs only to follow it and to honour it. The light will help him to walk and live with purpose, and in time, to guide others to do the same. He now understands the essence of his soul. He clearly recognises what he is made of; he knows and accepts without a doubt that he can be soul; he can become it while he lives his human life.

He stands up and feels taller, stronger, and healthier than he has ever felt before. Also, there is something wonderful about the way he feels. He feels special; he *is* special. He feels powerful—that power doesn't come from any physical aptitude, but from within the depths of his being. The power cannot be lost; it's his forever and always has been. However, he recognises that the power can be forgotten or suppressed, as it had been all this time up until a few moments ago. He hadn't known of his power, nor did he believe it, accept it, or trust it; he had been lost. But not anymore.

He will become the unique and divine expression of his power. From now on, he will ensure that he learns about the tools that are at his disposal, that he is deserving of, to walk on this wonderful planet as an eternal being having an expansive and evolving human experience. He has claimed what he really is: a divine expression of love. He is already on his journey.

CHAPTER 8

What is My Destination?

Today we will talk about destiny, destination, and purpose. People often question the existence of destiny or purpose in life. Many have doubts about it and believe destiny is just an excuse used to justify life situations; others wish to know about and be shown their destiny. Well, each human being certainly does have a destiny, which I prefer to call "destination," as well as a purpose. Destiny and purpose are often used synonymously; however, they have different meanings. *Destination* or destiny is where a soul is set upon going as part of its physical life experience. *Purpose* refers to who you are being, how you express yourself, and what you are doing while you are in the process of reaching that destination. Both destination and purpose complement each other and play together, hand in hand, in the process that you call life.

You are all here on a journey that will take you to many different places, but no matter how many places you go, there will always be a destination for you to ultimately arrive at. There is always a purposeful place that you must reach in your life. That place is the point of your existence. Yes, you were born with a destination to reach. The way you arrive at that destination is up to you. You have the free will to travel at your own pace and be guided by your own compass. Contrary to what many believe, the layout of that journey is not written out or predetermined; in fact, you write it as you travel along. You have infinite options for your journey. Your soul doesn't prefer one over another, nor doesn't approve or disapprove of your choices, nor judge turns as right or wrong, because the aim of your soul is to experience and expand through those experiences. *The only thing your soul wants from you is awareness of its existence; it wants you to connect with it and create experiences together.*

You can choose to ride the journey of life however you want. You do choose, all the time, whether you are aware of it or not. Even when you do not choose, when you do not take directed action, when you do not have driving desires, when you do not leave your comfort zone, when you do not form or voice your opinions, when you do not think about yourself, when you do not move—you are still exercising choice. Every time you do not choose, you are choosing by default. So then, why not choose the best possible ride? You can travel the easiest and most wonderful of roads by the power of your own conscious choice, which is the opposite of living by default. How? Being aware of and taking responsibility for the choices you make, learning valuable skills as you move forward in life, and using the helpful pointers provided in this book are some of the ways. On the other hand, you could also choose to travel without a map, following no particular direction and taking no advantage of your inner tools; you could choose by default and relinquish awareness. The outcome of this kind of choice will be a trip clouded by all sorts of delays, barriers, and unpleasant scenery.

Learning about who you are, connecting with your inner being, and finding about your purpose will set you in the right direction. Constant connection with your inner guidance will give you invaluable information on your life's journey. Trusting in your power to manifest how you want to travel will provide you with the means to have a perfect ride. Even before you were born into your human life, you had all you need to reach your destination in the most perfect and magnificent way, and to experience all that needs to be experienced by your spirit in human form. When the road gets difficult, painful, or even tragic, if you are connected to your soul, you will be able to access the support, love, and understanding you need to travel that part of the journey the way you intend.

If you are clear about your purpose, or at least have feeling you are walking with purpose, you will instinctively know where your destination is. As the director of your own life, you will choose to create whatever you need to achieve that goal. You can do it. You can do it! It is easy to see the stories of successful lives full of abundance and joyous experiences as examples of conscious, creative choice. However, it is not so easy to see the same conscious choices in the lives of those who, despite having experienced hardship, poverty, illness, defeat, and other tragic and devastating experiences in their lives, made the decision to make the most of what life gave them, and managed to reach their destinations with purpose and fulfilment. You can do the same. Of course you can. You need only to believe it. The people that you need, the places, the events, the circumstances, the resources—all can be manifested by the power within you. Set the intention to be a powerful creator of your life, and you will achieve it.

Don't not be held back by the worry that using your inner guidance and power to take the clearest, most empowering, and expanding way to reach your destination will make your life short because your purpose and destination have been fulfilled. Don't let your ego tell you wrong. Behind any purpose is the realisation of the effects of that purpose; within, there is always another, bigger purpose to determine and reach if so you desire.

You and only you are the one who eventually decides when you want to depart this human existence to go back to your light, the source. You will determine when it is time to return to your true form and replenish yourself to process and share your growth, to enjoy your expanded being until you desire again to have a new human life.

This is the joy of God, who gives us all the opportunity to experience life from many perspectives, many dimensions, and many points of view. Each expression of life allows us to discover and explore a different aspect of the source. You can be anything you desire to be. It is your choice.

Life is not just about reaching a destination and fulfilling a purpose. Life is about discovering yourself as you travel on your journey to reach that destination. Life is about clarifying your purposes, connecting with your inner being, learning to use and command your inner tools, being part of the whole, taking every experience as an opportunity to feel alive, and noticing the roads that constantly open up to you. Most importantly, it is about rejoicing in the abundance, beauty, and glory that greets you every day, with each new breath of life you take.

Happiness: The Ultimate Purpose

"Happiness is the meaning and the purpose of life, the whole aim and end of human existence."
                                                              —Aristotle

The ultimate purpose of life is to be happy. Many have expressed this truth in countless ways, and many more will continue to divulge it until there is complete acknowledgment of this universal truth. Happiness is very simple and much desired. The true journey is for you to discover what you have to do, who you have to become, and how you have to express your talents in order to achieve happiness.

It is everyone's underlying reason and silent desire to attain happiness that is usually masked by diverse situations and circumstances. In pursuit of some degree of happiness, you engage in all sorts of activities, undergo all kinds of emotions, interact with the most diverse of people, visit and live in the most extravagant and contrasting places, get involved in all type of experiences, and desire and acquire endless quantities of material possessions. Happiness is your driving force and your purpose, and you attain it through means that are unique to each human expression. Each person has his own definition of happiness, as well as his own experience of it. Each and every definition and expression of happiness is equally valid in the eyes of spirit.

You might wonder, if happiness is our purpose, our ultimate end, why are so many people on our planet unhappy? The answer is straightforward. It is so because you cannot understand or accept that you have such a simple purpose, that the beginning and end of your whole existence is just to achieve happiness by whichever avenue you choose. Then you go away, looking for other seemingly valid reasons for your existence, searching for other purposes, seeking to feel more complicated emotions that are actually lesser to happiness and usually bring misery, pain, illness, sadness, and heartache into your life. You tell yourself that life is meant to be difficult and painful, and furthermore, that happiness is only a matter of luck or a short-lived experience. As you convince yourself of this "reality," you see others with unhappy, unfulfilled lives. You find overwhelming examples in the daily news, your neighbourhood, your family, your work, your friends and acquaintances, even yourself, that confirm your "reality." Then, you cannot help but believe that it is fact.

The reason why you find happiness so elusive or short-lived is because you set your sights on the outcome of whatever you believe will provide you with that happiness. When that outcome is not as you envisaged, you feel unhappy. The term "unhappy" is used to encompass a whole range of emotions that are antonyms of happiness. Dissatisfaction, disillusionment, disappointment, sadness, discontent, frustration, annoyance, anger, jealousy, and confusion are just a few on the list. You know them all. When you expect happiness as an outcome to be provided by something or someone outside of yourself, you are completely missing the point. Happiness doesn't await you somewhere, but greets you along the way. Happiness shows itself on every step of the journey. As I said before: Even in the darkest night, there is always light.

By now, you will have realised that fear, doubt, anger, frustration, pain, jealousy, hate, worry, loneliness, sadness, illness, and all other lesser emotions will not serve you in your objective to achieve happiness. Moreover, when constantly experienced, they bring about only the kinds of actions and reactions that lead you away from living with purpose. Being weak will not bring you happiness; nor will feelings of disempowerment or inferiority. Ignoring or hiding these weakened states of being is not a good way of dealing with them, either, since they exist for a reason. They are meant to be wake-up calls to make you take charge of your life situations and make new choices to readjust your direction.

Not until you embark on your journey of light will you finally see that your "truth" about life is not reality. When you begin to walk with purpose, renewed awareness, and understanding, you will find happiness and gratitude in every moment of life, not as a result of some sort. Moreover, with your light ignited inside you, you will start building your power to inspire others to follow suit. Happiness lifts up your life, which becomes less heavy and brighter because light shines upon it. The universe offers you an abundance of opportunities to experience the feeling of happiness. Even during challenging times, you will always find a helping hand, a warm hug, or a kind word to bring peace and comfort to your heart, if you take notice of them. Do not overlook these opportunities any more. Do not dismiss them any longer. Start noticing them more and you will soon be able to appreciate a difference in your life.

Happiness is best experienced through creative ventures, since you are creative beings. Your creativity originates in your inner being, is communicated to your thoughts, and then is translated and exposed through your actions, words, and emotions. Therefore, a great way to experience happiness is to explore your creative talents and gifts. As good as life is to offer you infinite ways of enjoying happiness, you are ultimately the one who creates and attracts your own opportunities for happiness. This is an important point we want you to understand: if you see yourself as a powerful, creative being who chooses to be happy, then you can create a world—your world—that will provide you with everything you need to achieve that feeling of happiness.

Searching for Happiness vs. Choosing to Be Happy

It is important to highlight that there is a big difference between searching for happiness and choosing to be happy. Pursuing happiness is going about life the hard way, viewing happiness as something that comes from outside yourself: money, relationships, jobs, physical appearance, environment. Maintaining all that structure drains your energy and peace; you will always have an underlying fear that if anything is lost or taken away from you, your happiness will be affected in a negative way.

However, choosing happiness is easier and simpler to do because it comes from within; you can control your choice, work it into your life, take it with you wherever you go, and expand it as much as you desire. Even though the conditions of your life can greatly help or hinder your approach to happiness, the power to choose how happy you want to be is still within you. The choice doesn't depend on anything except you—that is much easier to handle, don't you agree? Do not search for happiness, but choose to be happy instead.

Start building your world of happiness today. What does it look like? What are you doing in your happy world? Who are you sharing it with? What scenery do you travel through on your happy ride? Start living in empowerment to reach your potential as the creator of your life.

Ten Steps to a Purposeful Life

How do you do it; how do you start walking in purpose? How do you experience happiness, no matter what? You can walk with purpose and thus enjoy happiness on the journey of your life by following this guidance:

1. *Acknowledge that your thoughts are creative* and that you create through thinking of what you desire, as well as what you do not.
2. *Transform the way you think* by devoting the majority of your thoughts to things that make you feel good and bring about positive emotions. Even in challenging situations, you can choose to think positive and proactive thoughts, thus creating your world from an optimistic and brighter point of view.

3. *Transform the way you express yourself* through your words, actions, and emotions to reflect the more positive, empowering, and happy self you truly are.

4. *Do not dismiss unhappy feelings or emotions*, as they are your wake-up calls to start looking for more empowering choices.

5. *Persevere with this new way of creating and expressing yourself.* Even when you do not see apparent results, transformation is happening within you. Delays are caused by the interference of your ego, which wants to keep you focused on the so-called reality of life.

6. *Do not get attached to certain outcomes or get hung up waiting for results;* instead, trust your inner knowledge and feelings that tell you that all you desire is here and now.

7. *Find constant ways to grow and express yourself.* Never stop wanting to become more than you are, and never stop showing the world the godly light that you are.

8. *Fill your body with life.* Love and take care of yourself by nurturing your mind, your physical body, and your inner being. Start each day by breathing in the divine life force that Mother Earth offers you. Let it fill your body and reach all your cells, and feel cleansed and whole. End each day by exhaling anything that doesn't serve you; let it be carried away from you so you can enjoy a peaceful and healing sleep.

9. *Be grateful and full of wonder* for all the amazing things that life gives you for free, which are also the main contributors to happiness.

10. *Feel purposeful and walk the path of light.* Set the intention to be consciously alive and connected to the energy of the Earth. Acknowledge that you are part of the energy, dancing with the rhythm of all life, both physical and nonphysical.

"My Happy Life" Exercise

All of us want to be happy. This book is the result of my seeking to restore happiness to my life. However, even though we all want to be happy, we usually struggle when we are asked to define what happiness means to us. How can we create something in our lives if we don't know what we want to create—what it looks like, feels like, smells like? I invite you to engage in the following activity, which is fun and will make you feel great.

Have you ever taken the time to think or dream about your life as a happy one? If you are not living a happy life, then I can assume the answer is no. If you are happily cruising through it, or you feel your life is okay, then you can strive for more. Doing this exercise should present you with new ideas.

When we think about a happy life, usually the first thought that comes to mind is having lots of money. If that is true for you, perhaps you would like to take a closer look at the wealthy people you admire. There is no doubt that money can bring happiness by making life easier, more comfortable, and more secure. However, a quick look into the lives of the rich and famous shows us that these supposedly fortunate people are not always as happy as we presume. Furthermore, many of them are miserable, lonely, depressed, fearful, have low self-esteem, and are even ill. But this is your exercise: by the power of your free will, you choose to have money in your happy life. Therefore, money is ticked off. The same applies to all the material possessions that you would like to have. House—ticked, car—ticked, clothes—ticked, holiday trips—ticked, this—ticked, that—ticked, those—ticked, and ticked, and one more tick. You have it all in your happy life. Now, what else?

———————————————————●

Now that all your material needs have been taken care of, take some time to think about what brings you happiness from within; think about what no one can take away from you, that you cannot lose, that you cannot waste, that you can always have access to. It helps to go back in time and see yourself as a kid again. Think about your happy life from your inner child's perspective. I guarantee that you will not have any problems coming up with ideas about how to have fun and laugh more, where to discover new things, and how to express your creative talents to feel joyous and alive. Use your imagination and think as a child does, with no restrictions or boundaries. What are you doing? What do you look like? Who is with you, sharing your happy life? Where do you live? What do you strive for? How do you feel? How is your health? How are your relationships? What are you hobbies? What places are you travelling to? What new skills are you learning? Do not think about the current state of your life now; just think about how you would like it to be.

After you spend a few minutes thinking and daydreaming about all that makes you happy, you will find yourself engulfed by waves of good feelings. You will feel refreshed, enthusiastic, hopeful, eager, even driven. In the midst of all these great sensations, ask yourself this question: what can I start doing today to move in the direction of my happy life? I'm sure there is something, even one tiny thing that you can start doing today to start shifting directions.

Let me give you some suggestions:

- Get active; take the stairs instead of the lift at work, start a walking routine, or join a gym.
- Set aside time to pursue a creative activity that you've always wanted to do; enrol in a course.
- Take cooking lessons and meet new people; get some cookbooks to prepare healthier meals and buy fewer take-aways.
- Refresh your environment; throw out the old to declutter your home, create more space, and allow the new to come in.
- Bring nature into your home; spend more time in the garden because being outdoors in nature makes you feel good.

- Save your pocket change; think of creative ways you could improve your savings for the achievement of a specific goal.
- Plan a holiday; it could be as close as your local beach or as far as an overseas adventure.
- Get in touch with someone with whom you haven't talked for a long time and would love to hear from.
- Learn something completely new and out of your comfort zone to boost to your self-esteem and show you your unlimited potential.
- Learn and practise relaxation techniques to reduce stress and calm yourself.
- Learn and practise meditation to start connecting with your inner self.
- Clarify and heal your relationships, especially the one with yourself.
- Get interested in life, people, and places; visit the library, museums, and other places of interest to see what you discover.
- Do service for others; volunteer, give away items, donate to a charity, offer help to someone in need.
- Take some "me" time; do something for yourself just for the sake of doing it.
- Spend some time with children and the elderly—they will show you how to laugh.
- Smile more often; you will soon discover that life smiles back at you.
- Consider doing something that requires a lot of courage, such as going back to university, moving to another state or country, or expressing your feelings to the person you love.
- Your heart knows what makes you happy; listen to your heart and let it guide you.

It doesn't matter if what you do today feels like a tiny speck of sand in the desert. What matters is that you start choosing a direction, a new road to take you closer to happiness. Once you choose, you have to keep on going. Where to? Well, as you follow the chosen path, the next step will reveal itself to you. Do not give up after the euphoria of the beginning fades. Remember that your ego will try with all its might to stop you. If you do continue, you will have a surprising realisation. Not only will you find happiness at the end of the journey, you will find happiness along the way as well when you are true to your dreams and to yourself. I hope that you enjoy doing this exercise, and that it gives you the incentive to start doing something today, now, even if all you do is set the intention to choose something new for yourself.

CHAPTER 9

Soul Partnership

Your inner voice constantly speaks to you with love, understanding, and guidance. With intention and practice, you can learn to recognise the way it sounds and feels inside you. The voice of your soul is warm, encouraging, supportive, and loving. It never criticises, judges, pushes, diminishes, or lets you down. It is always there inside of you, waiting to assist you with your endeavours and challenges. Once you become accustomed to recognising and trusting this voice, you will learn to quiet the other very different voice in you, that of the ego. This voice is the constant chatter in your head that wants to drive your life and is the complete opposite to the voice of your soul. Once you have experienced the voice of your soul, you will be able to easily identify when the ego is trying to fill you with its empty words.

Successful acknowledgment of your true voice is a joyous event in your life's journey, because it signals a very important milestone. It marks the consolidation and reaffirmation of a relationship that was created at the time of your physical birth: your partnership with your soul. Your soul partnership is the most important of all the relationships in your physical life. This is something that we cannot emphasise strongly enough; unfortunately, people's relationships with themselves are most often the ones that are relegated, forgotten, and misunderstood. But as you read this book, you are learning to give your soul partnership the importance it deserves. In return, this unique relationship will flood you with many gifts, such as a sense of purpose, feelings of joy, and inner peace.

Please, don't let the voice of your soul be drowned by your everyday endeavours. Each day, set aside a few minutes to have a conversation with your soul; check if you are on track, exchange ideas, and see how you are both journeying. This is a holy partnership. Your soul cannot achieve its purpose without your cooperation, total trust, and attention; neither can you have a complete and fulfilling life if you don't live it from your soul's perspective in a purposeful way.

When you live in isolation, disconnected from your soul, you experience life detached from the whole that you are part of. This way of living disrupts the free flow of universal energy to you, through you, and from you to everything else. Your dance with life loses its harmony and its glow, and no matter what kind of life you live, it will never be as happy, joyous, or enlightened as it was meant to have been. When you live in isolation, you are a diminished version of yourself. You are not accessing your true potential, that is, the immense power that is behind you, supporting you, and waiting to be tapped into. Please, honour your relationship with your soul; nurture it, respect it, love it, and rejoice in it. Live each day from the heart of your true, divine self, and see the difference it makes, not only in your own life, but also in the lives of those you come into contact with and those you don't.

Remember this: you never walk alone. Spirit is always by your side, waiting to be asked for help, yearning to assist, and brimming with wisdom and knowledge to share with you. Spirit is always with you, embracing each and every step of your path to make your life flow harmoniously through all the experiences you came here to live. Spirit is always with you, even when you ignore it. When you finally accept and understand this truth, you will open the doors for your soul to show itself. You will become less fearful as you accept and feel unconditional love for the power that supports you. You will find the way to summon courage and excitement to face any situation that life throws at you, even the challenging ones, knowing that at any moment you can go within and find all the compassion and strength you need to keep on going.

You will never feel alone or lonely. You will find the joy and power to live your life to the fullest, with purpose and in unison with the universal dance of the divine. Start today: reconnect with your soul, reignite your partnership with your inner being, live with purpose.

Ask Your Intuition about Purpose

Your inner voice is constantly guiding you through your everyday life; it knows your bigger purpose and destination. However, this communication usually goes one way. Your guidance speaks to you, but is not heard, or sometimes, you ask, but cannot hear the answers. As you strengthen your relationship with your soul, communication will become more harmonious and turn into a two-way conversation; you will ask and be able to hear the answers. This stage is what we call "developing the intuition." It means connecting with your inner voice, your inner being, your inner guidance, or your inner wisdom.

As the channels of communication become clearer, you will find yourself more relaxed and comfortable about seeking direction and assistance from the voice of your intuition. You can ask about anything: your concerns, the next step of your life path, some confusion, or even the outcome of a given situation. Your inner voice imparts its guidance in diverse and creative ways. During meditation, it communicates through combinations of images, symbols, voices, words, sounds, colours, and sensations. Outside of meditation, it communicates via myriad elements from the world around you, such as songs, books, conversations, signs, numbers, people, events, and so on. It also speaks to you through your dreams and physical sensations. Every individual will have particular ease in receiving messages one way over others; one person may be more visual, another may hear messages with more clarity, and yet another may be more apt to spot and interpret signs. Whichever method is easiest for you, each time you intend to communicate with your soul, a channel opens for that communication to happen. Therefore, when you ask for guidance, your request is *always* honoured.

However, there may be times when you don't seem to receive any messages, and perhaps feel that your soul is not helping you. Interference in communication is never due to your soul's lack of response, but to blockages and delays on your end. The most common reasons for this to happen are

- You are putting too much effort into the process, which hinders your ability to receive. This is a normal occurrence when you are still getting familiar with two-way conversations with your inner being.
- Your expectations about the answers you seek make you overlook or miss the real message.
- You are not ready to know what you are asking about.
- Your ego is sabotaging the communication.

Regardless of the reason, it is always good practice to remove any blockages in your energy before asking for guidance. One way to do this is by clearing your chakras with the technique provided in Chapter 6.

As you develop your intuition, you will gradually become more in tune with the dynamics of the process. As time goes on, you will be able to receive answers with ease and complete trust. You will also develop a knowledge of when you should ask for guidance and when you should wait for the events of life to unfold. If for any reason you feel that you are not yet ready to learn the details of the guidance you are seeking (for example, concerning matters of health), then it is better to focus on some other issue. Your soul knows what is best for you; it will never give you information that can upset you, confuse you, or make you fearful or worried about what is to come. Your soul will never bring chaos to your present life situation.

Listen to the Physical Signs

Your inner guidance is a powerful tool you have at your disposal. Use it wisely to find out about your direction in life. Powerful questions you can ask are

- Am I in the right place?
- Am I doing what I am meant to be doing?
- Am I employing my energy in the way that is most beneficial to me and the whole?
- Am I with the type of people who encourage my growth?
- Am I being the best I could be at this time?
- Am I making the best choices?

Even if you think you know the answers to all these questions, it is highly valuable to verify them with your inner guidance. More often than not, the answers you think you already have are just your ego telling you about your story and your reality. One way to know who you are listening to and whether you are going off course or are on the right track is to paying attention to how your body feels. Have you noticed odd sensations popping up here and there, or do you feel amazing and full of vitality? Any signs of imbalance in your body, from tightening of the throat, chest pains, heaviness in the stomach, anxiety, or fatigue, to severe illnesses, are means for your inner being to let you know that you are disconnected and not in tune with its guidance. At the beginning, these warning signs are mild, so they tend to go unnoticed or ignored. Only when you have developed an enhanced awareness of the self will you become immediately attentive to any uneasiness in your body and seek additional inner guidance.

If the symptoms persist and are not addressed, then with time, they will become louder and larger. It's fine to look for external ways of treating them; however, you need only look within to find their true cause. If you allow it to, the ego will convince you that there is nothing to address by masking your uneasiness with labels such as stress, fatigue, boredom, worry, loneliness, disconnection, and overactivity, to name a few. Too often, people unconsciously accept the ego's explanations and engage in all sorts of action to mute what they are feeling. This behaviour will be either futile or yield short-lived results.

The soul is persistent, and its nagging can also be experienced as dissatisfaction, unhappiness, discontent, disconnection, lack of purpose or meaning in life, lack of direction, unloving feelings towards the self or others, ungratefulness, or lack of appreciation. These feelings all create different degrees of confusion and upheaval in an individual's life, especially for those who seem to have a perfect life. Too often, we hear comments like these:

"I have everything that should make me happy, but I am not."

"I want to feel happy and content, but I don't know how."

"I feel that I am not doing what I am supposed to do, but I don't know what I should be doing."

"I have a constant feeling that I am not being myself."

"I don't know what my purpose is. I wish I knew."

Until you realise that the soul has a voice and is trying to communicate with you, the issues will continue to pile up; they will not go away. The very reason you experience those issues is that you are ready to go back on track and move forward. Sometimes, the soul gives you a respite and lets your inner feelings of uneasiness go quiet for a while. This truce allows you to settle down, to assess the situation you are experiencing, and to become a little more attentive to your essence. However, breaks like this don't usually last for long. The inner nagging will not disappear, but keep on resurfacing until it is fully addressed.

CHAPTER 10

The River of Life

The river is flowing down the mountains like a serpent, wiggling its way forward. The water is clear and fresh, producing a musical sound as it runs over the riverbed. The man is in the river, enjoying the delicious pleasure of bathing himself in this wonderful gift from nature. He is lying on his back, floating in the water, enjoying the warmth of the sun falling all over his body. His eyes are closed but he can sense the intensity of the sun's light painting his closed eyelids red. His arms are extended at his sides and his legs are spread apart.

He is letting himself go, gently drifting in the current, which cradles him in the slow-moving water. He does not worry about where he is being taken or what he has left behind. He has all he needs right here, right now, in this precise moment. He feels peaceful, serene and whole. He trusts that wherever the river takes him it is where he needs to go. He is enjoying the smooth ride with its turns and small ripples. He is relaxed and free of all thought; his mind is totally clear and at ease. His body behaves as if it were made of water, part of the river itself.

After a while, he opens his eyes and sees a beautiful place with tall, old trees surrounding the riverbanks. He swims to the riverbank, comes out of the water and lies down on the grass. *What an amazing place this is*, he thinks. He fills his lungs with fresh air, conscious of his action, and he feels light and refreshed. He caresses the soft grass, feeling it between his fingers while admiring the blue of the sky and observing the shapes of the clouds witnessing this delicious moment.

Now, for no reason and without hesitation, he gets to his feet and starts walking along a path through the trees. He is excited as to where it will lead him. As he walks along, he touches the tree trunks with open hands, as though leaving a trail to mark that he has been there—although he senses that he will never come back to this place again. He will never live these moments again. And he is happy, at peace, and connected to life. The man is flowing with life.

The Flow of Life

In every stream, in every river, the flowing water more often than not encounters obstacles: branches, rocks, even rubbish polluting it. However, the water juggles those obstacles and keeps on flowing. It doesn't stop, it doesn't stay stuck, it doesn't go backwards or upstream; it just keeps on going forward, sometimes calmly, other times quickly. Your life is the same. It is a fact that you will find obstacles as you go along in life. Nevertheless, you will continue to flow forward. The obstacles may make you stop, observe, question, evaluate, change direction, or delay, but you will still flow forward. Life never stops flowing; nor does it ever go backwards. Sometimes the flow will become easier, smoother; some other times it will be rough and fast in uninterrupted movement. Regardless of the pace of the flow, learn not to make obstacles a major concern. Instead, accept them, encounter them, jump over them, see what you can learn from them, and then keep on flowing. When you stop resisting and go trustingly with the current, you will discover that life takes care of you. Your ride will become the inspired journey that it is meant to be.

Life is like a river. If you let it take you on its ride without resistance, but trust, it will always carry you to the places you need to go, while nourishing you along the way. Most of your frustrations and blockages arise from your resistance to flow, from allowing your ego to guide you instead of trusting your soul to show you the way. Each one of you has a unique river of life mapped out by the soul. You are immersed in this river since the moment you are born into this world. When you allow life to be your guide, when you follow your soul's directions, you put complete and total trust into that river and travel in purposeful movement and flow. You will go wherever you need to go, you will stop wherever you need to stop, and when you need to do so, you will continue onwards without interference, doubt, or fear, but with love, trust, ease, and knowledge. You are not guaranteed a perfect life, but you are guaranteed the kind of life that your soul chooses to experience during its time in this human expression: you.

However, people often decide to map out their lives by themselves, because that is what they think they are supposed to do. "It is my life and I'll live it as I wish," they claim. Then, they go through life struggling to find their way through obstacles and barriers, amongst temporary successes and out-of-reach victories, crawling along day after day to try to reach somewhere. At some point, they finally realise that they will never get "there," despite all the struggle, all the ups and downs, all the effort. They will never be truly happy, nor satisfied, nor fulfilled. This is because they set out on their trip carrying the wrong tools, reading the wrong maps, without a compass or clear destination or pointers that indicate direction. They have a false assumption that they need to do everything on their own, without any help or guidance. The truth is, the only thing you need to do is show up, listen, ask, trust, and most importantly, to enjoy the ride, wherever it takes you. Know with certainty that your soul will always lead you to the right places, with the right people and at the right time.

Let's stop resisting life and instead, embrace it from the heart. Sit still and listen to your soul and the directions it gives you. Trust in your guidance, your intuition. If you feel unsure about anything, ask about it as many times as you need to feel comfortable enough to follow your guidance. Life is not meant to be a struggle. It is not a race, nor any other kind of competition. Anyone, everyone can lead a purposeful life. Life is meant to be joyous, to offer amazing opportunities to feel happiness, gratitude, awe, and glory. Life is also meant to empower you by offering you challenging times (and you will encounter many of those in life) from which you can grow and advance to new levels of personal evolution.

Happiness is not striving for a perfect life, nor seeing it through rose-tinted glasses. On the contrary, happiness is accepting all experiences: the joyous ones that make your heart swell with love and laughter, as well as the ones that shrink it with fear and heartache. You cannot grow if your ride is always smooth. You cannot know your power if you haven't got a chance to summon it. You cannot appreciate success if you haven't been presented with the opportunity to go for it.

Meditation: The River of Life

Allow yourself to flow with life. Any time you feel stuck, blocked, frustrated, or upset, know that if you continue in this way, it will only make the situation worse. The nagging feeling inside of you will not go away; it will only get louder and louder, calling for your attention. The best course of action is to take a few minutes to quiet your mind.

———————————————•

Sit or lie down in a tranquil place where you can switch off from the world around you.

Take a few deep breaths and relax your body.

When you are in a state of peaceful connection with your inner voice, picture yourself floating in the river of life. Feel yourself drifting, gently being taken downstream by the water, which runs all along your body. Listen to the sounds of the water flowing smoothly. Allow the sound to hypnotise you.

As you relax into the experience, ask yourself the following questions. "What do I do now?" "Where are you taking me?" "What do I need to know?" Ask any other question relevant to your present situation. Expect a response. Trust you will get an answer; be open to the communication.

Now see yourself emerging from the river and walking into a place, situation, or experience that reflects the next step to take regarding your questions. What do you see? What do you feel? What do you hear? Who do you meet? If you do not see anything, pay attention to words, sounds, feelings, or any other sign that comes up.

When you are ready, come out of the meditation.

———————————————

Write down in your journal any message or information that you receive. If nothing happened, do not feel let down or disappointed. The exercise has already fulfilled one of its objectives of relaxing you and making you direct your focus to your inner world.

You can and must practice this meditation when you wish to get some direction on any aspect of your journey, just as you would if you were visiting an unfamiliar location and needed help with your map. In this instance, the unfamiliar location is your life's next destination, and your map is your soul's guidance. Stop going upstream. Start floating—trustingly, effortlessly—down the river of life.

PART III

Inner Tool Kit:
Our Powers

The divine power that was given to us the day we were born can be described by a set of inner qualities whose only purpose is to assist, facilitate, and enrich life's journey. These qualities, which I call the "inner tool kit," are available to every one of us. However, only a minority of people are consciously awakened to their true existence and choose to use these invaluable tools during their transit through this physical expression. The rest, by choosing not to explore or learn about themselves, leave that immense power untapped and dormant.

These inner qualities are unique to human beings and set us apart from any other living entity on the planet. They are responsible for transforming our journeys from ordinary into extraordinary experiences. Imagine a painter with great resources at his disposal: canvases, brushes, paints, techniques, books, masters to learn from, and his desire to express himself. If he doesn't take the time to learn to use what is available to him, if he doesn't have determination to explore and exploit his tools, if he doesn't believe that he can create beauty through his paintings, then regardless of the quality of his resources, he will not produce the amazing art that he has the potential to create. However, taking the time to learn and explore, trusting and following his desire to paint, and deciding to seek expression through his art will make an enormous difference in his artistic creation. The way he applies his acquired and inner knowledge, the way he conveys his feelings with his paintings, and the way he employs the resources available to him all combine with an unrestricted partnership to his soul to transform simple paintings into masterpieces.

This is exactly what you can do with your inner tool kit. By discovering and learning about your powers, and using them wisely with full awareness and confidence, you can create a masterpiece of your life. The secret to our powers is not in knowing how to use them; we already possess that knowledge, as it is inherent to our inner being. We have all used our powers at various points in our lives, usually without realising that a special kind of magic was at play. For example, who hasn't

- Had a lucky break after following a hunch or after the voice of intuition guided us to act?
- Felt his heart expand when greeted by the smile of a child, or felt warmth all over while holding a baby? These are both clear expressions of the power of love.
- Played with visions of his dreams in his mind to see them later become real?
- Thought with positive and undivided intention of something that later became manifest in his life?
- Trusted a belief that helped him commit to following a dream, despite how crazy it seemed?
- Fell head over hills in love with someone for no apparent reason other than because it felt amazing?
- Attracted, like a magnet, good or bad experiences?
- Felt the urge to do something completely out of character, and later realised he has conquered a fear?
- Had a sudden desire to help a stranger selflessly?

I am sure you identified with one or more of the above examples, and could add many more to the list. I am also sure that each time those events happened in your life, you didn't give them a second thought, or recognised them as arising from your own creation. But they did, every one of them. The great news is that you don't need to wait for any of these events to "accidentally" happen in order to start experiencing amazing magical moments. You have the ability within yourself to shape your life the way you envision it by using your inner tool kit; you can command, use, and trust your powers.

So then, the big secret is not that we possess these powers—we have had them since the day we were born—nor how to use them—we instinctively and unconsciously use our powers all the time. The big secret is simply that we must *acknowledge* the existence of our powers, *accept* and *welcome* them as a gift from God to us, and *integrate* them gratefully into our lives. We do all of the above by using our powers with *full awareness* of what we are and what we can do, with *consistency* to strengthen and ingrain them, and absolute *trust*.

Become familiar with the words italicized above, because they are the keys that will open the door to your powers: *acknowledge, accept, welcome, integrate, awareness, consistency, and trust*. Engrave them on your mind and on your heart.

The Nine Powers

Our inner tool kit consists of the following nine powers:

1. The power within: the knowing
2. The power of inner guidance: the hearing
3. The power of love: the being
4. The power of intention: the desires
5. The power of visualization: the seeing
6. The power of focus and thought: the creating
7. The power of manifestation: the outcome
8. The power of self-drive: the forces
9. The power of perseverance: the belief

The sections that follow describe these powers and provide you with practical ways in which you can incorporate and apply them to your life. If you are just awakening to your powers, be joyous and grateful for this new beginning. Choose any power you feel guided to. It could be the one that spoke to you the loudest after you read this list. Or, you could start with the first one. If you are already consciously using one or more of your powers, then aim to develop the ones you are not familiar with yet. And remember that even when you think you know a lot about something, there is always room for improvement and growth. You can always expand your abilities even further, because that is what life is all about: a succession of stepping stones that lead us to personal greatness.

Once you have chosen a power, start becoming familiar with it. Read the notes relevant to that power and reflect on what they mean and what your understanding is. Practice the exercises; write in your journal about how you feel, what you think, what you are accomplishing, and how that power is manifesting in your life. Until you feel the chosen power is working within you, and you know that you have learnt its essence, do not move on to the next power.

Some powers will be easier to integrate into your life than others; this will vary from person to person. Make sure you do not rush the process. Be patient and take the time you need to understand and become aware of each power by exploring how it works within you. Enjoy this process of discovering yourself by knowing that you are opening your eyes to who you really are, as well as building a relationship with your soul.

As you progress in this journey, you will feel empowered, be in more control of your life, and see the evidence of its magic enhancing your experiences in ways that you never imagined. These powers are our birthright. They are at our disposal, waiting to be discovered and exploited to shape life however we choose. It is my wish that by becoming aware of, learning, and mastering your inner tool kit, you will stop going through your days unaware of the immense powers you possess, and start directing your life in the direction of your dreams.

CHAPTER 11

The Power Within:
The Knowing

This power represents *the knowing*: the invisible sensation in your being that makes your soul known to you. You are a divine being with a physical form. However, maybe before this moment you thought you were a physical form only; or thought, with some doubt, that you were made of something else that you could not fully understand; or firmly believed you were some form of spiritual being living inside your human being.

Now you are openly and plainly learning that there is a divine component of yourself that is not outside of you. On the contrary, this divine component is within all of you. Its power is within all of you. It connects all of you into one big, infinite being. The better you comprehend this concept, the more you acknowledge it, the more you feel this divine component within you, the more you will start living from its perspective. As a result, your life will start going the way you envision it. I cannot repeat this enough times: act from your divine perspective and enjoy your life through your physical rewards. This is the reason you were given a physical form, after all, was to be able to feel with your senses the achievements of your powerful being.

This book was written thanks to belief in your divine nature. Otherwise, it would not have been possible for the physical and nonphysical to establish a connection of acceptance and trust. You can expand this belief to other areas of your life, not only to connecting with your soul or spirit guides, but also to other life achievements or pursuits. There are no limits to what you can create. The world you desire can exist—go and build it.

Invoking the Power Within

If you were to choose only one of your powers to explore and utilise, then the power within yourself is all you need to gain momentum and start moving the wheels of your journey to self-discovery and inner knowledge. There is *nothing* that cannot be accomplished, *nothing* that is impossible when you summon your power within. How do you invoke that power? By taking the following steps:

1. Believe

Above all, you need to believe that this enormous power exists within you. You need to accept the concept that you have godlike power, that you are a creative entity. Unless you master this step, no amount of reading, studying, or self-growth will help you to change your perspective from outside-in to inside-out. Your power is your tool for working on all your masterpieces. If you don't believe in it, how can you create?

This step can take as long as you need. It could happen in an instant, during a critical event or a turning point; you might suddenly drop all your barriers and surrender to your source in such a way that this belief emerges with a force that hits you full-on. Alternatively, it could take years—even your whole life—depending on your readiness to accept, your resistance, your amount of faith, and your intention to believe that such a power is part of you.

Acceptance and willingness to accept are good starting points for moving in the direction of belief.

2. Feel

Once you truly, deeply believe in your power, you need to learn to feel it. Place your hand on your solar plexus and search for a unique sensation in this area of your body. Move your hand around, searching for signs of your power. Listen with your hand. Do not doubt, do not assume you are imagining things. If you believe in your inner power, it will want to show itself to you.

Once you have found the place, rest your open palm on it and discover how your inner power feels. Learn to recognise it. The sensation will differ from person to person. It could feel like mild palpitations, a feeling of pressure or fullness, a tickle or an itch, a warm sensation, or just a sense of knowing. Once you recognise the seat of your power in your body, it will always be found there.

3. Connect

Make it a routine to connect with your inner power at least once a day in order to acknowledge it and become accustomed to its existence within you. It is easy to forget or ignore something when it cannot be seen. Take the example of your body. All your internal and external parts exist and function without you being consciously aware of them. Regardless of your attention or lack of it, they fulfil their purpose and enable you to be alive. However, when you focus your awareness on any given part, such as your beating heart or the rise and fall of your lungs, you connect with it, and you might discover sensations that go unnoticed when you overlook the existence of those internal parts.

A similar concept applies to your inner power, except with a slight difference. Your power exists within you and is located in your solar plexus; however, in order to fulfil its purpose, this power requires you to be fully aware of its existence. Your power works at its peak when you consciously acknowledge and summon it.

4. Apply

Start using your power: listen to it, feel it, follow it, question it, seek it, trust it. Above all, love it; this power is, like the power of your source, a small piece of God beating within you. For the great majority, this power is dormant or underutilised. It's only awakened in moments of extreme change or need, in situations in which you are capable of acts and accomplishments that you can't explain—situations in which you are pushed to critical points, outside the boundaries of comfort. In those times, you lower your resistance and surrender to the flow of the events taking place in your life. It is in precisely these moments that you open up to your inner power.

You don't need to wait until such circumstances occur in your life. You can learn to tap into the power within at any time, and then you can work miracles. Your life can head in the direction of your desires. You can heal your health and your relationships, enjoy the blessing of loving friends, bring harmony where you thought it was impossible, work on something that fulfils you, and gain the abundance you have always wanted, as well as the time to enjoy it. In other words, you can have a glorious and magnificent life if you can just conceive of it and accept it.

This power is your birthright, given to assist you on the journey of your human experience. Your soul is constricted by human limitations *only* when it cannot access and express its power. Once you get familiar with your power, you will be able to access it any way you may require. It can be used as fuel for added energy and stamina, as an ideas generator, as a guide and illuminator, as a hunch provider, as a faithful friend during your lonely hours, as a sincere counsellor, as a source of healing, or as God's words speaking to you. Your power represents everything and everyone you need in this life to fulfil your purpose and reach your destination. It is for this reason that we constantly emphasise that you need only look within, and your truth will be revealed. *All you need is you, and in you.* The world you live in provides you with the stage to put your desires into practice. See the world as your playground and see your power as your master guide and enabler. Go now, and start living an empowered life.

How Inner Power Feels

I am in another of my meditations. I see myself walking along the beach, peaceful and relaxed. However, in this particular instance, instead of following the usual path through the forest on my way to the temple, I continue walking along the beach. Slowly the scenery changes, and the beach turns into a tunnel within the forest. The tunnel is made of an entanglement of the branches of very tall trees, which bend over the path and interlock. The tunnel is illuminated by the rays of sunlight that enter through openings between the mesh of branches. I continue walking along this tunnel, curious about where it is taking me. Darkness sets in the deeper I go.

After a while, the tunnel ends abruptly. I find myself standing at an open window. Through that window, I can see the universe, an amazingly beautiful and calm dark sky full of stars and planets. As I enjoy this view, looking at every corner of this bright, vast quiet, I start to grow. The window gets smaller, to the point that it disappears and I see myself sitting on top the Earth. Our planet is a small ball and I am sitting on top of it, floating in space, enjoying the view, losing myself in the silence.

Then, I grow even more, until my body disappears, the Earth disappears, and I become energy. I become part of the universe. It feels wonderful. This experience is showing me what we really are: energy of the universe contained in physical form. It feels amazing and scary at the same time. I am completely alone; there is no one else here but consciousness. I cannot feel anything else; only the silence, the other planets, and the stars, which seem to be light years away. I think: are we really alone? Is there only this silence? Maybe it feels lonely because we are all one. We are one eternal energy, silent, infinite. One becomes many when it goes down into lower consciousness levels.

Slowly, the process begins to revert. I materialise again, sitting on top of the Earth. Then I become smaller, and I go back to the window and into the tunnel. When I come out of the tunnel, I am in the field of wildflowers. It is day again, and I am walking towards the temple as usual. I start to run. I want to get to the temple fast and meet my guides to ask about this amazing experience.

What was this? I ask my higher self.

What you just saw and experienced was a glimpse of you as powerful energy. When you started your meditation, you put your hand on your solar plexus and your power showed itself to you. You are boundless, unlimited by human constraints, and one with the eternal universe's scheme. You can draw from this power anytime.

Why did it feel so lonely?

It is not loneliness, and it is. Loneliness is not a concept at that level of being. Loneliness is a human perception. At the level of consciousness of an eternal being, there is nothing but silence, perfection, and love.

I don't know if I'd like to be conscious at that level of consciousness, if you know what I mean.

I know what you mean; you expressed the same feelings when you experienced yourself as light in a previous meditation. My answer is the same as before. This is the reason we came to a lower level of consciousness: to experience ourselves in the physical realm, to evolve in our thinking, to know and expand our power, and in doing so, affect the higher levels of consciousness.

It is great to be able to go up and down the consciousness levels. It felt exhilarating to be sitting on top of the Earth and see the universe from that perspective. I imagine it might be a feeling similar to what astronauts feel when they observe our planet and space from their spaceships.

You don't need to be an astronaut to have those kinds of experiences. You can consciously experience it through meditation, as you did. It is called "transcending." Unconsciously, you go to higher levels of consciousness during sleep, although you don't realise it. Your soul needs that release, needs to go back to what it really is, to its source, in order to continue its journey within the physical form every day. Sleep, as well as dreaming, are very important aspects of your human activities. They rank highly in the scale towards well-being, and they need to be given the importance they deserve.

Thank you.

How to Use Your Inner Power in Everyday Life

Everyday life always manages to spoil, delay, infiltrate, and take over our dreams and desires. We are living in a time when our schedules are plagued by endless lists of to-dos and should-dos that leave little or no time to enjoy life, embark on imaginary adventures, daydream, or follow our bliss. For a long time now, most of us have relegated our dreams in favour of life's demands. However, as we learn about this amazing, unimaginable power within ourselves, it is fair to ask: how can we better use and apply our inner power in everyday life in order to change the way we live and have a more joyful and fulfilling journey?

By changing your perception of what joy and fulfilment are. By not expecting things outside of you to provide you with joy and fulfilment, but focusing your inner self to provide them. You use your inner power when you feel grateful, abundant, hopeful, empowered, when you trust life, have faith, believe in wonder, and experience desires. Notice the myriad signs of happiness surrounding you; smile to yourself and others; love your physical form; help others to grow; agree to disagree; understand that everyone is different; let go of the need to be right; focus on your intended goals; accept the darkness and know that there is light; honour the planet that sustains you; accept the existence of God within you; marvel at the world blooming in front of your eyes; take the time to be silent; never stop being more. All of these make for powerful miracles in your life.

You often think that life must be complicated; that using your power must be an act of great strength and importance. But in truth, it is not. Your power is effected through soul-based acts of these qualities: gratitude, love, happiness, hope, trust, sharing, acceptance, understanding, belief, awe, curiosity, desire, growth, healing, compassion, tenderness. Your soul makes itself known to you through these acts.

It is possible you are oblivious to the effects of your power because:

- You don't accept your power; the responsibility is too big for you to handle, so you unknowingly let your ego control you instead of claiming the power of the soul.
- You are waiting to witness big miracles as proof that you are powerful—it could happen, but it usually doesn't.

In fact, once you accept that you are powerful, you will start to notice the miracles in your life. They take place every day; you just haven't yet given them the value they deserve because you have deemed them unimportant or small. But miracles are not big or small; they just *are*. Accept the small miracles in your life and bigger ones will follow. The only one who can summon your power is you. The only one who can interfere with the expression of your power is you. It is within your control to be the powerful soul you are, living an amazing experience—or not. The time has come for you to choose.

CHAPTER 12

The Power of Inner Guidance: The Hearing

This power represents *the hearing* of the voice of intuition that guides you on every step of the way and lets you know that you never walk alone. I touched on this topic in Part II when I described who you are, and I am discussing it here to explain how it is one of your inner tools.

I am talking about light. It is your inner voice, the light of your soul, the flame of life itself, the light that silences the darkness. When you feel that light within yourself, everything is possible. You can accomplish anything.

Feel your light. Become familiar with it. Know your light. Listen to its whispers.

Place your hand on your solar plexus and visualize this light shining inside of you. See it flowing to all parts of your body. See it transcending your physical being and expanding through your aura, connecting with the light of other beings—until all lights become one light. All is *one*, and one is *all*.

When you focus on light, darkness ceases to exist. The two cannot coexist because light is the absence of darkness. So then, any time you have a problem; feel fearful, frustrated, doubtful, or anxious; or suffer pain, illness, or distress—all forms of darkness—

bring light into the matter. You will receive a solution, healing, peace, knowledge, happiness, determination, drive, or empowerment to disperse whatever caused the darkness. Look inwards for your light. Bring it to the outside by following its guidance. That is how this tool works. Remember the man in our metaphorical story. He doesn't want to live in darkness any longer; therefore, he starts his search to find and reconnect with his inner light. You can follow his lead.

Meditation: Connect with Your Inner Light and Inner Guidance

Sit or lie down in a quiet place with your eyes closed. Take a few deep breaths.

As you breathe in and out, feel yourself become more and more relaxed.

Your whole body feels calm and relaxed. You feel relaxed all over.

If any thoughts come into your mind, just let them go. Acknowledge them, but don't follow them. Just let them go.

Place your hand on your solar plexus and spend a few minutes breathing in and out, relaxing more and more, disconnecting from your surroundings and focusing your awareness on your inner world.

As you do this, bring your awareness to your hand. Imagine you are the palm of your hand resting on your solar plexus. Imagine you are your lungs expanding and contracting as your breathing becomes slower.

Now imagine yourself inside your body. You are walking in darkness, looking for the light. You cannot see it yet, so you continue walking. Something guides you in the right direction.

You feel safe as you walk in this darkness. You are not slightly afraid of stumbling, colliding with anything, or getting hurt. You walk knowing that you are protected and guided.

Now the darkness starts to dissipate. You are walking towards a beautiful glowing light up ahead.

Suddenly, all is bright, all is illuminated. You rejoice in this light, which engulfs you with its warmth. You welcome this light; you cannot help but trust it.

This light is speaking to you. *It is the voice of your soul.* Listen carefully to what it says. Pay attention to how it feels. This is the voice of your purpose, the voice that guides you every step of the way, your entire life. This voice is your truth, your essence, your source. It is love shining within you.

Now you can ask for specific guidance, or simply be at peace and listen for any advice your inner guidance has to give you. Give thanks and be grateful for the connection and the experience.

When you are ready to come back, slowly start to become aware of your surroundings, of your physical body. Gently shake your hands and feet. Move your head and shoulders. Feel a soft energy pulling you towards Mother Earth as you open your eyes.

This simple meditation gives you a way to connect with and use this powerful tool. You can ask your inner light any question and receive answers that are always in line with your true essence and life's purpose. No matter how big or small the issue might seem, how important or trivial the question might be, the answer will always be the best one for you.

The more you practice this meditation, the more and more your light will shine and expand in your body. Eventually, you will be able to know the answer you are seeking almost immediately, simply by placing your hand on your body (your solar plexus, or if you prefer, your heart). As your light expands, it connects with other lights, so the answers you receive will contain tips and information involving others, even if they are physically far away from you; in spirit, we are all connected.

It is natural to be connected to your source; not being connected is an unnatural state. Many have forgotten their link to the Creator, and need to remember it. In doing so, they will regain their power and their ability to walk in purpose.

CHAPTER 13

The Power of Love: The Being

This power represents *the being* of the pure and holy essence that lives within you, your soul. Love is your natural state of being, your purest form. Everything that you are, do, and create has its origins in a state of love—even if that is hard to see or understand. Love is all there was, is, and will be throughout eternity. You were born out of love—the unconditional love that is your source and your soul—and you will return to that love at the end of your life's journey. Between the beginning and end of your physical existence, you will experience infinite shades of love, from its lightest forms to its darkest. You might lose everything, even your physical self, but you will always have the love from your source, the loving energy that created you and everything else.

The power of love is the strongest of all powers; it overshadows everything else. Even the brightest and shiniest of lights is a dim sparkle compared to true, honest love. This clearly shows that darkness cannot exist in the presence of love. When you surrender to the power of love, it will save you, rescue you, heal you, resurrect you from your misfortunes, guide you, fill you, empower you, and most importantly, show God within you.

The Power of Love

Your heart radiates love, which is the most powerful energy in the whole universe. Love is what holds everything together. Nothing would exist if it not for the power of love. Love is all there is. Outside love, there is nothing, only emptiness. God is love in its purest form, and He is present wherever love is felt, spoken, or shown. If you feel love in your heart, you feel God in your heart. If you have God in your heart, you have His power to create, with the universe, anything your soul and mind can imagine or desire. There are no boundaries—there never have been, and there will never be.

In the very moment you open your eyes and focus on something, you are creating that something. Likewise, every time you look at yourself, you are recreating yourself. You are that powerful. With what inspiration are you creating your world? Is it powerful love or a lesser emotion? Do you look at the world around you only with your eyes, or do you see it with the love in your heart? Make the decision today to imbue everything you do, say, see, touch, smell, feel, and think with love; observe the magnificent ways in which your life changes. Even if you are challenged by unloving conditions, willingly surround yourself with love. Do not aim to change your conditions; they will change by themselves because love softens, lightens, sweetens, magnifies, straightens, strengthens, unites, and completes everything it touches. This is the reason feeling love is so wonderful: it enhances all aspects of your life. When you feel love, you are seeing your true essence and experiencing your true nature. Contrary to common belief, you do not feel this way because someone or something is giving you the opportunity to feel love. Rather, you feel this way because *you* are the origin of love; you radiate it into the world around you, which in turn reflects it back to you.

Being "in love" is a special state. It happens when you choose to direct your love to a specific person, the object of your affection. When you are in love, you feel radiant and vibrant, and enjoy a constant state of bliss. You don't look for imperfections, nor judge or criticise; instead, you see only grace, pleasure, and happiness as you love from the heart. The feeling of love is always within you; you can access it at any time. When you see the world with the eyes of love, you see it unfolding in all its glory. However, when you see it with eyes of hate, impatience, jealousy, despair, distrust, or greed, you obscure your world with a veil of darkness that prevents you from experiencing the abundance that is truly there. More often than not, the culprit that relegates love to a corner of your heart, to be remembered only on certain occasions, is your judgement about how life should be. Your perception of reality becomes overshadowed by darkness. If you only allowed love to shine from you, constantly and consciously, that darkness would be banished.

You possess this power. You *are* this power; that is why it is called "the being." You *are* love. If you cannot feel this to be true, it may be that circumstances in your life have made you temporarily forget and detach from the truth about who you really are. Know that the circumstances of your life do not determine whether you are worthy of love. Even if love has been invisible to you up to this moment, you are still capable of starting to feel it now. Know that you are love, and that you can love yourself without needing the approval or acceptance of anyone besides yourself. You are a perfectly divine being—how could you not love yourself for that?

Now is your chance to regain your awareness and reclaim this unique power. Now you can start looking at yourself and the world from this point of power, the eyes of love, and by doing so, begin to create yourself as your soul sees you. Your world will start changing to reflect love back to you. You can become whomever you desire because you are love, and you are loved!

Meditation: The Power of Love

Feeling love within yourself is the foundation of a wonderful, harmonious, and fulfilling life. You cannot radiate love or share it with others if you do not love yourself first. Love originates from you, extends to and permeates all that it reaches, and then returns to you, enriched by the interaction. When you learn to love and appreciate yourself fully, your life will flow whichever way it is meant to, and you will flow with it. Love empowers you to enjoy all the gifts that life gives you. It makes you strong enough to handle any challenges that come your way.

When you feel this power, you feel good about yourself and about the world around you; you feel confident, dynamic, optimistic, grateful, healthy, strong, and purposeful. You feel beautiful. Love makes you seek and connect with the essence in everyone and everything, allowing you to accept the world the way it is, to leave judgement and criticism aside and see the perfection in life, even when that what you see seems wrong or imperfect.

Practice this exercise to reconnect with the love inside you.

———————————————————•

Sit in a quiet place with your eyes closed.

Breathe peacefully, relaxing your body and freeing your mind of thought.

Concentrate on your breathing and detach yourself from your physical body and surroundings. Zoom into your senses and your focus on your inner world.

Once you have done so, direct your attention to your heart, to your heartbeats dancing in a slow rhythm. Love your heart: appreciate it fully because it sustains your physical life.

Now imagine that with each beat, your heart reciprocates your love and appreciation; each beat pumps love into your body. Imagine pink rays of love emanating from your heart and reaching every part of your body. If there is any area of your body in need of extra loving attention, send love there.

You can amplify the power of this exercise by saying an empowering thought, such as, "I love myself and I accept the perfection of my being," or "Loving myself heals my life," or "I am worthy of love because I am love." You can also use the word "love" as a mantra, repeating it while you bathe in the warm feeling it creates.

Stay in this joyous state for as long as you desire.

When you are ready to come out of it, bring your awareness to your surroundings, ground yourself, and open your eyes.

———●————————————

Set aside a few minutes every day for this exercise of appreciating and loving yourself. It is a common habit to seek and even demand love from others in order to feel valued and worthy. Unfortunately, this habit brings much heartache when that external love doesn't make present itself the way we desire it to. You need to become expert at loving yourself; you cannot give out something that you do not have. You cannot give quality love if you don't feel quality love for yourself. Incorporating this exercise to your already demanding routine could feel like a chore at first. However, after a while, not only will you start to look forward to that quiet encounter with yourself, you will also start noticing the difference it makes in your life.

The purpose of the exercise is to help you reconnect with the love within you. Some will find it easier than others—this depends on the number and kind of loving experiences you have been exposed to during your life. Nevertheless, love comes from within, and as such, you need only reach inside to feel it. Even if you feel that the exercise is not working, that you cannot love yourself, or your body, or any other imperfection you think you have, the simple act of regularly going through the activity shows your intentions. It is a big first step to getting acquainted with the love within. By acknowledging your heart, by feeling it beating inside you, you have started down the road to discovering the amazing and wonderful inner power of love.

Another point to mention concerns the areas of your body that might need extra attention. You might consciously send more love to a given area of your body if you know that it needs more focus or more healing. However, be aware of instances when the rays of love are directed to a specific area without your intervention. This could mean that your inner guidance is pointing out some issue that needs to be addressed, or an area that requires consideration. Do not dismiss this guidance; it could be highlighting a health-related issue, answering a question, or providing a sign. Take notice of your inner signs, especially when they are repetitive; this is one way your soul communicates with you.

Love and Forgiveness

I find it interesting that we seem to judge others and ourselves most intensely by seemingly unloving or unkind acts, at the same time forgetting all the concern, kindness, and love shown on other occasions. Think about it: there is probably someone—it could even be you—with whom you are upset, disappointed, or angry due to some action you deemed unloving, unfair, or wrong. You may not realise that you harbour those negative feelings; often, they sneak in and stay under the radar. However, a clue to their existence is that no matter how many well-meaning acts this person does, you still cannot bring yourself to appreciate or value them. Over time, unconsciously, your feeling of disillusionment grows; you continue to judge his imperfections and flaws, and continue to overlook what is great about him. The disillusionment gradually turns into intolerance. No matter what he does, says, or becomes, the "wrong" thing he did is a permanent stain that spoils everything else.

You might not realise what you are doing, but if you do notice, you tell yourself that your judgement, criticism, and displeasure are justified. You could be right—but is it worth it? The point here is not to determine the rightness or wrongness of your feelings towards yourself or this particular person, nor to accept or condemn what happened. The point is to realise that by telling yourself you have the right to feel the way you do, you:

- Have stopped noticing the light; you are focusing completely on the darkness in the target of your criticism
- Don't realize that you still feel pain, sadness, and disenchantment by holding onto those judgements

- Don't see that not forgiving is eating you up inside and preventing you from enjoying other aspects of your life
- Are not loving yourself; you are intoxicating your spirit with those negative feelings
- Will bring on more darkness if you don't stop dwelling on these faults and omissions and lack of love, and choose to let them go

You can use the Power of Love exercise to heal any unforgiving feelings you have, by sending love to heal yourself, any other involved party, and the situation that created those feelings. Choosing to forgive is letting go of any judgement about what happened, (which, in any case, cannot be changed). Choosing to forgive is relieving yourself of the burden of unloving feelings that has been affecting you in all sorts of negative ways. Most importantly, choosing to forgive is freeing yourself of a shadow that hovers over you and suppresses light from your life. Once you forgive and let go, you will feel relieved, contented, and in control. You will also feel lightness, both in terms of luminosity (the shadows have dissipated), and in terms of weight (the load has disappeared).

If you have some forgiving to do, now is the time to choose to release those negative feelings, kindly and one at a time. Do it for yourself because you choose to love yourself. Do it to free yourself of darkness and fill your life with light.

Sending Love Outwards

My wish for you is that you make the time to practice the Power of Love exercise, immerse yourself in the experience, and successfully heal whatever needs healing. If you don't currently have an abundance of love in your life, you deserve the time you spend uncovering this precious inner quality, which you may have temporarily forgotten and need to bring up to the surface to reclaim. If you are fortunate enough to love and appreciate yourself, and enjoy plenty of love in your life, practicing this exercise will still energise you—there is always room for more love. Once you have practiced the exercise enough, you will feel and acknowledge the love inside you with full awareness. You will cease to expect it from external sources only. Your experience of love will be a combination of love both from inside and from outside sources—but the master source will be you, yourself.

Once you have reached this point of feeling love naturally within yourself, you will be ready to focus your love outwards. Then, you can alter the Power of Love exercise, by not only seeing love flowing within you, but also seeing it expand and overflow from your physical body, and sending loving intentions from your inner world to the outer world. You may send healing love to other people, to a community, to a country, or to the whole planet. At this stage, your life will feel much better; you will be in harmony with everyone and everything, you will enjoy the beautiful experiences that life brings with amplified effect, and you will be able to endure tough experiences with a grace and strength that only love and trust can provide. You will stop asking for reasons or justifications about life and accept it the way it is, with all its perfect imperfections.

CHAPTER 14

The Power of Intention: The Desires

Living an Intentional Life

This power represents *the desire* for what you want to create and manifest in your life. This is your soul's vision of your journey together as one. You know how powerful your intentions are; you have used them before, consciously or unconsciously, and they brought about what you intended—whether or not it was what you really wanted. Do not underestimate this power. Regardless of how an intention is expressed—by word, thought, action, or feeling—the intention will take form in the very shape that was intended.

You constantly express intentions—most of the time without conscious knowledge. As soon as you open your eyes in the morning, you intend things, and that process continues every second of your day. In this way, day after day, you have intentions for your life. If you are not aware of what you are doing, you may end up living a life that does not reflect your true wants and desires, although it would be the life that you intended. Unconscious intention is the source of most frustration, disappointment, dissatisfaction, distress and disillusionment in life. It may seem that life is against you, continually giving you unwanted experiences, when the truth is that *you* are the one bringing about discontent by making careless use of this extraordinary power. Therefore, conscious intention makes for optimum choices. Intend every moment of your life to be how you want it to be, and see your life unfold in the most glorious ways.

The process of conscious intention does not need to be difficult or tedious. You don't have to create intention for every detail of every life situation; this would rob you of the pleasure of enjoying the gifts of life. Instead, just set an intention of the way you wish to feel in every moment. For example, you can intend to be prosperous, happy, harmonious, safe, or healthy, and let the universe work out the best way for the intention to be realized. If you go through your day and notice within yourself feelings of uneasiness, worry, fear, sadness, or distress, then set you intentions over again. Intend to experience content, peace, empowerment, knowledge, trust, and love, and see your discomfort and disharmony vanish almost instantly! Every moment can be set with an intention to feel good, in whichever way you'd like to experience it.

When you start using your intentions consciously, constantly, and trustingly, you will feel powerful and in control. Living a pure, intentioned life makes for an easy and joyous ride; you choose how you'd like to experience life and then let yourself flow along with those experiences, as opposed to working at them or trying to figure them out. Just let your life be; there is nothing you need to figure out. Live life as it comes, knowing that if you set your intentions the way you desire, life will work them out for you.

Exercise: The Power of Purposeful Intentions

Every morning when you wake up, spend some time in bed setting your intentions for the day. This exercise is very brief and should only take a few minutes.

At this time of the day, you are still in contact with your soul, so it is very likely that the intentions you set will come from the whispers of your inner voice.

You can set general intentions, such as to go through your day with purpose, harmony, and ease in every situation. You can also set some specific intentions, such as to prepare nutritious meals, to give good advice to whoever needs it, to have a productive meeting at work, to give a great presentation, to enjoy some quality time with your loved ones, and so on. If you cannot come up with any intentions, then just intend that whatever happens that day, you will be able to handle it. Then, get up and leave things to the universe; trust that it will take those intentions and make them happen. Spend your day confident that what you intended will come to pass.

———————————————————————————————

If your intentions don't seem to work, know that there is a higher reason at play. More often than not, it's because consciously or unconsciously you have set new intentions that affected your previous ones. Many times, your anxiety, fear, and insecurity make you intend things that you don't really desire. For example, your inexperience preparing a new recipe makes you feel insecure. That insecurity may make you unintentionally set an intention of failure—the result is that the recipe turns out badly. Or, your low self-esteem and feelings of inferiority may cause you to set an unconscious intention of not getting your message across at work, and for that reason, a meeting or presentation does not go as you expected. In these examples, all you needed to turn your experiences into positive ones were the intention to be confident and adventurous when trying a new recipe, and the intention to demonstrate your knowledge and hard work to your colleagues.

When working with this tool, and as with any of the others, it pays off to be focused in the present moment, in the "now"; by doing so you can be aware of how you are feeling and acknowledge from which point of consciousness you are setting your intentions.

Is it from your powerful divine nature? Or is it from the powerless perspective of your ego, which makes you choose things by default? Most of the time, your intentions are set automatically by your ego, by your routine, and by your habitual feelings. You are probably unaware of the untapped power you have within to create change and reach for your desires. Understand, acknowledge, and accept that *your intentions are powerful*; this is a highly useful tool in the tool kit for your life's journey. My intention is for you to use it well and make it work to your divine purpose.

Practice the power of intention. Give your intentions purpose. Conscious intentions that are made from the guidance of your inner being are the ones that will send you in a desired direction and set in motion the process of creation. Set your purposeful intentions daily: in the morning, during the day, and before you go to sleep. Think of your intentions as wishes whispered into the universe. See them working in your life. If you accompany your intentions with visualization (another one of your powers), you will imbue them with more power and strength. Use this tool with awareness, trust, and fun too, and see what you can achieve.

CHAPTER 15

The Power of Visualization:
The Seeing

Creative Visualization

This power represents *the seeing* of your dreams, fantasies of your perfect life in the ocean of your mind, where everything is possible and no boundaries exist. Visualization is another very powerful tool you possess. When used with awareness and purpose, it is a vehicle that moves you towards your desires.

As with your other inner qualities, you are constantly visualizing. Even those who claim they cannot do it are actually practicing it unconsciously. Every thought, every word, every idea you have it is first drafted in your mind as an image and/or colours; therefore, you are all experienced unconscious visualisers. The key to the power of visualization is to have full awareness so that you can direct it to go hand-in-hand with your intentions.

When you engage in the practice of visualization, you are creating mental pictures of what you desire. However, that is not the main purpose of this tool. You reap the intended benefit of visualization when you fully immerse yourself in the experience of it, seeing and also feeling the sensations of having, being, or doing what you want.

And when this happens—when images are accompanied by feelings that were in turn triggered by intentions—true creation starts to manifest.

Although you may understand the extent of this power, most of you do not know how to use it consciously to bring your desires into life. You are constantly distracted by day-to-day situations, trapped by your reality, and worried about the future. What with all of this distraction, your dreams and desires get forgotten in a corner, awaiting some day you will have time to address them. Well, the time to address them is not in the future; it is now. You can manifest the life you desire by means of this tool. The reason why you probably haven't noticed your progress is the tendency to give up easily when immediate results are not obvious. People are attached to outcomes; they expect and want habits and beliefs that took months and even years to become rooted in their lives to change immediately.

Understand that part of the joy of gaining what you desire is the process you immerse yourself in creating it. Therefore, you need to savour the time you spend visualizing your dreams. The more strongly you feel your dreams, the faster you will manifest them. I suggest that you spend time every day going through your visualizations; continue doing this until you start noticing changes. Do not give up. Whatever your desire is, it can happen. The key is to stay focused on one thing at a time, consciously, constantly, and trustingly.

How long do you have to visualize something before it comes true? We advise you to detach from the expectation of time in order to really enjoy and appreciate the effects of visualization. Hold the image of your desire in your mind. See, feel, and experience that image in your mind every day until it happens in whatever shape it manifests. What is required from you is the commitment to visualize every day and to trust that what you visualize will happen. Do not worry about when this will be; all will unfold at the precise time and place it should—unless what you desire does not actually line up with your life's purpose, or opposes someone else's life path. In these circumstances, your visualizations will go unfulfilled, and you will understand the reasons for that with clarity as you progress on your path of inner growth. In the meantime, enjoy the sensations as you witness the events that unfold in your life to create what you have envisioned.

If you are unfamiliar with the process of creative visualization, then you need learn about it. Many people have written books or give talks on the subject. It is not a complicated activity, but in fact, very simple and amazingly enjoyable. Unlike meditation, in which you go quiet and silence your mind with the purpose of listening, creative visualization is the active use of your mind and imagination to see and feel your dreams as vividly as you possibly can.

The Ocean of Your Mind

Your mind is an ocean. Look into the ocean of your mind. Don't force yourself to see anything special; just imagine an ocean—wide, infinite. The ocean breathes life into all. It is the source of your being reflected in your mind. When you picture this ocean, you are picturing the vastness, the immensity of your source. This ocean is the canvas for your manifestations. Anything that you desire can be brought to life in this ocean. Here, you can picture every detail, from every angle. Even things, people, and events that don't yet exist in your physical reality can exist in that ocean. From this ocean, you create reality. The power to create in the ocean of your mind is real and unlimited, and needs to be re-affirmed.

Many speak about the power of creative visualization, but not everyone uses it. It's not a tool that has been instilled as part of common practice, though it should be. Visualization is an immensely powerful tool to aid you in your life's journey. Why go about things the hard way? You can perfectly conceive desires in your mind, just as you want them. Why not utilize your ability to design and define even the smallest and intricate details of every desire before trying to produce them in your physical plane? Work at it in your mind; the more you see what you want and the more you enjoy it with your inner senses, the more quickly it will come into existence.

Practice visualization. Visualize your goals being achieved, all the details successfully accomplished. In the ocean of your mind, there are no problems or issues blocking your way. Everything is possible and feasible; just visualize and it will become a reality. Play with visualization. At your own pace, go from easy, small desires to ones that are more complex. Don't hold yourself back by thinking that your desires are impossible or inappropriate for your life. Anything you can imagine, you can create, from your mind into your physical world.

You must understand that everything that you can imagine already exists. All experiences, feelings, objects, and inventions exist in a state of untapped consciousness that you do not perceive when you are focused on your physical realm. However, when you turn your attention inwards, you start removing the veils from your eyes, and what you envision appears in your space, as if cast by magic. Believe in this magic! Fill your world with magical manifestations. Imagine what you want in your mind. See it and enjoy it, and it will become reality as you envisioned it. Don't worry about the hows or the whens. Just think of is—what you desire *is*.

Practice visualization every day and see with amazement what unfolds in your life. You can imagine changes to every aspect: physical, mental, spiritual, and emotional. You do not need to worry about whether what you desire is correct or right; the desires you visualize will always be in line with your higher purpose. You will not be able to persistently visualize ones that are not; they will fall into the ocean, become weak, and fade, and certainly will not come into existence.

The power of visualization is real. Once you have become skilled in its practice, I suggest you recommend it to others. It is an invaluable tool to explore and exploit on your life's journey, especially if you wish to follow the extraordinary paths with an easy flow.

CHAPTER 16

The Power of Focus and Thought: The Creating

This power represents *creating* the life that you build through the conscious and unconscious use of the power of your mind, along with your beliefs, habits, and inner growth. Let us return to the story of the man sitting by the stream. The man is lost in the current of his life, submerged in the reality he breathes and perceives. When he goes into his dream and drinks from the river of love, he removes the veils from his eyes and sees, with clarity, what truly *is*. He discovers that what he had previously perceived as "reality" was not real. Now he desires true reality, which is awaiting his belief, trust, intention, and action to become part of his existence.

In his dream, the light gives him clarity on his life. All he has to do is enjoy, rejoice, love, and in that state of being, fulfil his purpose. This purer state of reality is available to him to make the process of life comfortable and smooth. The man has accessible to him everything he needs to address any event in his life. In his dream, he is shown that he controls everything with his thoughts; whatever he thinks, *is*. He realises that all of his thoughts have been about the "reality" he lived and breathed. In turn, he devoted most of his thoughts to that "reality," and the more of those thoughts he was thinking, the more of that reality he was creating. That was the vicious cycle of his existence: what he saw and experienced, he thought about. What he thought about, he created; what he created, he saw and experienced.

But now, something has changed in his life. He has started on the journey to the light. Now, when he is in his dream, he can see with clarity what he does when he is awake. As this realisation takes place, something begins to morph within him. The shift inside him triggers a change in the way he thinks while he is awake; in turn, what happens in his "real" life starts to change too. His reality ceases to be perceived reality; it becomes a created one. Nothing that he doesn't wish to be, feel, or do will be part of his reality unless he thinks it into existence. He knows he possesses the ability to direct his thoughts.

This is the simplest way to explain the secret of your existence. You need only live your life consciously, knowing that you are the creator of it and that you have the free will to create what you desire. Neither your soul, nor the angels, nor the spirit guides, nor even God will stop you in the process, because even in the imperfection of your chosen life, there is perfection in the whole scheme of life.

Focus on your desires and see your life change before your eyes. Like a backdrop on a stage alters the mood and tone of scenes as it changes, as you change your thoughts, the undercurrent of your life changes with them. This is the greatest law: you are a powerful being, so powerful that you can create worlds! You already have proof of this in your ability to conceive of new life. You are creating a world in that perfect new life. You have proof of this in the amazing technological and scientific advances human beings have achieved. You have proof of this in the ability to experience magnificence and awe with the pure intent of your heart.

Once you see yourselves as creator gods in physical form, you will start making miraculous changes in your life. Start to focus your thoughts on how you want your life to be. Forget about the technicalities and go with the flow. No amount of worry, fear, sadness, illness, and other setbacks could be stronger than the divine power that resides within you. Once you reclaim that power, all the barriers that have prevented you from fulfilling your true purpose will vanish. Then there will be no other option for you but to create a fulfilling life fit for your soul's realisation.

Exercise: The Golden Rays of Light

•————————————•

Sit in a quiet place with your eyes closed. Breathe peacefully, relaxing your body and freeing your mind of thought.

Now cover yourself in golden light; paint yourself in gold. See this golden light going within you, through you, all over and around you. See yourself inside a golden bubble of this light. Let yourself disappear inside this bubble of golden rays until you feel you *are* that light, bright and shining.

See the light travel outwards, away from you, and let it permeate all things, all people, all animals, and all plants.

Now imagine the light become something else, something that you'd like to be, have, do, or feel.

Then let the light transform itself into some other physical form or expression. See the light slowly and magnificently changing, morphing into other forms.

Now you can see that this light has manifested into something else; it has transmuted into something you chose.

Now imagine that your thoughts are like this golden light. They originate in your mind, and by the power inherent in them, they can transform themselves into anything to create what you desire. Imagine thin beams of golden light that represent your thoughts. They come out from you in all directions, and create, at your own request, whatever world you think about.

What kind of thoughts do you choose to think, then, knowing that each one of these beams has the power to create, to change, to transform? Do you choose to think loving, positive, empowering thoughts? Of course you do.

•————————————•

This is a great exercise to combine with your visualizations. Start the process by following the Golden Rays of Light exercise, then extend it by seeing your thoughts, the thin beams of light, transforming into whatever you'd like to visualize. The purpose of this exercise is to bring your attention to the power of your thoughts. Every thought you have represents a thread of energy that shoots out to the world. The energy has immense power to affect the world by means of interaction, transformation, and creation at all levels of your consciousness. Therefore, you should be mindful of the thoughts you toss into the universe. You do not, however, have to set yourself to mindful thinking. Focus must not be forced; that defeats its purpose. Instead, understand and acknowledge the act of being focused is a constant confirmation and affirmation of what you desire. Integrate this simple, encouraging change in perspective into your life. Setting the intention to do so would be a great start.

Exercise: Inspired Focus

Stop for a moment and think: what are you focusing on at present? Perhaps your mind has gone blank, as your ego is being threatened by the question. If this is the case, then take a few days to observe where your focus lies most of the time. Whether or not you intend it, you are certainly focusing on specific things. You give them each different amounts of focus and action; therefore, they are all manifested at different levels.

Are you using your power to create wisely and to your advantage? Are you focusing on what your heart desires, on what will improve the quality of your life? Are you aware of the impact of your thoughts on the experience of your life? Are you impatient, thus sabotaging your creations? Do you need to declutter your mind of its chatter?

In your journal, write with honesty what you think about most of the time. Once it's all on paper, you can relate the kind of thoughts you have with past and current events in your life. Are you happy with the results? Do you feel that the quality of your thinking could do with a little (or a lot of) improvement?

Do not worry or fret about your thinking up until now. Now that you have become aware of your power, you can control what you think about and focus on, no matter what the circumstances or direction of your life are. Access to this power is not restricted by your life situation, but by your desire to change, improve the quality of your life, enrich your experiences, and bring hope, peace of mind, healing, forgiveness, truth, and love to your existence. Start taking charge by shifting your focus and looking for ways to think thoughts that will give you feelings you'd like to experience. Be happy, grateful, and enthusiastic about your future knowing that from today onwards, you can start creating the life you were meant to live.

CHAPTER 17

The Power of Manifestation: The Outcome

Manifestation is not a power per se, but it is *the outcome* of the conscious or unconscious application of any of the powers presented in this book. It represents what you experience as a consequence of interacting with life itself, so we thought it would be valuable and valid to give it its own section.

We provided you with the Golden Rays of Light exercise not only to give you a practical tool to use, but also to teach you, in a colourful way, what happens when you think. Every time you think, a shower of golden rays emanates from your inner light and is sent into the universe with the sole intention of creating what you thought about. In order for the manifestation to be physically visible and tangible, repeated thoughts, or constant focus, are required. Just a few weak rays of light don't have the strength needed to manifest in the physical realm. Only strong focus on and repeated thought patterns of a desire have enough strength to see that thought manifested. Some of the tools that we have highlighted in this book, such as empowering thoughts, visual aids, and repeated writing of dreams and goals, are tricks to make you focus on your intent to create what you desire. Eventually, you will discover that you no longer need these tools because you have fully realised the power of your thinking.

Even when you have reached this stage of understanding the power of your thoughts and deciding to direct your focus on your desires, you may experience discontent and unhappiness due to a perceived lack of achievements. You might also be hard on yourself by judging that you are still not focused enough, and easily distracted by unimportant matters. However, blaming and being harsh with yourself are not the solution. The solution is to observe your thoughts. Perhaps you are dispersing your focus on many things; you might have many creations in progress but not manifested yet, resulting in your feelings of dissatisfaction. Your focus is like a laser beam. If you concentrate on one specific area, you will see prompt results in that area. If you concentrate on several areas at the same time, you will not see results until a number of those small areas are completed and become visible. As always, it is your choice how you use your powers. Dispersing your focus is one way that your ego tricks you out of your power. Don't buy into what it says; learn to focus on what is important to you, and let the rest take care of itself. Once you stop erecting barriers of doubt and fears in order to explain or justify your lack of focus, and once you start trusting in your own ability to manifest, you will start seeing more evidence of that ability. You have nothing to lose and everything to gain.

Do not use time, size, or value to measure the probability of something coming to you. Using any external condition to justify why your desires are not happening is only an excuse for your inability to complete the only action required from you: to *choose what you really want and to focus on it.* As creator, you have everything you need to create your masterpiece; you only need to decide what it will be! All your excuses and delays are only walls erected to separate you from some feared truths: What if this is all true? What if, just by thinking and focusing on something with all my attention and pure intention, I can make it manifest? What do I do, then, if there are no barriers, no limits? The answer is as simple as everything else that I share with you here: just give it a try, with honesty and trust. Set yourself a goal to reach—anything—and stay with it until you have manifested it with focusing and intention. Then, set yourself another goal to manifest, then another one, and another, until you are confident that there is nothing you cannot manifest. See what you can do with that newfound power.

I can give you some idea of what might happen. When you reach total realisation of your power to manifest, you will have become a different person: someone who is living or starting to live in a purposeful way. You will not be afraid. You will not feel that you have reached the end of anything; on the contrary, you will feel that you are at the beginning of a new way of life. You will be empowered to start manifesting a life originated from the purest intentions of your heart, and you will also endeavour to share this newfound knowledge with others so they too can become aware of the power of their golden light to create their desires.

Please, do not be afraid to walk a path different to the one most people are walking. Do not be afraid to speak words of change or miracles because you assume people will ridicule you. The more you spread the word, the more people will be reached, exposed, and tested. Do not give up if your focus and intention do not seem to get results. At the beginning, it may seem that all your efforts are useless—but please, do not give up. It took a long time for your present habits and traits to mould you into who you are, and for your patterns of thoughts to monopolise the way you think. Therefore, overnight change is extremely unlikely (although not impossible). As with everything we share with you here, the joy is in the ride, in discovering your inner qualities and experiencing the transformation within yourself; outer manifestations are just an added bonus. Change usually happens in silence, and only manifests when it has the perfect conditions. Once you succeed for the first time, you will realise that it was not your ability, but your doubts that prevented you from succeeding.

As divine beings, you are perfectly capable manifestors who have all the required knowledge within, but who need to trust and believe again. Start today. Choose any desire—big, small, simple, or complex—set your focus and intention on it, and see what happens. Just remember that often, your ego's interference distorts the way you picture your desires in your mind, but what manifests in your life is what your inner light envisions. Therefore, sometimes your desired outcome is different from what you expected. Accept that there is nothing wrong with this. Accept that whatever manifests is for your higher good, in line with your higher purpose. You will see in hindsight that it all fits perfectly into the big picture of your life. Rejoice in your powers! Use them, become accustomed to them, and new experiences will open up in your life. Anything you desire is only a thought away.

What If We Create Our Reality?

I was going over the material in this section, lost in contemplation of all these insightful messages, when, surprisingly, a question flashed in my mind, disrupting my peaceful state: What if we create everything in our lives and all that we experience, but in reality, nothing exists? Another question followed immediately: What would that mean? And another: What if our whole lives, including ourselves, are a projection of our thoughts and desires?

I knew I was onto something and I didn't want to stop the train of thought taking course in my mind. I wanted to know where it was heading, what it was going to show me, what I was going to discover. So my monologue continued: What if we can change anything, have everything, and be anyone? If this is the case, are any fears worth having, or risks not worth taking? Is failure a terrible enough thing to stop us from trying, to stop us from living? What if it really doesn't matter what we are, what we do, or what we have? What if our lives are like a movie or a stage performance, and we are the writer, director, designer, and protagonist, designing everything, including the casting, setting, and script? What if, at different stages of my life, I myself created the scenarios that I thought I needed to experience? This would go against the existing theory that the scenarios that surface as life situations are that ones that determine our experience of life.

What if the secret of living is to understand that we have the power of choice? That we can choose to let go of things that don't align with what we want, and instead concentrate on what we want to create in order to move forward? That we are each running our own shows, with our own guidelines and destinations, and no one can manipulate or change them but ourselves? That a person's life is his own movie, not ours? That we have power only in our own movie? That in order to play our part in our own movies, from the moment we are conceived, we need to decide on our appearance, behaviours, qualities, strengths, weaknesses, lessons; on the important places and the people who will play supporting roles?

How would life change if we saw it from that perspective, if we knew that no matter what happens, we never lose? If we finally saw ourselves as an expression of the source of all creation? We create our own stages to live out our own existences, to perfect parts of ourselves, to express our divinity through our experiences. The sooner we understand this, the sooner we will walk with purpose, and the more fulfilling and joyous our lives will be.

Nothing that happens in life is outside of us. Everything that happens is within. What we see and experience outside is the reflection or projection of our inner world onto the canvas of infinite possibilities that is life. We have nothing to wait for or to be divinely offered. We can make it all happen ourselves, consciously or unconsciously, by the use of our free will and our inner powers.

During these glorious times, darkness is dissipating and light is being shed on our awareness. During these glorious times, we are learning truths about life and about ourselves. By understanding these truths, we are becoming aware of the tools we possess, and that we can deliberately choose to change anything we desire through the power of our intention and attention; we ask for what we want (intention) and then wait with joyous expectation for it to be manifested (attention). In this scenario, there is no place for doubt, as it will only bring delays and disappointment. In this scenario, we are literally the creators of our own lives.

The Secret of Manifestation

I'd like to talk about manifestation and its relation to the collective consciousness, which is, the minds of a large group of people thinking or working on related topics as one. When you start manifesting from your soul's perspective, you will become more focused on what you want to achieve in relation to your purpose and destination. You will notice a shift in your attention from an egocentric point of reference to a global one. Increasingly, your desires will relate to areas that matter to your soul specifically, and also to more universal issues such as the prosperity of the planet, the welfare of the community, love, peace, harmony, fulfilling relationships, empowerment, appreciation, honesty, simplicity, truth, and service.

The more you engage in these universal desires, the more your vibrations will grow and expand, until you become a light-worker. As your aura extends, it reaches high levels of consciousness and connects with the vibrations of others who are focusing on similar matters or patterns of energy. Vibrations at high levels of consciousness are purer, cleaner, clearer, and lighter than those at lower levels. These high-level vibrations originate from soul-based desires and intentions. There are no ego-driven desires at high levels of consciousness, because ego-driven desires are low in frequency and always close to the physical level, usually giving the bearer feelings of heaviness weighing him down.

The speed at which everything travels increases the further away you move from the physical levels. Energy, vibrations, thoughts move very quickly at high levels of consciousness, travelling on universal highways where connections are quickly made to produce near-instantaneous creations. However, delays in physical manifestation occur because the desire has to break through the barriers of the lower-level vibrations; it has to transform from the ethereal into the physical. For that transformation to take place, intention and focus are key. However, you often sabotage your manifestations by withdrawing intention and focus after a period of time. You may think that you have given a reasonable amount of time to your desire, but the withdrawal of energy impedes and interferes with your desire's process into the physical world. You must understand that a request for creation is not an isolated event; requests or desires travel all over the universal consciousness community network across the planet and across the universe to bring you the best outcome for your purposeful life path. Therefore, you must appreciate the immeasurable number of connections and processes that take place in order to bring together resources of all kinds, synchronize all parts involved, and make not just yours, but everyone's desires possible.

Very rarely do people think about what happens in our ethereal domain. People complain that their desires or requests are not fulfilled for various reasons: because the universe doesn't hear them, the universal laws do not work, their desires manifesting is an impossibility, and so on. The more they focus on the nonfulfilment of the desire, the more they lose focus on the desire itself. As nothing happens, they feel disappointed. Their trust in their power weakens, and they shift their focus onto something else. At this point, when they shift their focus or they feel distrust, all the mechanisms that were in process to make the manifestation possible will stop, become dormant, or even be lost. When and if focus on that specific desire is resurrected, the process will have to restart. It may or may not pick up where it left off, as circumstances may have changed, and new mechanisms may need to be arranged. Again, be aware that thoughts are setting off chain reactions on all levels of consciousness to create reality. The more you go back and forth, or change your mind about what you want, the slower the manifestation process is.

But here is the secret, the key to successfully manifesting what you desire all of the time: make the basis of your thoughts of a more general nature, about things that enhance your life, regardless of what you are doing, having, or being. Make your thoughts about love, peace, gratitude, harmony, health, abundance, growth, giving, allowing, service to the planet and its inhabitants, and happiness in your well-being and all your endeavours. This way, your thoughts will always be consistent and focused, making the process of creation flow continuously. The gates of abundance will effortlessly open wide. Everything that represents happiness, love, harmony, peace, and purpose will be manifested in your relationships, work, health, material prosperity, inner growth, and all other aspects of your life.

As you progress on your journey of inner growth, you will realise that focusing solely on success, money, relationship status, material possessions, outer appearance, prestige, fame, and even pride (all, by the way, ego-driven desires) will not always make them happen in your life in the way you envisioned. Focus instead on the way you feel when you engage in any activity you love, on how purposefully you are walking in life, on being happy and healthy, on being grateful and finding opportunities to smile more, on being of service to others, and on the general growth of the planet. Basically, focus on your true heart's desires. When you do, then the rest will not matter that much. You will find that all kinds of amazing experiences manifest in your life without you even asking for them. They are secondary outcomes of living from your soul's desires.

Physical Desires and Worthiness

Is it wrong, then, to want material things or ego-driven desires such as money, success, possessions, and prosperity? Does it mean that we are not focusing on our purpose?

We do not place judgement on the objects of your desires, so it doesn't matter to us what you want in your physical world. Remember that your purpose, above all, is to be happy and to find ways and experiences to achieve that happiness. Your physical world offers you a rich smorgasbord of experiences and states of being that constantly grab your attention and entice your desires. Experimenting with that smorgasbord is part of your human experience. By all means, you should want things that will make you happy. All your manifestations, ego-driven or not, give you the opportunity to experience life. They allow you to decide whether they were what you expected or not, and therefore give you the chance to continue manifesting them or move on to something else. What truly matters to us is not the kind of manifestations you produce, but the quality of the relationship you build with your inner being. Opening up a partnership with your soul, putting trust in its guidance, gaining confidence to walk with purpose, and acknowledging that you are a powerful enabler of your soul's mission is what truly matters to us. We give you all your heart's desires and you give us your loving self.

There is another common issue regarding manifestation and feelings of worth and correctness. Sometimes people sabotage their intentions to manifest because they feel it's unworthy to want what they desire. Some have a belief that if you are living with purpose, you have to be humble and not desire anything material or in excess. Let me clarify: this belief is incorrect and unfounded. Everyone is worthy of desiring and manifesting things. Humility is an attitude unrelated to the amount of stuff you have in your life. You are all worthy of your desires, and of happiness as well. As always, we emphasise that happiness will come not from material abundance, but from inner richness and purposeful work. As long as you keep focused on this mindset, your happiness will not be dependent on outer prosperity. Everybody wants to lead a free, simple, prosperous life, and why shouldn't they? It is all in your mind. You can have anything that your mind can imagine: the good, the bad, the great, and the ugly.

Now that this is all clear, I'd like you to affirm the following: *I am worthy of all good in the universe: material, spiritual, emotional, and ethereal. I am a divine being with the power and ability to create the world I desire, and I invoke all the power within me, and the infinite love of God to fulfil my desires. I am blessed.*

The Stages of Manifestation

You are constantly bombarded by things, experiences, and sensations from a world of infinite abundance, where everything is on offer: good and bad, right and wrong, safe and dangerous, kind and unloving, restricted and free, and so on. There is nothing that cannot be experienced in this world, and as such, you have the freedom of will to choose from everything that is on offer, the experiences that will be part of your life's journey. You attract them to your life with your intention and focus, as we have explained. At any given moment, you desire many things; this causes confusion. Can you focus on all of them and have them manifested in your life? I tell you that you can, by giving some things *focused action*, and others *focused intention*. These are two different states that comprise the process of manifestation.

The first state, focused intention, is when you put mental and visual focus on something you desire in order to attract its energy to you. As the energy builds up around you and becomes strong, events, circumstances, resources, and people start working in synchronization to make it happen. Once you start noticing the synchronicity, knowing that it is the product of your focused intention, you can engage in the next stage, focused action. This is the action that you need perform to bring what you desire into your physical reality.

Let me explain this in a more graphic way. All your desires already exist in the vortex, a universal catalogue of everything that anyone has ever or will ever desire. You constantly browse through this catalogue and highlight what you want to have, be, feel, or do at a given point in your life. Once you have identified the things that you want from all the available ones, you start bringing them closer to you by engaging in the stage of focused intention, in which you use visualization, positive attention, and thought to see them as possible, attainable. These acts cause the universe to start rearranging reality in order to bring about manifestation.

However, to bring about physical manifestation, you usually need to engage in physical action, which is the second stage. It can be as simple as buying a lottery ticket or changing your route to work, or as radical as having a "sea change." You will know when you need to take obvious action by the appearance of signs, feelings, and hunches that will guide you in what to do next. It is up to you, and you alone, to be attentive, ready, and courageous enough to follow through.

Nothing is impossible; you just need to understand the process. You can focus on more than one thing at a time, but you must understand that the manifestation process goes through these stages. The length of each stage depends on your amount of focus in the first step, and on any delays in your engagement to take action in the second step. Those are the two main factors that determine how much time passes between original desire and physical manifestation.

One word of advice: during the stage of focused intention, you don't have to become obsessed with your desires. This will not help the manifestation process, but will in fact have the opposite effect. Feelings of anxiety and obsession inadvertently show your distrust for having those dreams come true.

During the first stage, you need to develop comfort, confidence and joyous expectation that whatever you want is possible and will happen at the proper time, under the best conditions for you. In reality, the focus must be based on your happiness for being the creator of you own life with the power to determine its quality. Once you become aware of that feeling within you, your goal is to feel it consistently all the way through. Being focused is not only thinking about what you want, but also experiencing the wonderful feeling inside you that puts you at the steering wheel of your life, thus setting you free.

CHAPTER 18

The Power of Self-Drive: *The Forces*

The power of self-drive represents the combination of two *forces*: the force of your soul inside you and the force of the whole universe outside you. Both push you forward on your journey of life. You have a soul that has manifested in this physical world to fulfil a purpose. A soul is not an isolated entity, but part of an infinite universal energy that works its way to evolution through a perfect, harmonious, and balanced plan. Everything and everyone in the universe is ruled by these driving forces that direct the flow and rhythm of expression, expansion, and creation. The power of self-drive harnesses the power of these divine forces. It is always working within you, silently and slowly without your conscious awareness, or loudly at full strength when you are empowered in the driver's seat of your life.

You can relate your driving force to your inner truth, the purpose that is engraved in your heart and in the depths of your being. Most people acknowledge, even unconsciously, that there is a truth, a purpose for their existence, and although one might not be able to explain it with words, comprehend it, or even imagine it, it is nevertheless there. At some point, you instinctively came to know that truth. Think of a time when you were lost in contemplation, flowing with life, or briefly disconnected from your ego. Recall those fleeting moments: you experienced an eerie sensation, a complete, profound peace, and a feeling of letting go. Those inexplicable but wonderful sensations were produced by your self-driving force as it gently directed you to your inner truth, which then seemed to show up on the peripheries of your being. It is in these precise moments that you felt you "got it," that you could give your purpose a name. However, as soon as you examined it, as soon as you broke the spell you were under and tried to grasp it, your awareness set it loose again, and you were left wondering what had just happened.

This truth, this self-driving force, is what many describe as the "calling." It is the reason for your very existence, and may or may not emerge at a conscious level for you to express in words. It is what you are called to do, be, or achieve in this life, sometimes without any clear explanation of why. When you begin your search for the light, what you are really doing is embarking on a journey to discover what your inner truth is. This is a one-way road; once your awareness awakens and becomes inquisitive, you cannot go back to your previous state of ignorance. Once you start walking the path to the light, you can only continue walking. This is the natural process of inner growth and evolution. This is your self-driving power in action.

Right from the start of the journey, you must commit to what is required of you. Irrespective of what stage of your journey you are at—blissful unawareness, grasping what life is all about, discovering the self, gaining clarity about your next move, working to align with your self-driving force—you need to be committed to the process through continual searching, asking, learning, attempting, growing, and evolving with the aim of fulfilling your truth, making it happen. Embarking on the journey to the light triggers a chain reaction of events and changes in your life whose primary intention is to push you forward. These events have an impact on your experiences at all levels, and take place at specific times and with various degrees of significance. The process can be long, tedious, and full of obstacles and vicissitudes; it can also be enlightening, empowering, magnificent, and full of adventure. Your experience of it depends on your awareness of your inner powers and your relationship with your soul.

Often, staying committed to your inner truth may seem demanding and difficult to sustain due to the changes in beliefs, habits, patterns of thought, and attitudes that are usually required as part of the journey. For that reason, some may attempt to go back to ignorance to solve their uneasiness; they try to ignore what their enhanced awareness tells them and pretend that nothing is happening, that the nagging inside them is not real. However, this is an impossible task, as once you have become aware of your true nature, your purpose, your light, once your awareness has been stimulated and enticed by the surfacing of one or more of your inner powers, you cannot go back—you can only keep on going.

You can temporarily stop where you are and delay the process, but this will only lead to discontent, misery, disillusionment, even illness, and in the long run, death, until you finally acknowledge that you cannot go back to your previous, smaller self. You have changed; your spiritual and physical composition has morphed into a more evolved expression. Wanting to revert to a less-awakened state is like wanting to go back to being a foetus in your mother's uterus. It is not impossible in our realm, but it is definitely not possible in yours.

Using the Power of Self-Drive

This power is not so much about what you have to do to put it in practice as about what you have to let go of to allow it to flow through you at its full potential. It's about letting go of resistance, doubt, fear, baggage, and old layers that weigh you down; and ridding yourself of beliefs that no longer serve you, unhealthy patterns of thought, and disease. You need to submit yourself to a cleansing process that not only purifies your physical being (body, mind, and energy; your soul is always pure), but also weakens and eventually eliminates the barriers erected by the ego. During this process, your driving force will progress from being silent and slow to being loud and strong.

You can perform this cleansing through any of the exercises presented in this book, as well as by other methods, activities, and therapies that draw your focus onto your inner strengths, powers, and talents, and aim to connect you with your soul. Examples of these activities are meditation, balancing your energy centres, journaling, positive self-talk, self-empowering activities, expansion of your comfort zone, visualization, determining your true desires, decluttering your life, and focusing on the present, as well as physical, creative, and self-expressive activities.

The act of acknowledging your truth, whatever it might be, and of opening yourself to the driving force living inside you is like a birth, or more accurately, a rebirth. Committing yourself and working to fulfil your truth is like peeling away layers of your awareness that have been weighing you down up until now. If you feel powerless where you stand; too scared, full of doubt, critical, and weak to honour your inner truth; you can call upon your faithful companions—your self-driving force, your spiritual guidance, and your divine nature—to overcome any difficulty. They will act as catalysts that transform your journey from arduous and impossible to joyous and glorious. In the same way that a baby needs his human family to nurture, look after, feed, protect, and love him, in this rebirth, you need the support of your spiritual others to do exactly the same for you.

Spirit takes care of you from within you. When the light of your soul is vibrant and strong enough, you can walk by yourself as a soul in this physical land. In order for this to happen, you need to accept this rebirth, to acknowledge your inner powers, and to commit to what is required of you to achieve your purpose. This process can be related to one that takes place in the human domain: a person is required to accept and commit to the established social laws of human interaction in order to be accepted and acknowledged as part of a given society and to flourish within that domain.

When you finally surrender to your inner truth, accept who you really are, and let yourself be guided by the forces that govern the whole, you will be rewarded. The first reward is a delightful sensation of relief caused by releasing many layers and baggage from your energetic body, as you take on new resolutions and embark on new ways of living life. The second reward is an unmeasurable feeling of excitement and openness to whatever may come, without any doubt or fear about the source or your purpose. The third reward is feelings of love and happiness; your life gains more meaning and sense, despite the fact that you may not know where you are going. You feel awe and detachment.

Once you commit and stay focused, all divine laws start working in harmony to move you forward on your path, and no matter how simple or intricate the flow of life may seem to you, you will always flow forward, knowing that you are travelling in the direction that you are supposed to go. Doubt and fear have the effect of delaying the flow of life, even bringing it to a stop. They don't serve you at all; as divine spirit, you are perfect and powerful, fearless and all-knowing. Your inner truth should always be your guiding, driving power. When doubt or fear cast a shadow over you, remain focused on your inner light; it will clear away the shadows. As the darkness dissipates, the clear path will show itself again for you to walk confidently.

CHAPTER 19

The Power of Perseverance: The Belief

This power represents the determination and resolve that naturally exist in you and are inherent to *belief* in your inner self and your sense of purpose. This sometimes inexplicable tenacity is what keeps you going, what makes you follow your dreams and persist in your mission, whatever it might be, regardless of others' opinions, and despite the obstacles, doubts, hesitations, and unknowns. Perseverance is the power that makes you reach your destination, that whispers in your ear words of encouragement, comfort, patience, and trust in what you are doing.

Many of you ignore this power and choose to give up when the road becomes difficult or uncertain, or when the boundaries of your life are tested and your confidence affected because you cannot see the physical manifestation of your efforts. How often have you started an enterprise with drive and enthusiasm, only to stop working on it when you can't see any results and are disheartened and disappointed? You live in times that, due to your technological advancements, expect instant results. This has contributed greatly to the loss of patience as a virtue. Don't underestimate patience, which allows you to wait gracefully for events to take place in their due time and course without suffering stress, frustration, disappointment, sadness, or anger. This point is especially relevant to life situations in which events cannot be controlled by man, nor achieved through technology. Most of you believe in technology, whose precision, accuracy, and near-perfection provides you with everything you desire, and from which you demand and expect results. However, you probably fail to notice that it is an external provider run by complex and advanced programs. You are so accustomed to this modern way of interacting and living that you aspire to apply the same expectations to yourself and other people, to nature, and to the laws of the universe, which orchestrate everything with unsurpassable wisdom. You want not only to see the results of your actions immediately, but also, perhaps, to know the outcomes of those actions before they even take place.

In some situations, these wants can be met—you can see some results and outcomes early on at a level that will please you. However, in other situations, you will not achieve your immediate wants; there will be unknowns and variables outside of your control. Instead of persevering, continuing to follow the drive that originated your action, you might then engage in negative self-talk to justify the lack of results. You might say things like, "I am not doing things right"; "I am off track"; "Something is wrong"; "I am wrong"; "I am not good enough"; "I cannot have, be, or achieve what I want"; "I don't deserve it"; "I am not worthy"; "I am useless"; "I am not qualified"; and so on. None of that is real. In truth, you are not seeing the results of your actions because all that negative self-talk and all those doubts are blocking your vision. More than anything else, our saying, "Believing is seeing," is applicable to this subject; when you believe then you will see.

In the physical world, things take time to manifest (refer to the stages of manifestation in Chapter 17), especially when they relate to the emotions and the spirit. In these areas specifically, outcomes and results are for the most part intangible, because they relate to the way you feel, think, and behave. Changing or improving these aspects of yourself takes time, determination, and commitment. Therefore, persevering is a key component in your life journey, in relation to not only your physical desires, but also your emotional and spiritual ones. What makes you keep on going, regardless of any apparent result, is belief in yourself and what you are doing.

Your heart is the flame that pushes you to embark on any path involving your physical, emotional, and spiritual life. Slowly, this flame turns into faith, which is the seed that germinates and transforms into strong belief. If you believe in yourself, if you embrace your values, if you persevere on the chosen path of your light, if you trust in your power, if you have faith in a divine Source that lives in you, then you will start feeling the changes inside yourself. Soon after, you will be able to see those changes reflected in the outside world. The changes might not be visible to other people's eyes, and for that reason, they might criticise you or call you a dreamer—but the changes will be visible to your eyes and heart, and that is what truly matters.

Giving up keeps you stuck, unsatisfied, and repressed. You know that the only option is to move forward, to try, even if you do not think you will succeed. The truth is that you have already succeeded, as a result of trying. Time exists only in your dimension. It is a concept that the ego created to control your drive. Therefore, when you disempower the ego and detach yourself from its command, you regain your power, and with that, your ability to control time. You will discover that you can make things happen faster as you engage the wisdom of your soul. You will find that lack of perseverance is no longer an issue. You will also find that, even if you can't see your path, the answers and steps will unfold along the way. If you take a wrong turn, you will always find some valuable lesson to be learnt from that slip-up. Even when you are not completely confident, you can take another step forward, believing in yourself and trusting in the universe.

As you use your power of perseverance, you will detach from the expectations of time and start cooperating and working in harmony with everyone and everything. You will soon realise that you have all the time in the world for things to happen when they are ripe to bring the best outcome for all those involved, not when your ego says they should happen.

Using the Power of Perseverance

Take some time to determine your level of perseverance. Remember that everyone has this power. However, it will be more active in some than in others. Some people have a natural tendency to persevere, while others will have to work at it until it becomes natural. Also, you could persevere more in some aspects of your life than in others.

Do you drop out of things quickly when the road gets tough, or you do not attain quick results? Do you have a tendency to continue indefinitely, even when what you are doing doesn't seem to yield any results, nor has a clear objective or benefit? Or, do you persevere and constantly evaluate your progress? You probably do a bit of all of these, depending on the situation.

Identify with clarity and understanding what is sabotaging your efforts in any given activity. Is it your lack of belief or faith in whatever you are doing? Or is it something else that you are not yet aware of? More often than not, we blame our lack of perseverance to cover for other issues that are the true offenders spoiling our efforts and desires. For example, inner blockages, old beliefs, unhealthy self-perception, high expectations, perfectionism, low self-esteem, lack of interest, self-criticism, and fear to success are often masked by a supposed lack of perseverance.

When you find yourself in the kind of situation that usually makes you give up, do not be quick to label yourself as impatient or not persevering. Instead, spend some time evaluating the real reasons for your actions. It could truly be that you don't have much heart for what you are doing, or it could be some other issue altogether that is interfering with your undertaking. These issues need to be addressed and cleared up in order for you to regain your power, to feel in control, to achieve whatever you intend, and to be fulfilled.

The same applies to those who persevere too much, continually working on something that never seems to end nor yield the intended results. This is another type of mask to cover issues like the ones mentioned above and some others, such as avoiding important life situations, wanting to get a return on investment (although it may never come), inability to accept lack of success or defeat, lack of purpose or direction, and loneliness. As in the previous scenario, the issues behind performing never-ending activities without any results must be identified and addressed before the person can feel empowered.

You know you are using the power of perseverance for your own benefit when you

- Are engaged in your endeavours
- Allow them to develop at their own pace and rhythm but without dragging them out
- Are driven by desire and belief
- Frequently check for progress and outcomes
- Assess what you can do to further your progress
- Evaluate how satisfying and fulfilling the activities feel
- Are not afraid to change course or put an end to what you are doing if that feels right

Remember that perseverance is invaluable when you are working on something new and moving through new steps; there might be many unknowns in the process, and you probably won't know what to expect. You are most vulnerable in these new beginnings; the ego uses this fact to its advantage by presenting fears, doubts, and other obstacles, with the objective of making you hesitate and remain where you are. During times like these, be honest with yourself. Evaluate the reason you continue to do what you are doing, talk with your soul, release the baggage slowing you down, and silence your inner critic. If, after this reflection, all signs tell you to believe in yourself, then keep on going. Continue doing what you feel you must do for a little longer; know that all is evolving and moving at the right pace. In the end, you will be rewarded with results, and you will feel happy and proud of yourself for having trusted and persevered.

PART IV

Outer Issues, Inner Challenges

In this part of the book, my soul voice wants to bring to our attention some of the key issues that we face in life. Exploring these issues will shed light onto them; with clarity and understanding, we can change our perspective and perceptions about them.

Soul wants us to understand without a doubt that the outer issues that often disturb, push, shake, stretch, rock, perturb, and confuse us, as well as enticing, seducing, bewitching, and distorting our lives, are nothing but disguised challenges to help us grow as we travel our life's journey. Times of abundance are accompanied by times of loss; times of happiness and joy are accompanied by times of sadness and distress; times of fulfilment are accompanied by times of emptiness. In other words, we cannot have high times without low times; that is the essence of the dance of life. It is during the low times that we discover and test our strength, our perseverance, and our will power. We are not meant to experience only the upper parts of the spectrum of life; neither are we meant to experience only the lower ones, either.

Life is a succession of ups and downs that push us to evolve spiritually. How long we spend on each side of the road depends on our inner evolution. Life presents us with an infinite array of opportunities in the most diverse scenarios to help us learn and relearn our life lessons, test and retest what we have learnt. It is in this constant flow of trials, failures, successes, and lessons that we progress and move forward on our path towards fulfilling our life's mission on this physical plane.

Soul wants us to understand that all the issues of the world outside are really challenges to our world inside. The only way to tame the issues is to acknowledge, understand, and accept who we really are, by recognising and commanding our inner powers. We will not tame life by seeking and claiming external power. It flickers like a candle flame, and it is an illusion that can be snatched from us as quickly as it was given.

Issues will always show up in our lives so we can prove, repeatedly, that we have the ability and power to overcome them and continue on our journey. The sooner we understand this, the shorter our low times will last, and the swifter our ride will become.

CHAPTER 20

Experiencing Life

The Illusion of Life Today: Who We Have Become

We want you to become aware of the fact that you have stopped experiencing life from your inner perspective. You are mostly experiencing life from a physical perspective to satisfy the needs of your senses: sight, smell, taste, hearing, touch, and the dominant desires of your ego, power and control. Your lives have somehow become cold and devoid of true emotions, those coming from your soul.

These days, almost everything can be done from the comfort of your couches by means of a computer or similar electronic device. You are immersed in virtual worlds where you can have any kind of experience without even moving. By means of electronic gadgets, you can talk and interact with people, even people you don't know and might never meet, without actually being in the same room. You can listen to music, hear the news, watch movies; you can read books without holding them in your hands or feeling their pages; you can travel and have adventures in places that don't actually exist, and enjoy an adrenaline rush by playing video games set in dangerous situations. You can kill and you can die in these virtual places. You can be bullied and tormented by complete strangers to whom you have given the power to have a say in your lives. You can also bully and torment others, sometimes not even realising what you are doing. You can make these places as real as you want to believe they are, and still have the sense that you are in control—but are you? You can lose yourselves there. Could it be that you have lost control and are allowing these virtual worlds to take over your lives? Could it be that you are driven by your modern lifestyle, moving through your days on autopilot? Could it be that you have lost your self-drive and inner guidance, which has profoundly affected your desire to explore what life is really about?

Your present lifestyle, with all its technological advances and fast communications, is responsible for many of the issues troubling society today. You have lost patience for allowing things to move at their own pace. Many of you feel isolated, segregated, and lonely despite the great worldwide network of communication available to you because you have become anonymous entities interacting at superficial levels. You are less and less likely to discover what you really are, need, want, and feel. You are faced with startling rates of ill health on the planet. Not only human beings are affected by physical and mental diseases—the wellbeing of the Earth is also in danger. Plants, animals, and the environment itself are suffering as a result of your issues. You are becoming alarmingly obese due to sedentary habits and unhealthy diets. Other kinds of diseases are also on the rise, and new ones are surfacing too. Stress and depression are normal components of your modern lifestyle, while malnourishment and unhealthy living conditions adversely affect underdeveloped areas. You use drugs to treat your illnesses and feelings of confusion; deep down, though, you are trying to silence the nagging of your souls, who want to help you. You satiate your need for control with violence and war. You have lost your connection with all that surrounds you, with the essence of life, with your own essence. Thus, the pictures of your lives are not turning into the masterpieces they could be.

Instead of using progress in your favour, you are using it to your detriment. Instead of utilising technological advancement as an additional valuable tool to aid you during your journey on this beautiful, abundant planet, you have made it the ruler of your lives, and become addicted to its commands. You have muted your souls, made yourselves servants, and crowned the ego the master. Every era has had its challenges and rewards; however, today, you are paying a high price, in every aspect of your lives, to satisfy the ego's needs and wants.

Look back to your ancestors, your grandparents, your parents, or even your own childhood. Don't you think they were happier, more content, more in tune with the whole? Despite the limitations of their technology and scientific and medical knowledge, they still experienced life more fully. They had to work hard to provide for themselves and their families by cultivating their land and producing food, or working in factories for long hours and little pay, yet they still shared what they had with relatives and friends. They performed chores and everyday activities using manpower: their own energy and capacity. They built their own homes and furnishings, they made their own clothes, they read aloud to others. Their hands were rough, not just from hard work, but because they experienced life. They had wrinkles in their skin carved by emotions, work, and life challenges. They visited and talked with each other; they spent time together. Parents passed on their knowledge, experiences, stories, and traditions to their children by teaching and sharing with them, the same way their parents had taught and shared with them. They had a strong sense of community, of belonging, and of being part of the environment they inhabited. They trusted their instincts, and many of their decisions were based on intuition and God's guidance. Through religion, they interpreted their connection with their Source and their belief in a higher being, to whom they prayed. They respected and honoured Mother Nature; she was their partner, providing them with the prime materials to build, create, produce, and generate what they needed. They accepted the ups and downs of life: they played, laughed, suffered, discovered, fought, shared, communed, prayed, endured, hoped, celebrated new life, and bid farewell to the dead.

In contrast, these days, you give great attention and importance to the accumulation of material possessions, the status and momentum of your careers, your finances, your connections, your achievements, and of course, your appearance. All of these are constantly threatened by an impartial and unfriendly foe: time. The majority of you work hard to obtain and maintain all your possessions, which you believe reflect who and what you are. You are so busy working your days away that you hardly realise how little time you have left to enjoy and savour what you possess, let alone to stop for a moment to evaluate whether all that stuff is really worth the effort. Are you happy or miserable? Do you really need all these things? The same applies to your jobs. Many of you pursue certain careers because you are told to, or because it is financially beneficial, even though these are not the occupations you honestly prefer. Others of you remain in unfulfilling jobs for the good income and career prospects, not because they fill you with drive or enthusiasm.

You spend much energy on building all sorts of relationships so you can be surrounded by people and involved in activities, with the true conscious or unconscious objective of avoiding being alone. You believe that doing nothing is lazy, unproductive, and a waste of time, and that spending time alone or being selective about who you spend your time with are signs of selfishness, loneliness, or being a loser. You put great pride in what you do and achieve because it feels good to be applauded, admired, and appreciated. Thus, you are pushed to constantly do more; you even become critical of those who choose to go through life at a slower pace, doing less and living more.

However, the biggest problem of today's society is your fixation on your appearance. It absorbs, immerses, and sucks you into a whirlwind of obsessions. No one wants to age. You try to maintain immaculate hands, luscious hair, wrinkle free skin, and toned bodies; many managing to keep young and healthy for longer, thanks not only to medical and scientific advances, but also to the cosmetics industry. People go to great extremes to look great and feel young. You are driven by yearning to be approved of and loved by others, rather than by your own desire to feel happy and healthy in your own skin. Weight is a constant concern. Both adults and young people use fad diets, slimming shakes, diet pills, vitamins, and supplements to try achieving slim bodies, not for health reasons, but for aesthetic ones. Beauty and perfection are seen as a guarantee of acceptance. People who don't fit the current aesthetic trends cannot lead happy lives because they are constantly reminded of their shortcomings. Naturally, these expectations push them to try, by whatever means possible, to fit in.

You have become outwards-oriented, and as such, you allow yourselves to be constantly interrupted and distracted by things, even though not many of them contribute to your purpose or growth, but instead eat up your time without your being aware of it. You have accepted that outside forces tell you how you should be, feel, and look; what you should and shouldn't do; and whom you should be friends with. You believe it is your job to work tirelessly towards eliminating (or hiding) your uniqueness and your differences in order to fit in and be accepted. The message society sends is that the better you conform to its expectations and dictates, the happier you will be. This is the reason people live their lives trying to be the same as everyone else; "everybody does it," so it must be right.

Many resort to drugs—alcohol, tobacco, prescription and illegal drugs—to deal with the uneasiness and conflict (both inner and outer) that you don't know how to face. You have also befriended your internal foes, negative internal chatter and defeating self-talk, to try to overcome your feelings of not fitting in, and your lack of motivation or purpose. Your souls yearn for experience and growth that your physical selves do not have or allow. If you just stopped and listened, you'd realise that your souls have solutions for your external issues—they could help you overcome your misery and unhappiness, and put you on course.

Life Is Just the River and Us: Who We Really Are

Everything has a balance, an equilibrium that must be maintained to create harmony in every order of life, not only at the individual level, but also on the planet and in the universe. Too much or too little of anything can be damaging, and negatively affect the order and flow of your lives. Could you have lost your balance, and no longer be flowing harmoniously in the river of life? Could you be doing too many things that affect your lives adversely, and too few things that empower you with love and fulfilment? Perhaps the reason for this imbalance is that you have temporarily forgotten your connection with your inner light; you have stopped listening to your souls and bringing spirit into everything you do.

The recipe to restore balance is simple and gratifying: *reconnect with the light within, unmute your soul, and restore its voice.* In this book, your souls are speaking to you to awaken you from your slumber and make you see things for what they really are—this will restore harmony and peace to your lives. The purpose of the book is not to condemn your present society, nor to imply that technological advances are bad or wrong for you or the planet. After all, the advances of your physical world are a reflection of the progress of your spiritual evolution. No, we are trying to make you understand that nothing in this world can replace the wisdom and knowledge of your feelings and your inner guidance; no one can tell you what is good or right for you. You possess the inner tool that knows what you need in order to feel great and function perfectly. You have to learn over again to use everything available to you for your advancement, advantage, and happiness. Not doing so will only lead to your own detriment and the deterioration of your race and planet.

Regain control of your lives. Combine the best of all times: yesterday's chances to experience life, today's opportunities provided by your advancements, and the future's creations born of a more soul-based nature. Live life using all the modern gadgets and tools to aid you, not as substitutes for your own experience and interaction. Go back to the river of life and allow yourselves to drift downstream without resistance or worries about where it might take you. All that really exists is the river and you. The rest is at your disposal and can either help or hinder your journey; it all depends on the wisdom of your choices and actions, whether you use opportunities to push you forward, or abuse them and end up stuck.

Read these pages not only with your mind but also with your heart, that part of you where your soul resides, and the place where the words on these pages originated. Your heart is the place where every concept and message in this book will resonate the clearest and loudest to awaken you, transform you, and raise your awareness of its truths, all of which will remain with you forever.

Let's Flow with Life: The Way Forward

Learn to enjoy life to the fullest. Learn to appreciate all your experiences as opportunities to explore your inner talents and uniqueness, and in doing so, allow your soul to show through however it chooses. Learn to walk more slowly in every aspect of your life, and take in the small things, even if the building blocks of your existence are, sometimes, not pretty. Remember that there is always a hidden meaning in everything placed in your way. When life moves at a slower pace, you can appreciate results and outcomes with more clarity. You can also observe the details of the processes and events of every moment. Learn to listen more, and you'll discover hidden languages that you didn't know you could understand, such as the language of nature, which is constantly communicating with you; the language of the universe, which talks through us; and the language of your movements, actions, expressions, and silences, which tells you more than a million words.

Learn to give value to what really is valuable, to give your time to things that deserve it, to fight for your desires if your heart, not your mind, is truly screaming for them, to love openly, starting with yourself, and to pursue what brings you joy and fulfilment. Most importantly, learn to be happy; then, see the world change around you to match that feeling. Also, learn to accept that whatever is valuable, worthy of your time, desirable, important, loving, joyous, treasured, beautiful, and fulfilling today may not be so tomorrow. As you decrease the distance between who you truly are and who you are becoming, you change your perspective and appreciation of life.

Learn to accept that deterioration of the body is inevitable, regardless of how hard you try to keep it young, and that human life follows a cycle of birth, growth, and death. However, deterioration of the soul is impossible, as the soul is eternal. Please, experience life and let your soul express itself and grow. This doesn't mean that you shouldn't look after yourself and take care of your physical body—of course you must. Your body is the instrument that allows your soul to be here, on this plane. Take care of your health, love your body, and honour it, because it is the temple of your divine being. If you love yourself and are proud of your physical form at every stage of your life, those feelings of appreciation will have an enormous effect on you—you will have no choice but to feel rejuvenated, healthy, and strong.

Look after yourself by eating properly, exercising, resting. Pamper yourself and tell yourself how wonderful and perfect you are, as you would to someone precious to you. However, do not become obsessed with aging or your appearance, because it is just that—your appearance, an illusion. Don't focus solely on your outside, but work on keeping young, happy, and healthy on the inside. I promise that if you do, your outer self will show fewer years than you really are. Everything ages, everything dies, everything follows a cycle, and everything has a beginning and end on this plane. Do not waste precious time worrying about ways to delay or stop that process— they will not work. Instead, use your energy to enjoy to the utmost each phase of the cycle of life.

Does a rose, knowing how beautiful it becomes in the glory of its blooming, try to stop itself from dying? Does it want to keep that beauty forever? It doesn't. The rose accepts that it is born to give immense beauty and delightful perfume only for a short time, and that after the splendour, death follows. When it is time, the rose dies effortlessly, without resistance, knowing that other roses of even greater beauty will come after it to continue the process of life. Observe nature. Nothing in nature shows resistance to the inevitable progression of life. Nature is connected to the rhythms of the universe, to the higher intelligence that creates and orchestrates all. Nature flows with the river of life easily and joyfully; it celebrates being alive and its reason for being. Learn from nature, and flow with life.

CHAPTER 21

Being In the Present: The Power of Now

Being in the present moment is something that all spiritual and personal growth teachers talk about and recommend. However, I am sure that even among those who have learned about this concept already, there are plenty of people who haven't yet fully understood what it means to be "in the now," and hence, haven't yet been able to put it into practice. If you are one of these people, don't worry, there is nothing wrong with you. Not appreciating the now is just a habit that needs to be dissolved. Once you understand this concept, you will be able to put it into practice easily, and in your own time.

I, myself, still struggle sometimes to be in the present moment. I have to be very firm to stop my mind from wandering in ways that do not serve me. Other times, I consciously choose not be in the present moment, as a need for a break or time-out from what is happening around me. I am, however, fully aware of what I am doing in those instances. Once the need to escape is satisfied, I can come back to the now. However, the majority of people do not have this control. They are not even aware of where their minds are, most of the time. Most of the issues in their lives arise from that fact. Let's not forget that our thoughts are creative, powerful, and magnetic, attracting experiences that match the vibration of what we constantly think about. Hence, one can unconsciously recreate situations in his life that may reflect a past he refuses to let go, or a very uncertain future.

The Past and the Future

Are you someone who spends too much time thinking of the past? Do you like to indulge in reliving past events, even ones from a long time ago? Do you prefer to reminiscence about negative experiences rather than happy ones, as a way of justifying the present state of your life? What happened in the past cannot be changed. However, perhaps you don't want to acknowledge the fact that you have no more control over the past than anybody else. The more you replay the past in your mind, wishing it were different, the more distorted your memories become, and the more wrongs, injustices, and pain you see. While you are submerged in these mind games, these sensations envelop you and play up your feelings—this affects you and your life now, at the present moment! As I mentioned before, this unhealthy habit needs to be dealt with in order for you to regain control, and thus live a more joyous and fulfilling life. You can heal the past only by immersing yourself in inner work and forgiveness, so you can break your bonds with that past and move forward in life.

There are, of course, positive, joyous past experiences too. Thinking about them is a great way to attract positive vibes and feelings to the present time in order to keep you happy and motivated about life. However, this habit is beneficial only if done with some measure or for a specific purpose, as part of internal work for example. Realise that your aim is to continue creating more of these great moments in your present, not to live your life through your memories.

Similar issues arise when people spend large amounts of time chasing the future. In their minds, depending on their experiences, beliefs, and perception of the world, the future looks magnificent and glorious, or terrifying, painful, and dark. Thoughts of the future can create within us feelings that immobilise, scare, and depress us, or feelings that excite, motivate us and make us do reckless things. To varying degrees, these feelings all have an effect on our present.

Remembering the past and dreaming about the future not only take away our attention from the now, but also shape our present by transferring the feelings created by those thoughts into our present. Thus, we miss what is going on now, at the present moment. Our present becomes clouded and coloured by thoughts that prevent us from seeing, acting, behaving, and even thinking with clarity. Clarity comes from being present and acknowledging what life is offering to us *now!*

When we are not in the now, we are physically present, but mentally absent. We may miss out on opportunities and fail to pay attention to things that could give us answers, relief, joy, peace, and help. We are not present for everybody and everything we are interacting with: loved ones, friends, co-workers, acquaintances, strangers, animals, plants. More importantly, we are not fully present for ourselves, let alone for our inner being or the spiritual guides that are eager to assist us. Sometimes we consciously choose to live in our heads. There are various reasons, for example, life is too challenging and we need a respite, we need to feel justified by relieving a past event, or we need to bring some excitement to a boring existence by daydreaming. Consciously or unconsciously, our inner chatter constantly wants to monopolise the flow of our thinking. It fights very hard against any attempt on our part to revoke its control. We can win that battle if we understand that it is acceptable for thoughts of the past or the future to pop up here and there and distract us, as long as we are not hanged upon them.

Worry, resentment, pain, anger, and blame about the past are not only unhealthy to our being, but also darken our present. The way to heal our tendency to live in the past is to accept that nothing that happened can be changed—it is all out of our control. The only wise actions to take are to observe, with detachment, what happened, to learn the lessons offered us, and to move forward, all along acknowledging the feelings that may arise. All this should be done within a reasonable timeframe. Your whole life is not a reasonable timeframe.

Mostly living in the future, whether it is dreaded or anticipated, is not a better option. Nothing can replace the opportunities that life constantly offers us in order to put us on track to manifesting our desires. The way to heal our tendency to live in the future is to claim back our passion, to rediscover what moves us, to engage in activities that entice our senses, to work on what we can control and change, and to find clarity in order to dissipate thoughts of doom and gloom.

Once we bring healing and liveliness into our present, we won't feel the need to live in the past or the future. We will be eager to experience the now.

We Create Our Lives in the Now

You may know that the only thing you have in life is this very moment. However, few of you appreciate what this really means. Everything is true and real in the now. The second before this one has gone forever; the next second might never come. What you intended, focused, thought, felt, said, or did in that last second created your experience of life in that moment of time. You will never have that same exact experience again, because the conditions that created it have changed.

When you think of the past or the future, you are living in your mind. It is a virtual setting where you create all the conditions, dialogues, actions, and behaviours with the sole purpose of giving you some kind of relief. However, none of it is real; you are not physically experiencing those events, though it might sometimes feel that way. Similarly, when you watch a movie, you might relate to some of the characters or the story. For the duration of the movie, you become the character and immerse yourself in the story. You gain satisfaction from imagining yourself living those experiences; you might feel validation of some sort, have fun, overcome danger, enjoy love, embrace challenges, succeed, earn money, or merely have a chance to forget about your real life. The difference between watching a movie and living in your head is that once the movie is over, you come back to the present moment, but when you live in your head, you may get lost in it for a long time—sometimes for a lifetime. While you are experiencing artificial feelings, there is an amazing world out there. It is a real stage for you to experience everything you desire.

When we tell you to be present, we are asking you to open up your senses and feel your environment. Notice your feelings and your body's sensations as you experience the stage you are on. As you move through your day, walk in different settings and interact with different actors notice how you feel, how you react, what vibrations you give, what feedback you get. Then you will be able to determine, from an unclouded perspective, what you like, who attracts you, which things you wish to experience or avoid. When you are in settings that are unappealing to you, remember that you can intend for the experience to be smooth and fast-paced, enabling you to move on sooner to a scene that excites you. When you are fully present, your character absorbs what it is experiencing, and changes according to the experience. As you change, the stage and other actors change as well. The movie you are directing and acting in changes and moves in the direction you want it to go.

Make an intention to be in the present for a few days—a new world will open up to you. You are not in yesterday, nor you are in tomorrow; you are in the now. By giving your attention to the now, you affect it, create it, and give it your full energy.

How to Be In the Present

Stay focused. Engage your mind; make it tell you how you feel, what it hears, what it tastes, what it sees and smells, what it currently likes or dislikes. Also, be attentive to messages from your body, which is in constant communication within itself and with you. Are you tired? Are you hungry or thirsty? Do you have pain in any part of your body? Are you paying attention to it, or disregarding it? Do you feel stressed or down? Do you feel upbeat or happy? Does your mood change depending on where you are and whom you are with? Does that change make you feel empowered, or powerless? If you are in the present, you will notice all these feelings and be able to act on them to restore balance and harmony to your being. Stay focused on the now and change the present as you go along by ordering it to change. Remember that if what you are focusing on is not something you like, you can change your focus to whatever you'd like it to be. Manifestation will follow—maybe not on your first attempt, but with practice, you will start to notice miracles around you.

Uncertainty is the reason many choose to daydream about their past or future instead of taking action to create the life they desire. Uncertainty immobilises you by keeping you stuck in a life that you'd love to change if you only knew how. Daydreaming (created by the ego) keeps you locked where you are. Uncertainty manifests in various ways, as a result of different issues.

- *Anxiety, depression,* or *stress*: You can't find the path that will take you from where you are now to where you dream of being. You don't use your inner compass or inner powers for guidance or support, and end up getting lost in the intricate labyrinth of choices that leads you away from your path, or not choosing anything at all. As a result, you lose hope and enthusiasm, and become stuck.

- *Failure* and *giving up*: You think the journey to your dreams will be tough, unpleasant, lengthy, or even impossible to achieve in this life. You don't realise that you need only move one step at a time, or that you don't have to do it alone, because your soul is always walking along with you to show you the next step and offer help if you need it.

- *Powerlessness* and *lack of control*: You see past events as a prediction of the future. You are ignoring the facts that you create your life in each moment, and that past experiences don't have any power in the now. You fail to see your past lessons as experiences that provided you with wisdom, knowledge, and strength, and that shaped the person you are today, yet do not determine who you might become in future.

None of these uncertainties reflects true causes for concern; they are only excuses posed by the ego to keep you where you are, in your mind. The truth is that anything you can desire, you can achieve. However, you must go through the journey to fulfil your dream.

Many people fail to reach their dreams—or if they do reach them, they fail to keep them alive for long—because they resort to shortcuts, trying to avoid the full experience that sees the seed transformed into the flower, pain replaced by healing, and faith building up through discovery of and trust in the inner self. They would rather have a garden full of instant flowers than go through the process of planting the seeds, watering them, feeding them, and nurturing them before finally seeing them blossom. I tell you right now that the flowers of an instant garden don't last. People who take shortcuts have desires in them, but they are not yet ready to change or grow, so they cannot achieve their goals; their goals will stay mere dreams until they are ready to become those dreams. If they do manage to realise their dreams, then they cannot sustain them for long, because their changes are false, superficial; their internal make-up is the same as it was at the beginning of the process.

Let me give you an example with which you may relate. Let's say someone wishes to lose weight, either to feel good about himself, to be healthier, or to be more attractive to others. He really desires to achieve this dream. He can see himself feeling slim and wonderful, but he sees the path to get there as a burden; he would like to skip it altogether. He doesn't want to learn to eat properly, or to exercise or move more, or to deprive himself of the foods that have given him comfort for so long. In other words, he doesn't want to change his patterns of behaviour and thought. He may also feel defeated already by past unsuccessful attempts to lose weight. If he decides to try, he might lose weight using quick-weight-loss methods—however, the weight will come back. Unless he goes through the whole process and changes his internal physiological functioning by learning about the nutritional values of foods; incorporating enjoyable exercise into his life; wanting to be healthy and feel great for its own sake; and examining his relationship with food and with himself; he will not fully succeed.

You can choose to live your dreams and adventures as a movie in your head, or you can choose to go through the journey and live your dreams for real. If you dream all your life, not much in it will change—but if anything does change, your life will probably take you down paths in the opposite direction of your dreams, making things uncomfortable or dull for you. This disillusionment is a way that life pokes you, trying to get you unstuck, moving, and on the road again. Unless you engage yourself in the now and work consciously on your desires, your dreams will only ever stay dreams. Life is always giving you chances to wake up from the slumber of daydreams and start living to create that dream.

Visualization is a great tool only if it is accompanied by action. Dreaming on its own will not take you anywhere. Being in the now will ignite your spirit and make you aware of opportunities that will move you along on your journey. Being in the present will keep you active, awake, and attentive to the next step, which you must follow with faith and trust while, of course, still dreaming.

Daydreaming Is Good, But Don't Lose Yourself in It

Thinking of the past or the future is beneficial, especially if it generates feelings of joy, pride, and wellness, and is done in moderation. But all too often, people get lost in their daydreams; they use daydreams to avoid the present and as excuses for not taking responsibility, regaining control, finding solutions, growing from experiences, or moving forward. The ego makes it appealing for you to stay into daydreams. After a while, you don't even realise you are immersed in them, and you don't notice that your life is passing you by. Then, daydreaming becomes like any other addiction; you get caught up in it, lost in it, and you avoid sorting out your life. You stay with the status quo, not dealing with or healing the past, nor addressing how to manifest your desired future. You are stuck, hiding your head under the ground so as not to have to face what must be faced at some point.

It all comes down to how much pain you are willing to undergo before you decide to take action. Do you really want to spend months, even years, on the road to reach a destination when you could make it in a few days or hours? Wouldn't you prefer to take the shortest and most scenic route, so you can sooner enjoy the place you are going? Life is no different. You make excuses only because you are trapped in your own comforts, habits, beliefs, and rules.

Those who succeed in life leave their comfort zones to reach for their goals. A success is the same as an achievement, although the exact definition of the word varies between individuals depending on who is manifesting the achievement and who is observing it. A success could be big, small, material, spiritual, internal, external, good, bad, positive, negative, lawful, or illegal. Those who succeed are driven by their desires, regardless of what those desires are. Their life journeys are extraordinary, usually full of ups and downs, fears to overcome, beliefs to change, talents to discover, and pain to endure, but also full of rewards such as the freedom to be themselves, joy over never giving up, feelings of accomplishment and satisfaction, abundance, fame, and even eccentricities. Above all, those who succeed teach us that in order to achieve what you want, to make your dreams come true, you need to go wherever that dream can be made real. You have to elevate yourself to the place where you vibrate at the same rate and with the same intensity as your dream.

So wake up, and get up! Make amends with the past, clarify who you truly want to become, and get excited about the future. Your present moment is a step on the journey of life. Come out of your head and start living your life in the present. Engage in whatever you are guided to do. Everything you need is available to you. Sooner than you think, you will be living your dreams.

Simple Rules for Being in the Now

These are some simple rules you can apply to be more present in your mind, body, and soul.

1. Don't be hard on yourself if you find that your mind is wandering. Allow it a bit of playtime before you bring it back to the present; it is usually during those travels

that you uncover important things. However, be aware that you need to control your mind and not allow it to take over at will.

2. Use all your senses in the present moment to be connected to your surroundings. Your senses transmit feedback, signs, and responses; use them as anchors to keep you in the now.

3. Stop your inner chatter and listen to your inner voice and guidance. If you don't hear anything, then stay attuned to your sensations.

4. Be strong and determined to gain control. Persevere, and you will see change.

This is the best advice I can give without getting into too much detail. There is not much more to it than these simple rules. If you follow them, they will open the doors to a new way of perceiving life and reward you with gratitude, peace, and awe.

Smell the Flowers

I'd like to share with you this quote by Alfred A. Montapert, a philosopher and author who summarised in just a few words the wisdom of living in the present.

People spend their lives in anticipation of being extremely happy in the future.
But all we own is the PRESENT . . . NOW.
PAST opportunities are gone.
FUTURE opportunities may, or may not, come.
NOW is all we have.
We must enjoy each day—one at a time.
Be sure to smell the flowers.

I first read this quote many years ago in a healthy living newsletter distributed where I used to work. I felt that it was not only inspiring, but also full of truth, so I cut it out and placed it on my fridge amongst our photos, my daughters' collages, and all of the magnets and affirmations that try to find a place there. Afterwards, I came across the quotation many times, even translated into different languages, often sent to me as part of inspirational messages from well-intentioned friends. However, I think most of them just passed it along without really appreciating the significance of its meaning. I wish they had all decided to put it on their fridges too. I read it as often, or whenever I feel the need to be centred and present. It puts things back into perspective for me every single time. I hope that it does the same for you. Please make sure to smell the flowers.

CHAPTER 22

The Perception of Life

Essence vs. Perception

What is it life? Is "reality" real, or is it only imagined in your mind? As I have mentioned, life is a stage on which you act out your thoughts. You are born into form onto the stage that you chose to be part of before you entered the physical realm, with the people and in the surroundings that you decided were best-suited for you to work towards your purpose. Being born into the physical is an occasion full of joy and grace. The soul is eager to start its new life and live it. However, somewhere along the way, for most people, life stops being the adventure it was meant to be, and instead becomes a task that must be endured. Actually, the essence of life remains unchanged throughout the whole journey; the essence of life is and always will be love, happiness, inner peace, harmony, and wholeness. What changes is not the essence, but the perception of life.

At the beginning of your life as a physical being, you are a child simply desiring to live, enjoy, and experience life. Everything is magnificent, an adventure, a mystery. It doesn't matter what happens in a child's world. As a child, you find many opportunities to smile, play, make friends, trust, love and share. Even in the worst situations, through tears and pain, children are able to trust. They do not need reasons or explanations; they just live the lives they have chosen and willingly accept how events unfold. As a child, you are still close to your soul, and you live in partnership with it. Without consciously knowing it, you live from your soul's perspective, as a soul having a human experience. Children have a thirst for doing, learning, experiencing, trying, testing, and discovering; there are no boundaries or dangers in their minds. They know that they are safe and they trust in life; they are full of life!

But at some point on your journey from childhood to adulthood, something happens that causes disconnection between you and your soul. At that point, the child begins to function as a human isolated from his spiritual source. It is at this stage that the questioning starts; you lose your sense of identity and start to become confused about who you are and what you are supposed to be doing. You lose individuality and start feeling a need to fit in. Fears surface, walls are erected, boundaries are set, and life stops seeming like a place of infinite possibilities and starts feeling like a chore or burden, a thing to be endured, a restless race that has nothing to do with socioeconomic status, but with an individual's internal conflict.

These issues start to emerge when you enter adulthood, and will each crop up at key points in your life until your lessons are leant, your wounds are healed, and your soul can move on to the next phase of the journey. Your detachment from your divine nature makes you lose the voice of your soul; it is silenced by a new voice, that of the ego. This voice tells you who you are, what you want, where you must go, what you need to do, what you can or cannot do or be, and as time goes by, it becomes stronger and louder. This voice becomes the dominant ruler of your mind.

If you could be led by your inner child's heart all of your life, life would be completely different. You could be engaged in adult endeavours but guided by your soul's calling. You would have dreams that weren't truncated by the rules of what could or couldn't be. You would laugh more, worry less, and be fearless in the face of the unknown, seeing in everything an opportunity to discover something new. You would be less concerned about your physical appearance, the colour of your skin, your social status, or any other differences. You'd call your divine Source and Creator by whatever name you wanted, knowing that regardless of name, there is only one creator of all. You would share what you had, and you wouldn't want any more than what you needed to live. You wouldn't be concerned about tomorrow, or even later, because you'd be too busy creating the now. You wouldn't need to be more or have more than others, as you'd understand that everything is available to everyone, that resources are endless, and that every person can claim what is his by birthright.

Why don't you all live from a childlike perspective, then? Why do you reach that point in time when you lose connection with your soul? This is a pivotal point in your life that you also agreed to before birth. It gives you the chance to relearn and rediscover that you are a soul in a physical experience. Through this process, soul grows and expands. On its journey, the soul needs to first experience being pure human disconnected from its source, and to learn how limiting and frustrating that is, before reaching the point at which the search for answers begins. Questions such as, "Is this all there is to life?"; "What am I really here for?" and "What is my purpose, if any?" are triggered by feelings of emptiness and disillusionment with life.

The next turning point is when you realise that you possess an immense power within, that by finding and acknowledging that power, you will find the answers to your questions. You discover the light that will guide you to the truth that you are not your limitations, barriers, boundaries, and fears; that nothing is the way you thought it was; that you are a divine being with unlimited power to create. Once this amazing discovery is recalled—and you know it is truth because it resonates deep in your heart—you start the journey to remember how to be a creator, how to start living the life you once set out to live, and how to be constantly in the light.

You, who are reading these words, have awoken from the illusions of the ego. You know that you are spirit in the confines of your human form. You know your truth—or at least you can sense it vibrating inside your being. Now you must remember how to be light, how to be a creator, how to live with purpose, and how to live the life you came here to live. You can learn all that from the messages of this book. All you need is a *willing heart*, a *burning desire* to be a soul in physical expression, and a *persevering force* driving you. All you need to do is follow your inner guidance without fear or hesitation, knowing and trusting that you will never be asked to do or be anything that you cannot handle or that you didn't agree to.

We are all on this journey together. All people on the planet agreed to be here for the growth of our divine universal lives. We are all contributing to the process of evolution, so the sooner people realise their divine nature, their power, and the importance of their existence, the faster the process will unfold. However, since the timing and pacing of the universe are perfect, only those who need to awaken will do so. The ones not yet ready will stay in the shadows until their time comes. There is a correlation between manifestation and readiness; no one is able to manifest from his soul's perspective until he is ready to recognise his power, and that he is a soul in human form. All is perfect, and the process will not be forced.

The Way Life Really Is

I am in another one of my meditations, going to the temple to meet my spirit guides. I am walking along the beach peacefully, enjoying the experience, but something peculiar is happening. Wherever I lay my eyes, the scene becomes enlarged, as though I am looking through a magnifying glass. I can see every detail clearly. The blue in the sky is bluer, the water is so clear that I can spot the smallest rocks on the sandy bottom, the trees are gigantic and greener than ever, the sand under my feet is fine, smooth, and almost white. I can also perceive the aura around everything, even around my hands and fingers.

I am definitely seeing life through different eyes. It feels great. Everything seems more alive, brighter, and more vibrant. As I scan the surroundings, whatever I focus on comes alive and seems to be talking to me, grabbing my attention. I keep walking, amazed by the experience, relaxed and peaceful.

I walk through the field of wildflowers towards the temple, which for the first time is not just grey but also has golden patches. It is as if the grey in the walls has receded in some places, giving way to golden tones. It seems that the temple has become alive too!

Once I reach the temple, I walk up the stairs and inside, which is, as always, empty and bright. However, there is a different feeling about it this time. The energy seems different, but I cannot describe why. It feels as though there are things there that I cannot see, but can sense. I see one of my guides standing by a window, looking outside. Just before I get to him, he turns around to welcome me with a smile on his face and open arms.

This is the way life really is. The reason most of you do not perceive it this way is because your eyes are clouded by illusions of what the world looks like. Mother Nature is amazing and bountiful. You see only a fraction of all there is to be seen. Discard the illusion of how things should be. Try to discover something different about the sights you set your eyes upon, and you will be amazed at what reveals itself to you. See and experience life from the perspective of infinite possibility. Each time you look at something, it is different from the way it was the last time you looked at it. Everything is constantly changing; everything is constantly being created. Nothing is the same as it was the last time, even if that was but a second ago. Every day, set your intention to see life as if it were new to you, as though it is just being created while you observe it. Set your intention to discover life each second.

This is the way you are too. You are recreated with every breath, every heartbeat, until one day, the creation process will end with your last breath and last heartbeat. Make every breath worthwhile; make every beat count. Free yourself from worry, fear, burden, and illness. Stop creating these negative things by giving them your focus and attention. Instead, create what you desire and live a life of meaning, purpose, appreciation, and joy.

There have been times when you experienced the wonder of creation, even if it was for a fleeting moment. However, most of the time, you don't observe or even notice what is taking place. You do not create from a point of power; you recreate your life mostly from the memory of how it was yesterday, what you think it should be, or what you were told it should be. You don't realise that yesterday is gone, and today—now—is a new opportunity to create everything differently. I am telling you this because you have the power to create every moment anew. Any interaction can be refreshed, any situation can be renewed, anything can be recreated by the will of an open mind and new outlook. Use your ability; start seeing with the part of you that is not being used, from the point of the divine creative energy that you are. You can create a wonderful life, every moment, by looking through different eyes: the eyes of the soul. Practice this and reach new levels of happiness.

The Power to Recreate Life

How can I apply this gift? How can I recreate something different from how I know or think it is?

You recreate life by

- Not asking how to do it, but just doing it from instinct, your intuitive self.
- Not accepting that whatever it is on which you are focusing your attention is or has always been the way you think it is.
- Not seeing life filtered through your memory bank. Instead, see it from a different perspective, as though you have never seen it before and you are learning about it at this precise moment.
- Not basing life on your learnt assumptions or ideas. Use your inner knowing to guide you regarding the way something behaves, feels, tastes, and sounds now, not in the past.
- Taking a different action and offering a different attitude to the way you behave.
- Forming it the way you'd like it to be, then seeing it all unfold before you.

It might take some practice, but soon you will start noticing things here and there that were not the same before. You will know then that you are making these changes happen; you are using your power to create the now. See and experience your life from a point of wonder and rejoicing.

CHAPTER 23

Slow Down and Simplify

Slow Down

I am in one of my meditations, going to the temple to meet my spirit guides, but today I am moving in slow motion, as if I were walking underwater. As I walk through the forest, everything else moves very slowly, too, and I can appreciate every single detail around me: my hair flowing in the air, my slowly advancing steps, my arms swinging gently beside my body, tree branches stirring from one side to the other, and butterflies suspended in mid-air, dancing amongst the flowers. Everything moves very gently.

I walk out of the forest and into the field of wildflowers. I look at the temple, which appears to be far, far away. It takes me a long time to get there—or so it feels. Everything is still strangely slow. It feels like I will never get to where I am going.

Once I reach the temple, I walk inside and take the stairs to the upper room, where I meet my higher self. "That was different," I say. "It was a bit difficult for me to walk that slowly."

It was, indeed! The experience felt odd because you are always running, rushing, trying to get somewhere. You fail to notice where you are and what is around you. There is so much you miss out on seeing. If you were forced to walk through your days at a slower pace, you would then appreciate and become aware of the changes that take place every moment. You would notice changes in your body, in your mood, in the way you express yourself, in the way you think, and in your surroundings, and you would appreciate those changes in others too.

People so often make remarks like these: "How did this happen?"; "How did I get here?"; "Last time I checked, things were different!"; "Why is it that I feel this way?"; "Why is that I don't feel that way anymore?" Your lives have become so much about *doing* that you have stopped observing your *being*. You have lost the ability to notice what is happening *now*, which is really all there is. You could learn so much from noticing, paying attention, being in the now. Appreciating small details would give you a different picture of reality, which, in turn, would cause you to act differently too. Life unfolds a certain way when you live from a perspective of being; it unfolds in a rather different way when lived from a perspective of doing. If you start moving at a slower pace, you will begin to appreciate the details that usually go unnoticed when you are rushing around.

Let's use a movie as an example. When a movie director wants to emphasise a certain scene, he sets it in slow motion. In that way, he can artfully show every single detail of that scene: the millions of droplets in a splash of water, the cascade of colours in daylight, the moving flesh and splatter of fluids in a physical encounter. All these small details would be lost in the background if the scene were in normal motion. Likewise, when you are in doing-speed as opposed to being-speed, you fail to see the miraculous details around you; they fall into the background, pushed away by the speed of your ventures.

These details are what make your life beautiful, amazing, and exceptional. How many times have you failed to see the flowers blossoming in your garden? How many times have you ignored the grace in a child's dirty face, and automatically cleaned it without appreciating its magic? How many times have you dismissed a recurring pain in your body? How many times have you disregarded an expression of love or life itself because you were not really looking, listening, seeing, or sensing? You miss these things because you are not really here, but are instead one step ahead of now, or many steps behind, in the past.

You could appreciate that even in a meditative state, it was difficult to move slowly, to take the time to really see and feel the beautiful forest, the field of flowers, the temple that is so much loved. All it was wanted was to get to me. I am telling you now that you always get to where you are meant to go, whether quickly or slowly. However, slowly is the only way to appreciate and blend with life.

Live at a Slower Pace

Each day, make an intention to walk slower, to act at a slower speed, and to pay attention to the small details that make life a miracle and are all telling you something. Notice the changes taking place inside you. Become aware of your essence; you will discover an amazing universe. You may argue that in these times, it is very hard to slow down, but I want to remind you that you are in control of your reality—that reality is what you perceive. Your set intentions will determine and shape that reality. Make the decision to live in slow-motion and tell me about the *now* that you discover. You might notice the shape and form of new colours, the beauty of a day after the rain, the brightness of the stars in the sky, how your body changes from one day to the next, or how your feelings change when you are with one person or another. Make your intention to pay attention to life, and life will reward you in infinite ways.

As you go through this process of slowing down to observe life, try to breathe more deeply as well. Fill your lungs with fresh oxygen and send renewed energy to your brain. Fill yourself with prana. Healing and rejuvenation will be your reward. Look at the world from a child's perspective. Have you ever heard a child say that he is running out of time? There is always plenty of time to do, be, or have anything, in a child's world. Are you living in the same world that children live? If you don't think you are, think again. When you are involved in any task—interacting with someone, talking to yourself, immersed in nature—always allow yourself to be there, present, in your heart. Imbue any physical interaction with the power of your divine nature, and the communion taking place in that moment will make you see the world from the light, from the point of view of the observer in you.

In our metaphorical story, the man by the stream knows the truth, and he has started to apply it in his waking life. His days are becoming as bright as his nights; when he lives, as well as when he dreams, he is set free. Make an intention from now on to observe more and judge less, to allow life to unfold slowly, to let life flow through you.

Exercise: Slowing Down

Practice this exercise to reconnect with life, yourself, and with everything around you.

Every day, set the intention to live in slow-motion, at a slower pace. Intend to stop rushing from moment to moment, but to really be present every second of the day. As with any new habit, you will need to get used to the idea and then practice slowing down. It might be difficult at first; you will probably start by doing it a bit here and a bit there. Eventually, though, it will become your new way of being.

If you find yourself slipping into the old way, just stop—breathe in and out deeply a few times, then continue whatever you were doing in a more present way. As your life slows down, you will be able to observe it more closely. What do you hear? What do you feel? What do you really see? What new things are you discovering? Set the intention to make your doing-speed less relevant; concentrate more on your internal senses. What is your inner dialogue about? What is your inner guidance telling you? As you practice the intention of being present, you will start to discover another world that you have never seen before.

The purpose of this exercise is to help you focus on the present and allow yourself to discover and savour the simple gifts of life. A wonderful side effect of reducing all your rushing around, multitasking, inner chatter, and excessive *doing* is that your health and well-being will enormously improve as you become more relaxed, in control, balanced, and harmonious with what is happening in your life.

Simplify

Your lives are cluttered with too many things, wants, haves, and dos, and even with people. Simplify your life! Examine your life with an honest heart and determine what is truly essential. Most of the time, your lives are cluttered with to-dos and to-haves that are actually someone else's impositions. You have accepted them because of your need to fit in and be accepted, and because everyone else does the same. Look at your life from your heart's perspective and see what you can get rid of to make it simpler. In this way, you will create the space to be able to walk more slowly and observe more, because there will be less to take care of, think about, and worry over, and there will be less stuff absorbing your energy. As a result of this decluttering, more of what you want and desire will come to you.

Be at peace with yourself and with your life. Do not be afraid that you won't get where you're going if you slow down, or that you will be left alone if you detoxify your relationships, or that you will miss out on something if you don't do, have, or be what everyone else is. This is not true. On the contrary, you will achieve more. You will get to wherever you are meant to go faster, you will enjoy more fulfilling, joyful relationships, you will be more appreciative of what you have, and furthermore, you will be more refreshed, healthy, happy, peaceful, and you will live in a more purposeful manner. Be at peace; observe the beauty of life that unfolds daily in miraculous ways all around you. Love, appreciate, and enjoy.

Life is a present for you. Appreciate and acknowledge it by being present in life.

Exercise: Simplify Your Life

When our lives are cluttered or complicated, the energy inside and outside of us cannot flow easily or freely. Hence, we may develop feelings of confusion, heaviness, or dissatisfaction. We may get lost or stuck, or even become depressed and ill. We cannot flow harmoniously with life in a cluttered state of being. That is the reason for this message: simplify your life! Clutter and overly complicated lifestyles affect all areas of our lives and have a direct impact on our physical, mental, and spiritual well-being. The more simple, clear, and light our lives, the better we feel at all levels. We feel as though a heavy load has been lifted off of our shoulders. This load is all of the stuff that we think we need or want—it consumes a great amount of our energy. Therefore, my advice is to take a look at your life and find ways that you can make it simpler. With an objective eye and with your heart's guidance, identify the clutter and complexity around you and clear it up.

You can approach the exercise gradually and make only a few changes here and there, yet still notice a difference in the way you feel. This feel-good state will definitely in turn prompt you to make more changes. Alternatively, you can take a more determined approach and spend time reviewing all the aspects of your life. Then, simplify, simplify, simplify!

Simplify Your Physical World

You can start by assessing your physical world, which is the largest aspect of your life and usually the most cluttered. It comprises the place you live, the place you work, all your possessions (including your car, clothes, and furnishings), your physical body, the people in your life, your finances, and your schedule and to-do lists. The physical world is everything that you can sense with your physical senses and that has a direct impact on your physical well-being.

Go around your home and inspect every room inside and outside, including cupboards, drawers, wardrobes, boxes, and the fridge and pantry. Look for ways you can make space. Simplify by throwing away, recycling, donating, or selling all your unwanted or unneeded stuff. You are making space not only to receive renewed and refreshed energy, but also to allow new things to come into your life in whatever form they manifest.

Do the same in your workplace. Does it lift you up or drag you down? Do you have everything you need to perform your job? Do you have a cluttered workplace that affects not only your performance but also the image you portray? Do you have clear and simple lines of communication with your co-workers?

What about your car? Is it in perfect working condition, or are you always worried that is going to break down? Does it look like a rubbish bin or is it clean and well cared for? Some say that your car is an extension of you.

Your body is next. Do you follow simple routines to care and maintain it? Do you have a simple diet that is rich in nutrients to make you feel vibrant and strong, and that does not cater to addictions and toxins? You do not need to be a chef to prepare healthy meals. Simple foods prepared with fresh and unprocessed ingredients are good for you and can be made easily and quickly. Over the years, as a busy working mum, I have become expert at preparing easy, quick, yummy meals that my family all love. Do you engage in simple exercises to keep your body moving and in shape instead of trying to fit in long gym sessions that you never attend? Do you carry excess weight, or suffer any illnesses or chronic aches? You can take simple actions to rid your body of these problems by deciding to be healthy and feeling good. Do you use vitamins, medicines, power drinks, and caffeine? Could you get the same effect by resting more, doing less, spending more time outdoors, and engaging in activities that connect you with your soul?

Do you love and appreciate your body, regardless of its shape, size, colour, and age? Love and appreciation for your physical being is the first step to a harmonious and positive relationship with yourself. Love the perfect body you were gifted with!

Don't forget to assess the people and relationships in your life. Do you have relationships that support, fulfil, and enrich who you are and what you want to do? These are the ones to keep and nurture. Are there people who bring you down, diminish you, or drain your energy? Are there people you don't know well or don't care for much, but still interact with because they are part of your network of friends? Do you have a few good friends who understand you and are there when you need them? Or do you have a large group of friends who share shallow and have meaningless relationships with you? Is your intimate relationship loving, nurturing, empowering, and fulfilling? Do you need all the people who are in your life? Do you enjoy healthy relationships with all of them? Simplify your relationships by terminating those that do not serve you and spending less time with the people you don't care for but can't let go of completely, such as certain family members, co-workers, and acquaintances. Do not be afraid to suddenly spend time on your own. On the contrary, you should cherish this opportunity as a chance for you to know more about yourself, and to get in touch with your inner being.

Simplify your schedule and to-do list. You are probably doing too much. Remember to slow down and enjoy life more closely. Do you delegate tasks? Do you say yes when you really want to say no? Do you allow others to use and abuse your time? Do you accept all invitations even if they do not align with your interests or you are not in the mood for them? Are you living from your doing perspective more than from your being perspective? Do you set priorities? Do you give yourself realistic deadlines? Simplify your schedule by asking for help, delegating more, not taking on more than what you can cope with, having realistic expectations of yourself and others, knowing your limits, saying no more often, and allowing yourself "me time." A less complicated scheduled will give you more peace, freedom, control, and much more free time to spend with those you love (including yourself) and to pursue activities that lift your spirit and make you happy.

Finances tend to bring much complexity to our lives. Do you follow simple rules for handling your money? Do you have hard time managing your various accounts and numerous credit cards? Do you have an easy method for tracking your income, expenses, savings, and debt? Is your financial situation worrying you and clouding your life? Do you spend more than you earn? Do you know where your money goes, regardless of how much you have? Simplify your financial life by knowing exactly where you stand financially, learning about savings and investment strategies that may reduce worry about the future, addressing problematic spending habits, and seeking advice from professionals. If you ignore financial issues, you will only make things worse. A simple step in the right direction could put you on track to be in control of your financial well-being.

Simplify Your Inner World

Once your physical world starts feeling lighter and working better, you can look at your inner world: your mind, emotions, and spirit. Start with your mind: spend a few days observing what kind of thoughts you think. A cluttered mind is dominated by negative inner chatter, which focuses on worry, fear, doubt, panic, criticism, judgment, complaints, and gossip. Is your mind clouded by negative beliefs? Are you constantly judging or criticising yourself and others? Are your conversations often about gossip? Do you overanalyse or overcomplicate matters? Do you seem to see problems everywhere? Is your mind always racing with thoughts that make you tired, unhappy, and confused? Do you procrastinate and lack the will to actively do things to improve your wellbeing? Do you feel you don't know where you are going or what your purpose in life is? All these are signs of a cluttered mind.

A cluttered mind is fearful, and gets in the way of positive change. It results in cluttered emotions such as distress, grief, exhaustion, sadness, inferiority, and confusion. Decluttering your mind, and consequently, your emotions, gives you clarity and amplifies your ability to listen to your inner guidance. It enables you to see solutions instead of problems, and gives you a more positive outlook of life. It also allows you to be in the present more by focusing your thoughts on what you are experiencing. Having emotions based on a clear, peaceful, and loving mind makes you feel better. With a clear mind, you feel more confident and have the energy to take action and work towards your goals. Clarity and simplicity also enhance the way you communicate and interact with others. A clear mind allows you to accept and embrace change in a positive and natural way. Clear your mind and emotions by identifying, analysing, and clearing up your belief system (see Chapter 34 for tips on this), engaging in creative activities, learning new skills, using affirmations and visualization, immersing yourself in any type of art, being outdoors, meditating, exercising, reading inspiring material, and spending time with people who uplift you.

Simplifying your physical, mental, and emotional worlds has an immense effect on your spiritual realm, as you start flowing swiftly and smoothly with the river of life. A cluttered spirit is a selfish one that doesn't believe in a higher power or God, doesn't show or share love, and feels empty and lost most of the time. In essence, a cluttered spirit is disconnected from its inner being and from the whole. You simplify your spiritual life by believing in the existence of a universal loving power and in your soul, and by building a relationship with them; by understanding that every person is a unique, magnificent being with a purpose on this planet and in the bigger scheme of things; by being involved with the community and showing the love of spirit in everything you do. Practice activities that nurture your heart and soul, and make you feel love, kindness, compassion, friendship, joy, laughter. Prayer, meditation, playing, and servicing others are some examples of this kind of activity.

Leading a Simpler Life

It doesn't matter where you begin the decluttering process as long as you realise and accept that your life needs simplification. At the beginning, you might find it challenging to get rid of your stuff, your habits, your practices, and your beliefs—even though these old things do not serve you anymore, and you are replacing them with space, clarity, positivity, and inspiring activities. Your ego will not want to relinquish its power and control, and it will resort to any trick to keep you where you are. It could put you in denial of the fact your life needs to be simpler, filling you with old attachments and surrounding you with diversions to distract you from what really matters in your life.

I intended the questions that I posed in this exercise to act as triggers to get you started and asking more questions, and also to guide and help you keep on going. As you persevere in your decision to lead a simpler life, you will find yourself more driven and empowered to carry on with the clean-up. As a result, you will enjoy increased free space, energy, lightness of being, peace, direction, time, connection with your inner world, and positive change in some or all areas of your life.

Some time ago, I read a beautiful little book on clearing clutter: *Clear Your Clutter with Feng Shui*, by Karen Kingston. It is a short book that is easy to read and understand, and I enjoyed it very much. It clearly explains why people keep clutter and how it affects their lives, and it provides guidelines and tips on how to implement the decluttering process. The author's techniques are based on *feng shui*, the ancient Chinese philosophy that addresses the flow and balance of energy to achieve harmony with the environment. It is sometimes called the art of placement. The principles of feng shui, teach us that the energy in our surroundings directly affects our physical, mental, and spiritual well-being. You don't need to be an expert on feng shui to understand the book's content. If you have the opportunity, I recommend you read this useful book when you reach the stage of simplifying your life.

CHAPTER 24

Sleep Well

The Importance of Sleep

People always disregard the importance of the sleep process. What with the lifestyle most people have these days, sleep deprivation and insomnia enormously affect the ability of the soul to communicate with its human side. Sleep is required to not only regenerate the body and support crucial bodily functions, but also as an indispensable means for the soul to free itself from human boundaries and recharge by interacting with other souls. During sleep, all body functions slow down and the interference of the conscious mind is paused; this gives the body the chance to repair itself, to regenerate what is damaged, to check what needs attention, to work with the life force running through the cells, and to heal what needs healing. All this is performed by the internal mechanisms of your magnificent body.

When a person is asleep, the body also engages in the task of balancing the energy centres, or chakras, in order to dissolve any blockages preventing the free flow of life energy. These blockages are usually generated by the constant sabotage of the mind's games. It is essential to the well-being of the body that this divine universal life energy reaches each and every cell of the body. This energy is like a gush of fresh air that refreshes, repairs, rejuvenates, and heals all it touches, while at the same time carrying stale, damaged, tired energy out of the body. Blocked energy centres prevent this renewal process to fully take place. Not only does the flow of energy circulating from outside to inside, and from inside to the outside again, allow you to be connected to the energy network that surrounds you, it also allows the energy to flow into every cell in your body. Thus, the cells, which each work as part of the whole, receive much-needed nourishment and direction.

Unfortunately, the natural balance of the chakras lasts only until the next limiting thought comes along to put a latch on the door of free energy flow. If a person is constantly engaged in negative inner chatter, or has limiting beliefs, or needs to work out some issues about himself, the natural mechanism of repair and balance during sleep will not be fully effective. In this case, the process must be supplemented by meditation, by natural healing techniques performed by a skilled practitioner, and most importantly, by the person's conscious work to dissolve boundaries and unhealthy beliefs in order to support the cleansing of his energy channels. As you can see, the clearing of the energy centres is of the utmost importance.

The other activity that takes place while the body refreshes and heals itself during sleep is the soul escaping its confines and leaving the body. The soul needs this release in order to stretch, expand its wings, and fly freely to where other souls congregate; there, it receives direction, enjoys silence, feeds from the source of all creation, and breathes life and light. This process enables the soul to come back into the body for another day, ready to start afresh, to create everything from scratch, to seek adventure, to tackle new endeavours, to love deeply, to laugh loudly, to learn and grow, indeed, to do or be anything—but only if the human body it inhabits wants to. The soul has seen everything in dreams; in dreams, anything is possible. What is broken can be mended, what is dead comes alive again, what has failed is a success the next time. The old can be young again, the sick can be healed, peace can be achieved, and harmony on Earth can be maintained. The planet can be saved, and life on Earth can be like it is in heaven. In your dreams, you can be, do, and have everything—you must continue to believe it is possible after you open your eyes.

Do not disregard your sleep time as unnecessary; make it an important part of your day. You are not missing out on life when you sleep; on the contrary, if you don't sleep, you are missing out on becoming stronger and wiser, healed and balanced. Each time you go to sleep, you immerse yourself in a long, deep meditation in which you receive guidance, register your subconscious mind's answers to your questions, assimilate the events of the waking day, record anything you have learnt, and let your body rest and recharge. Accept sleep both as a much-needed bodily requirement and as a spiritual tool. It is as important as eating and breathing. When you go to sleep tonight, give thanks for all the processes that will take place while you rest, and when you get up in the morning, be grateful for having the chance to open your eyes once more. Set the intention to make the new day one worthy of being lived.

Exercise: Sleeping Well

This exercise will be beneficial to anyone who practises it, but it is mainly directed at those who have difficulty in getting a good night's sleep. Practicing it will reward those who sleep well with even better sleep, and those who have trouble sleeping with restful nights. If you find it difficult to fall asleep each night, you probably worry about it for a while before bedtime, or perhaps even all day long. Of course, this only worsens your difficulty sleeping. Therefore, take the time before going to bed to relax and dispel any worries you have. You might practice some affirmations to help you ease tensions and anxiety about your sleep issues. Some example affirmations are, "I can easily drift to sleep"; "I enjoy a good night's sleep"; and "Every day, I awaken rested and refreshed."

When it is time to go to sleep, get into bed, close your eyes, and welcome sleep whenever it comes. It might be challenging to do so at first, but worrying about the matter will not improve your chances of sleeping well. The best action you can take is to let go anxiety and become aware that your soul is a prisoner of your lack of sleep. Make it your desire to set your soul free. Use this as your incentive. While you are in bed, perform the following exercise.

———————————————•

Lie down with your eyes closed. You can listen to soft music if you wish.

Imagine healing light entering your body through your head. Gently, it goes down the length of your spine, on its way opening and clearing your energy centres, before coming out of your feet. See the light continuously flowing, from head to toes, easing any pain or discomfort, dissolving any blockages to your energy as effortlessly as if it were opening doors. See the powerful light spreading through all parts of your body while also relaxing you more and more.

If your mind is active and full of thoughts, do not fight them or stress about them; just let them go. Acknowledge that your mind doesn't want to rest, but don't follow its command. Without resistance, let your thoughts go and focus on your intention to rest and sleep.

Continue to see the light. Focus all your attention on the slow pace of your breathing and the soothing feeling it produces in your body. With your eyes still closed, let yourself be. Enjoy the peace and quiet until, without noticing it, you fall asleep.

•———————————————

Practice this exercise every night; after a while, you will notice that you can go to bed without the fear of not being able to sleep. You'll feel more relaxed and confident of having a good night's sleep. Feel trust and let yourself flow. You will sleep better that night, much better the following night, and so on. It is acceptable while practicing this exercise to use other aids for sleep, such as herbal teas, warm milk, and in severe cases, medication. With time, your need for additional aids will wane to the point that you will relinquish their use and sleep naturally. Make this exercise a nightly ritual, even when you think you will not be able to sleep. Please, do not deprive your body of rest.

Regaining Your Sleep

If you have sleeping problems, please be aware that your problem is not physical, but mental. You are being controlled by your ego's games; this has a physical effect. While the ego has power during your waking hours through its constant inner chatter, the whispers of the soul are heard without interference during sleeping hours, when your conscious thinking is temporarily dormant. When you cannot sleep, your ego expands its domain to sleeping hours, depriving you of the spiritual refuelling that you should be getting from your soul while asleep. The tension, anxiety, and headaches of insomnia are all physical responses to the body's lack of rest, which the mind's games have taken away. In a situation like this, you need to consciously desire to overcome the ego's control and set a firm routine in order to recover your sleep. This will enable your soul to regain contact with its human partner, you. Once this step is successfully completed, that is, once restful nights are regained, you will need to practice other exercises to eradicate the ego's chatter during the waking hours as well.

Sleeping problems, as well as some other physical illnesses, result from the separation of the individual and its spiritual self. When the connection is re-established, when you begin to trust in the existence of a divine life force running inside and around you; when you begin to be love, see love, give love, and receive love; then the illness is no longer necessary. If it does not serve any other purpose, it will leave the body for good. Whenever you feel an ache, any kind of discomfort, or the need for love, just breathe in deeply the life energy surrounding you; love and healing will fill you up. Now close your eyes and relax. Feel as though you are sleeping. Go to sleep, and rest. Good night.

CHAPTER 25

Cutting Bonds

What are Bonds?

Bonds are invisible but powerful links of energy that connect us with the whole. People build bonds with everything, physical and nonphysical, that surrounds them, and with everything they connect to, in any shape or form, across time and space. Consciously and unconsciously, they build bonds with other people, things, events, emotions, behaviours, states of being, and circumstances. Once a bond is created, it never ceases to exist, not even when the physical representation of that bond has terminated. As long as a person has memories and feelings, the bonds linking him with other things remain alive without his conscious acknowledgment. The bonds between him and an event that happened long ago in the past, or between him and someone who has passed, could still be vibrating. However, the intensity of a bond's vibration varies depending on how relevant or current that bond is in the person's life, and on the strength of the feelings attached to it. Therefore, a bond between two lovers could have equal strength and vibrancy to someone's a bond to a childhood memory, if that memory has significance and relevance to the adult's life. People are generally more aware of the bonds they have to other people; however, the bonds built through attachments, behaviours, thoughts, actions, and interactions are also significant and powerful.

It is important and helpful to understand that your creating bonds with everything you connect to can be explained by the nature of your being. You are a vibrational energy that interacts with this physical world through the multitude of energy links that are your bonds. The effects of your interactions are reflected in every aspect of your physical world. You are part of the universal network of life, connecting, feeding, breathing, learning, growing, and building through the power of your bonds. All bonds exist for a reason. They help you to communicate and interact within your spiritual and physical worlds. Bonds shouldn't be evaluated as being big or small, important or unimportant, valuable or valueless. Bonds must be appreciated from the perspective of the feelings that they produce.

Soul- and Ego-Based Bonds

Bonds that connect to your inner being enrich and empower the lives of those connected. This kind of bond can sometimes challenge you in order to trigger growth and evolution while still remaining healthy. Soul-based bonds can be identified easily because they produce feelings of happiness, love, empowerment, strength, determination, peace, joy, openness of heart and mind, unselfishness, union, courage, health, optimism, focus, independence, and awe. However, when the ego gets in the way with its mind games, some of your bonds might become unhealthy. They can create feelings of guilt, dependence, worry, jealousy, greed, and distress, in one or more of the people connected by them. For this reason, the bonds that people create from an ego-driven nature are a major source of stress and upset. When someone is affected by an unhealthy bond, he usually feels confused, guilty, even judgemental of others because he doesn't know how to deal with the connection. When this happens, that person is moving towards darkness and walking away from the light.

The key to cultivating healthy, soul-based bonds is to be aware of what is going on within you and around you—in other words, to be present. This will allow you to recognise when you are being affected by an unhealthy or ego-driven bond, and to work towards bringing yourself into the light again. The truth is that all the unhealthy feelings generated by ego-based bonds are created by you, and exist only in your mind. Most of what you believe is happening around you, what you think others are saying, doing, having, or feeling, is not truly the way you perceive it. The truth is, what you feel and experience is fed by your own thoughts, your version of the story, and that is usually distorted by the ego.

Even when you recognise you have an unhealthy bond, you might not be ready to heal it yet. Your fear of losing the bond, even if it is hurting you, could be stronger than your desire to heal it. For example, you might be holding onto some old beliefs that you continue to replay through your bonds. Messages or lessons that later in life become limiting beliefs are most often received during childhood. When you become an adult, these beliefs shape the types of connections and interactions you build. One strong message you receive as a child is that you must honour your parents' and elders' values and beliefs. Even if you're not aware of what you're doing, you probably act on that belief. When you fail to reinforce these values with which you were brought up—and when you try to alter or break the bonds tying you to your existing relationships—you feel guilt and anxiety about separation. We want you to understand that you need only honour those beliefs that move you towards the light, and that empower and strengthen you. No belief, regardless of its origins, is worth having if it drags you to the darkness.

To be fair, though, when other people influenced you during your childhood, they were only imparting the beliefs and values that their parents and elders raised them on. This is important to understand and acknowledge. Also, understand and accept that each person in your immediate world connected to you through bonds—including yourself—lives in his own shades of light and darkness. This understanding will allow you to accept both the way everything is, and that you have the right and the choice to be the way you are, and who you want to become. If you surrender to the beliefs of others, no matter how important they are in your life, you are surrendering from the perspective of your ego (wanting to please, avoiding conflict, needing to conform) at the expense of your own self, your soul.

We want you to acknowledge that you are your own unique being, with a mission to live your own life in your own unique way. You have the power to change and heal any unhealthy bond by letting go of guilt and replacing it with empowerment. Allow yourself to be you, in control of your life. By doing this, you are showing and teaching those around you that there are other ways of being, and you are choosing new, healthy ways.

How to Heal Unhealthy Bonds

Once you recognise that you are involved in an unhealthy bond, you must acknowledge that although the bond cannot be dissolved, it can be healed—at least on your end. Bonds exist for a reason: to teach you about yourself, to make you aware of your inner powers and gifts, to assist you with your personal growth, to help you connect and interact with the environment, and to make you into an instrument to help others learn, discover, and grow. You heal an unhealthy bond by bringing light into the situation. You can achieve this by

- Being connected to your inner being and trusting its guidance
- Not succumbing to inner chatter
- Not letting worry, guilt, blame, or any other upsetting feelings cloud a clear mind and loving heart
- Not taking matters personally
- Letting things flow
- Letting others take charge and responsibility of their own lives, and letting them move in the direction they choose

- Not interfering by making other's issues your own
- Listening to what others think and say, but ultimately following you own inner voice—and making sure that you can distinguish between your soul's voice and your ego's chatter
- Freeing yourself of the need to please everybody
- Just letting go
- Giving up the need to be right
- Clarifying your external world's distorted view of value and worth
- Correcting your distorted view of your own value and worth
- Evaluating your exaggerated need for possessions and attachments
- Addressing and avoiding addictive behaviours
- Allowing yourself to be the unique being you are and accepting all aspects of yourself
- Focusing on your life, your mission, and your dreams

Exercise: Cutting Bonds

Close your eyes and spend a few minutes breathing in and out. Relax your body and disconnect from your surroundings and thoughts.

Now feel the soft, healing light of your inner being resting gently on top of your head, like a nurturing hand giving you comfort and love.

In this state of calmness and grace, release any guilt you have. Release any feelings of doubt, anguish, or pain that are restricting you. Release any bonds to emotions, things, people, thoughts, behaviours, or situations that drag you down; these could be physical or nonphysical, and could include your parents, partner, children, relatives, friends, acquaintances, even yourself.

As you let go of any unhealthy bondage, see the ties around you loosen up, and feel the heavy load you have been carrying lifted off of you. Now, cut those bonds. Release any negative emotion that weighs you down.

You are free of unhealthy bonds now; you are light. Breathe deeply and feel yourself expand. Feel pleased and at peace. Within the feeling of peace and love, send light to surround all that you have detached from. Stay in this feeling for a while, enjoying the lightness of your being.

———————————————

This is a simple and yet very powerful exercise, even if it doesn't seem that way. It enables you to bring light to any unhealthy bond by clearing the energy of those bonds and recharging them with positive vibrations. By practicing this exercise, you are not dissolving the bonds, but you are healing them. This enables you to feel unrestricted and at ease with all that surrounds you, including life itself.

Do the exercise for a few minutes each time until you can sense feelings of release and relief within yourself. Repeat the exercise until you have refreshed energy and a refreshed attitude towards yourself, others, and situations. You will know when you have healed a bond when you experience these feelings about it.

We Are Teachers and Students

All the bonds that you create in life, especially those involving other human beings, have a purpose, a reason to be. All the people in your life are your teachers; they are here to teach you to use and apply what you have learnt so far and to help you grow through the process. At the same time, all the people you are around are students too, and you are here to help them do the same—to learn, apply what they came here to learn, and rise to the light. Bonds are two-way roads; the connected parties are both teachers and students at the same time. The road gets bumpy and unhealthy if anyone involved becomes too attached to what the outcome will be, what is happening, what is being said, and what is being done within the bond. The big lesson here is that we all have different opinions, points of view, and perceptions; no one is right or wrong.

When people are presented with challenging life situations, difficult relationships, unfulfilled desires, illness and loss, they desire the negative things to disappear, to be smoothed away. They hope to be surrounded by people who share their points of view or are at the same level of personal and spiritual evolution, so that can life be easy. But what good would that be? How would you grow? How else would you move towards your empowerment? You seek solutions and answers in order to rise above the challenges of life, by understanding different points of view, and by appreciating and evaluating different ways of thinking and living life.

You are all teachers, and you teach by example. As you are pushed by your discomforts and difficulties to look for resolutions, as you change, as you achieve, as you move forward with your dreams regardless of the issues you might face, as you slowly discover your inner gifts and talents, as you let life guide you, as you show determination and courage, you are teaching. Those around you learn and grow through your lessons and your growth, but only in their own time.

Live Your Life

When you learn new ways of living life and put those lessons into practice, you are assured to provoke waves of reaction in those closest to you. This happens because you are changing the rules within your bonds, and upsetting the established harmony of those bonds. The intensity and extent of the reactions will vary depending on the quality of your bonds; they will range from positive, constructive, encouraging, supportive, loving, or understanding to negative, critical, demoralizing, unhelpful, uncaring, or indifferent. However, you need to be strong and stand your ground. Do not be afraid of causing disagreements or distress; if you think or behave the way others want you to so their lives will be as they want, you are upsetting and hurting yourself. Stand your ground and follow your heart, knowing that you can always change the course of your life. Those who try to stop you are acting out of fear, but they will become aware of this when they are ready to do so.

At any given point in time, you are surrounded by people who connect with you on various levels of personal and spiritual development. Do not expect all of those connections to be the same—if they were, you and they wouldn't be doing the job. When someone doesn't need you immediately, he may move away or put some distance between you, only to come back when his need arises again, and vice versa; when you don't need someone in the immediate future, you move away or distance yourself from his life and only return if you need him. These are the true dynamics of a bond; the best you can do is to let go of feelings of guilt, disappointment, strong attachment, or any other emotion that wants to turn that bond into something static. Bonds are energy links that are meant to change and flow as the intelligence of life moves freely through them.

Give only the attention and time you feel comfortable giving, and then focus on what you want and desire. The people who exist in your life are there to reflect aspects of you that need work, as well as to bring you opportunities. They are links to other people and to things and events; they are doorways to new experiences and possibilities. Don't fight them, don't resist them, don't try to change them. Don't be afraid to spend time alone. The truth is that every person in the world is engaged in living his own life, so please, live yours. You need only be with yourself to be complete. Let everyone and everything flow, and let yourself flow; it is so simple.

PART V

The New Way

If you have come this far in the book, then at least some of its content has resonated with you and made you keep reading to continue discovering new ideas. The concepts, knowledge, and revelations within these pages—which up until now have been partially or completely dormant in your subconscious mind—have surfaced to your awareness and connected with you in some extraordinary way. You know that this connection has taken place because you feel good, empowered, and most importantly, you feel happy for no specific reason. You can feel that your zest for life has reawakened, and the drive you once had to live life to the fullest is burning within you once more.

You rejoice in the idea of infinite possibility, of doors waiting to be opened, and you feel young again. You understand that you do not need illness, doubt, procrastination, fear, blame, or guilt to act as barriers in your life any longer. As you explore your new connection between your spiritual and physical selves, you feel a beautiful sensation enveloping you, whispering words of change, telling you that you can live life differently and at the same time, feel happy. You know that you have awakened to your inner voice. You have discovered the voice of your soul, the voice of your divine inner knowing. Now you are ready to take the journey to the light and let your soul be free in its physical expression of you.

There are no more excuses. You have all the tools you need for a joyous journey. You now know that everything you need to live this new way is within your power; you just have to make the decision to take the first step and let your soul guide you in your new beginning.

Your soul is rejoicing in the knowledge that you are ready to live life in a new way—so am I.

But what is this new way of living life? What does it mean? The new way of living life simply asks you to experience life from a different perspective, a different point of power, and with a new attitude. This new way of living is really a new way of being, in which you

- Believe that a new era is brewing, and that in fact, it has been doing so for a long time. We call this new era the Era of Light. Love, happiness, peace, harmony, and oneness are at its core. The new era provides us the stage to create a new world based on a more evolved consciousness, where we are more united, more in tune with life, and understand and rejoice in the knowledge that we are unique expressions of the one energy creator of all and connecting us all.
- Are connected to your true self, who you really are, and you participate in the awakening process as a teacher, leader, or student. No role is smaller or more important than any other; everyone has a worthy mission to fulfil in these glorious times.
- Discover life from the eyes of your soul, seeing through spirit the life you are meant to live, and allowing yourself to be spirit enjoying this human experience.
- Accept that you are part of a soul community working towards similar goals, and rejoice in the feeling that you are never, ever alone. Spirit is always walking by your side, waiting to assist you in any life situation, reminding you that everyone and everything is an active participant of the creation process through the dance of the soul.
- Consciously choose the frequency at which you vibrate, and the vibrational network you are connected to, because you know that these choices can make your life move in the direction of your desires, or the opposite way. You have free will to choose how you live your life; by choosing the vibration of love, you flow with the river of life and live with purpose and in awe.

- Embrace being part of everything, being one with the whole; letting go of the feeling of separateness enhances your life in ways that you never imagined. Seeing and treating everyone as though they are you opens up new perspectives and points of action for living life.

In summary, the new way of living life calls for increased awareness. It requires you to acknowledge that every thought, every deed, every word, and every emotion, no matter how big or small, has a unique impact on the consciousness of the planet, so much so that even as you breathe life force in and out, that consciousness expands. The new way of living asks you to appreciate how magnificent, powerful, important, and unique you are; it instigates you to live from your soul's empowering vantage point, and in that way, to enjoy the journey to the light that is at the core of the new era. Choose to be who you really are, and there is nothing else you need do, but be you.

CHAPTER 26

Awakening to the New Era of Light

"The power of one" is not just a phrase; it is fact. It is a concept that spiritual teachers and conscious living individuals and groups are talking about and putting into practice. The power of one is the power of the universal consciousness channelled through a person or persons. It can be manifested at many levels:

- The collective level: many working together towards one goal, with one intention and one conviction. This level of oneness can be expressed and experienced in both the physical and the spiritual worlds.
- The individual level: the power of each individual connecting to his higher self, and through the higher self, to his Source.

When a person becomes aware of his inner power, and uses it with awareness and purpose, he is invoking the power of one. When a person prays, meditates, takes inspired action, trusts, loves, appreciates, is mindful of his intentions and thoughts, he is connecting to and applying the power of one. Each time the power of one is summoned, the entire power of the universal wisdom and grace is embraced, to make a difference, to bring change, healing, joy, and flow. With that power at your command, you could never feel powerless. How could anyone choose to feel or be powerless? Awaken to the power within, the divine light that is burning within your being, just waiting to be put to work for whatever purpose you need it.

This power can be moulded to any level and any task; it shouldn't be reserved for grandiose or meaningful endeavours. Wake up to your power of one and for all. We need people to realise their power and their divine nature. Souls have patiently been waiting for a long time, silently witnessing how humans live small, restricted, repressed lives. Only a few here and there have surfaced with sparkles of light igniting the interest of another few. But their voices were not loud enough, since the masses still lay dormant. The majority still remains unaware of the power living within them. But now, this is no longer an option. The time has come that all must know and acknowledge that you are born in the likeness of your source, and possess its same immense power to create. This is a magnificent time. This is a time of change.

More and more are rising, bringing awareness of the light within. More and more are knocking on doors and opening them. More and more are walking their paths with purpose, or at least searching for the purposeful path. More and more are focusing on happiness than ever before. More and more wish to heal. More and more pray and want peace. More and more ask for equal distribution of resources, for equality amongst races. More and more demand freedom at all levels. More and more are speaking words of truth and revealing their true nature without fear of judgement. More and more are brave enough to face the consequences of being who they really are. More and more are connecting with their inner wisdom.

Many are still living in the shadows, but they will soon awaken, as the time has come; the Era of Light is upon us, and no one will be blind to this divine light. Those who choose darkness will not find a place on this planet. Those who choose darkness will be lonely, isolated, and will suffer the fate of their own choice. A new time is coming, when joy, happiness, life, love, and oneness will be at the core of everything. Be happy to be part of this new time. Rejoice!

The Awakening Process

The present time is a wonderful and joyous one, for an awakening is taking place in different parts of the planet. People are expressing these awakenings via different means: global forums to express gratitude, worldwide group meditations, prayer, messages channelled from spirit, analyses of prophesies, songs, videos, seminars, movies, articles, and books (such as this one). Everyone is helping to disseminate the message that a new era is upon us. We are constantly sending validations to all of our light workers that they are on the right path. We are constantly providing them with ways to connect to the awakening energy so they will be more aware and in tune with all that is taking place on the planet. The bonds that have been created everywhere are strong, radiant, and overflowing with love, compassion, trust, faith, and enthusiasm for this awakening. Everyone is part of it; everyone is connected to the awakening energy!

These are glorious times because a new era is rising. Millions of people are awakening to new concepts that have lain dormant in their subconscious minds, waiting to surface. This is not an end to the world that is approaching, but an end to a time, an end to a way of thinking, an end to a way of seeing life. A new beginning is blooming. It started some time ago, led by those who were willing enough to open their channels and receive the messages of change. The work done by those pioneers spread and injected the universal consciousness in such a way that others started to be awakened and to become change, themselves. You are part of this wave of change sweeping the Earth in a most positive and glorious way. Do not be afraid, as there is nothing to fear. This new way of thinking will take all of you to new dimensions of existence. The Earth will enter a new phase of evolution. Humanity will enter a new stage in the process of enlightenment. Those who understand and find the light within will teach and guide the rest, and at their own pace, everyone will join this evolution; it will take hundreds of years to come.

Rejoice, as you are part of this crusade of change, of love, of evolution. Rejoice because you are open and accepting of the message from your source. Rejoice as you come closer to the one, closer to the all, and closer to you. There is nothing you cannot achieve when you become one and connect at a conscious level. You can heal the planet, you can feed the starving, and you can bring richness and splendour to life. You can bring paradise to Earth. Do not be concerned about the process. Do not worry about how long it will take, how it will be accomplished, or how difficult it will be. Do not despair if you will not be physically present to see these changes take place, because when the new conscious way of living is implanted, all will know and all will benefit and celebrate—both the living and the spirit. We will all be blessed.

How to Participate in the Awakening Process

There is plenty you can do to actively participate in this awakening from your inner being's perspective, allowing your soul to show you the way:

- Focus on your purpose, which will direct you to your role in the process of awakening. Do not doubt.
- Walk steadily on your path as we Spirit Guides walk by your side, showing you each step of the way.
- Do not focus on the impossible or on the obstacles; focus instead on your faith and willingness to see spiritual growth rampant on the planet. Make that objective the shining light that keeps you on track.
- Ask for help and you will get it; ask for support; ask for burdens to be lifted; ask for strength of will. Ask for anything you need in order to keep walking as an awakened being, and you will receive all that you ask for and much more.

- We—the Higher Selves, Spirit Guides, Angels, and the Source of all creation—are working together in this new stage of evolution.
- Believe in miracles; see them happen every day before your eyes.
- Understand that your life is a miracle that must be honoured and worshiped.
- Respect your life and understand that you have a role to play—it is as important as anyone else's.
- Believe in the magnificent source of energy that runs, breathes, lives within you. Live your life, day by day, from that perspective.
- You are creators. You are manifestors. You are perfect expressions of love who are awakening to a new level of consciousness. Accept this truth and life will flow smoothly and open up to you.
- Think thoughts that empower you, that aid you in whatever you are doing.
- Send thoughts of happiness, of peace, of love, of healing to everyone and everything, to Mother Earth and to the universe.
- Use the power of your mind to achieve whatever you intend, and let the doing be a result of the power of your thinking.
- Live effortlessly, do not worry, live with ease, and trust the process and the force that has put you on this physical plane. This force is wise and all-powerful; this force controls all the rhythms of nature and life itself, not only on this planet, but also in all the universe.
- Trust life; flow with it, and life will make you flow in the direction of your desires.

As you can see from these examples, there are myriad ways in which you can walk as an awakened being, in partnership with your soul, in community with all other beings, to participate in the awakening process.

These Are Glorious Times

This is the best time in the existence of humanity. You are a witness to amazing events. Rejoice in being part of them. Actively be part of them; spread the word. Do not be afraid of what it might happen; everything is taken care of. We love you all immensely in a way that none of you have yet experienced in your physical form. In that love, we send you our appreciation for your being the instruments of this change. With love and humility, we thank you for being partners and becoming one with us. The beginning is already here. This book is one of the many examples of it. Our message to the teachers and leaders is to keep on doing what you are doing. Continue to be guided by your inner light. Our message to those opening up to the awakening process is to celebrate this event in your life and support your leaders; the work of everyone combined will manifest the world that you desire. The new era is upon us. Rejoice!

CHAPTER 27

Spirit Having a Human Experience

The Suit of the Soul

Your physical form is to your soul as your clothes are to your body. When your soul decides to come into this physical plane, it chooses the physical "suit" that will best help it to accomplish its chosen purpose. In the same way, you choose which clothes to wear in accordance with the needs and requirements of your circumstances. Once a specific need or requirement is fulfilled, you change your clothes for another outfit more appropriate to your new circumstances. When your soul's intention to have a physical presence is no longer applicable, it discards of its body in the form of physical death; however, the soul doesn't die. It is eternal, living in spirit form until it decides to be born into the physical realm once again.

We Are Spirit Having a Human Experience

Let's go back to the story of the man sitting by the stream. The day is starting in the quiet of the mountain heights. The darkness is slowly giving way to light. The man sits at the peak of one of the mountains. He is looking at the horizon marvellously changing colours—black to blue, then orange and yellow, and finally, a brilliant white. The man gradually feels the warmth of the sun growing inside his body. He is at peace, he is free, he feels weightless, almost ethereal. There is no sound to interrupt this moment of the birth of a new day. Everything is perfect and complete.

This new birth brings the man infinite choices. It brings him the possibility of a new choice; after all, it is a new day. When the sun is high up in the sky like a huge fireball against an endless canvas of blue, the man stands up, opens his arms, breathes in deeply to take in the grace of the new day, and leaps into the air, soaring into the sky. The eagle is free again to fly into the infinite soul.

Then the man awakens from his sleep. He doesn't want to, he doesn't feel like it; being awake means leaving the freedom of wings for the boundaries of his form. He needs to learn how to be free and boundless during his waking hours. He needs to learn how to retain that unlimited nature as he experiences his physical reality. He needs to learn how to start each day afresh, with renewed perspective, without sinking into the automatic, familiar way of living.

He knows his soul speaks to him during his sleep. Each night, his recollections are more real; each day his ache for release is stronger. Now that he has awakened to this revelation, to the incredible knowledge of his divine essence, he doesn't want to live within the boundaries of his humanity. He wants to infuse his human life with the power of his spiritual nature. And so he seeks excitedly to connect with his soul. He wants the wings and the conscious awakening of his spirit so he can learn how to be, feel, and experience that divinity on Earth. He knows it is possible because his soul has told him so. He just needs to listen, to remember, to trust, and to act on the wisdom that is imparted to him when he is at the peak of the mountains, during his sleep.

In the silence of the vastness of the mountains, all souls meet and commune with those who, like him, want to know more. The congregated souls share with him these whispers of wisdom.

"Go within as often as you can, because it is there that all answers reside. Once you have the answers to your questions, go back to the outside world and experience your life based on the guidance provided by those answers. When you look for answers outside of yourself, they are not real because the outside is only a perception that you have created based on past experiences. The accuracy of the perceptions that you call reality depends on the nature of the facts that you used to create it. The more you look outside to gather facts and answers, the more distorted that reality is. By starting to seek facts and answers inside, you automatically start to perfect your reality without even needing to act on anything.

"As you look with the eyes of your soul (this is what happens when you go within), your life will reflect what your soul envisioned seeing and being in this human experience. The more you practice seeing from the eyes of your soul, the more your surroundings will change. The more you practice being like your soul, the more empowered and happy you will feel. The more you practice seeing and being as soul, the less you will need to do; doing will become so effortless that it will not seem doing at all. When you become more a human *being*, in turn, you will become less of a human *doing*, and the need for having so frequently associated with human doings will become irrelevant. At that point, when having is not so important anymore, you will have and experience all that you could possible desire without seeking it, and you will fully appreciate and enjoy everything life gives you.

"That is how to live your life from your soul's perspective. When you allow yourself to be a spirit having a human experience, when you experience life from the inside out, your life becomes perfect, whichever way it unfolds. Nothing is right or wrong; there is no good or bad, big or small, more or less, better or worse. Everything simply is the way it is. All experiences are valid ways for the soul to experience life in universal perfection and oneness."

Exercise: Spirit Having a Human Experience

You may wish to practise this exercise every day in order to become more connected and in tune with your human being nature. This means you will

- Connect more closely to the sensations and emotions you experience as you go through your days
- Be aware that you can always choose emotions that give you better feelings, regardless of the situation or circumstance
- Acknowledge that you can choose to create each day as a new day, and act upon that knowing by asking yourself simple questions, such as, "What can I do differently today?"
- See every life situation with new eyes, from a new point of view
- Enjoy the thrill of entertaining outrageous, big, out-of-your-comfort-zone ideas, and notice the impact they have on your being
- Not being afraid to try different options and think of more possibilities
- Discover and explore what feels natural within you, even if it defies any logic or anything you have done so far

Most people live in autopilot mode, processing, evaluating, and functioning in an automatic way. They react to what is happening in life instead of choosing what enhances it. They avoid changes, even small ones. They do not realise that this way of living makes each day almost exactly the same as the day before. You can come out of this sleep by freeing your soul and letting it show you how to live life. When you allow yourself to see life from the eyes of soul, you will rediscover the innocence and zest of the child living within you. Life will become a magical experience where everything is possible if you desire it and believe it.

Each night before you go to sleep, set the intention to be open to hearing whispers from your soul. Think about what answers or wisdom you are seeking. Ask to be given them to you during your sleep. Then, go to sleep, knowing that you will receive your answers and that you will remember them. Go to sleep in the knowledge and awareness that you will connect with your soul, as you do every time you drift off to sleep.

Then when you wake up in the morning, set the intention that everything you were given during the night will be revealed to you, at the right time, through words, signs, events, actions, people, or whichever medium is appropriate for your understanding.

Go through your day *being*. Feel your soul in your human body and live from that perspective. Act as though you already know what the whispers told you last night. If you consciously remember or notice anything that feels special or resonates in a unique way within you, stop for a few minutes to think about it, write it down in your journal, or share it with someone.

Pay attention to what comes up during the day. Be more present. Give thanks when you notice something divine taking place. Take a few minutes to meditate if you feel the desire to do so.

At night, again, before you drift off to sleep, give thanks for your awareness, any signs or messages you received that day, for any miracle you had the joy to witness, for being you.

Set your new intentions, as you did the night before.

Do this exercise for a period of seven days and notice the wonderful changes in your life. Notice how you become more of a spiritual being having a human experience. Notice how you start seeing life from a different perspective. Notice how your reality becomes clearer and less cluttered. Notice how some things disappear to give way to others that are completely different. Notice how you and your life transform and blossom. This is a powerful exercise that you might like to do for the rest of your life. Once you know how to let your soul show, not just during the night but also while you are awake, you will rejoice. You won't be able to live any other way. It is a blessing for your soul to shine constantly from within; it is having and experiencing God continually in you and with you, and being aware of it with all your human senses. We bless you.

CHAPTER 28

High-Level Consciousness

We Are Never Alone

I am enjoying another one of my meditations. I am, as usual, walking along the beach towards the temple, feeling peaceful and enjoying the walk.

As I think about how much I love my meditations, I realise that someone is walking beside me, holding my hand. It is a spirit showing itself in the form of bright light. I can sense that it is someone I haven't met before. We continue walking, holding hands, but I don't talk; I just look at this beautiful light as if it will suddenly show itself to me in human form. I can't be sure, but I feel it is a male energy, maybe because it feels strong, powerful, and radiates a warm vibration that extends far and gives me the impression of a very tall being. Its presence makes me feel safe and peaceful.

I continue walking, looking over sideways, as though I were looking into his eyes, like lovers do. I am enveloped, immersed, in a blissful sensation that I can only compare to a state of deep love. I lose track of my surroundings, but I don't need to look where I am going. I don't need to pay attention to the path I am walking, because intuitively, I know I am being guided. I am safe.

We walk all the way to the temple in silence, connected by the invisible energy that radiates out of this being. I'd like to ask many questions, but at the same time, I don't want to break the perfection of the moment. When we reach the entrance of the temple, we stop at the base of the stairs and the spirit being lets go of my hand. I look at him and once more, straining my eyes trying to see a form. However, I can see only light.

Now, as I sense his departure is imminent, I dare to talk to him—not with words, but with my thoughts. I ask him to come up to the temple with me, but he tells me that I must go alone. His company ends there. Then I ask, "Do you have a name? Who are you?"

"I represent the many to whom you are connected at a higher level of consciousness. I am not just one, but many. Like you, we are working at the same level of personal evolution, with the same objectives, and moving in the same direction. We are all connected by our thoughts. We all encourage each other, we all support each other, and we all help each other on our quest for answers that will allow us to unveil the path to the light. We are spread all over the planet, but as we operate at a higher level of consciousness, we do not struggle with distance, time, physical constraints, or the need to know anything about one another. We are connected by our values, our desires, our bonds, and our purpose. In essence, our soul mission connects us all.

"We came to you today to remind you that you are never alone, and to emphasise some things that you already know. First, what you think, every single moment, matters. Second, what you focus on allows you to connect with us through the high-level vibrations produced by the frequency of your thoughts. Therefore, we ask you to keep that connection alive, clear, and strong by not disturbing or interrupting it with thoughts of fear, worry, anxiety, or the like.

"By keeping yourself centred with your knowledge, your mission, your personal growth, and your path ahead, we can all work together harmoniously, flowing down the river of life at this higher level of awareness. We make a difference in your life and you make a difference in ours; all of us are connected by intention and thought, which makes a difference to the whole, not only in the physical realm, but also in the consciousness of the planet. Do not for a moment think that you are alone. You are always guided by your spiritual guides, by your teachers, by God, and by us, your human counterparts who have learnt that we are all connected through the power of our thinking. We are using that power for the well-being of all.

"Let's continue working together towards the new Era of Light. Everything that you are doing is related to what we are all doing; nothing lives in isolation. Everything functions harmoniously, happening at the proper time and place. Let the ones who know and understand the bigger picture guide us, and let us be their channel on this joint divine mission. Let's be grateful that we are taking part in this amazing enterprise. Let's rejoice in the knowledge that we can work with purpose and awareness of our actions and our power. Let's put the focus on what matters and move together, as though we were physically close to each other—many of us actually are.

"Any need to know anything about us such as who we are, what we do, what our abilities, knowledge, age, or background are, or any other ego-driven question is not only irrelevant, but serves to separate and disconnect us from one another. The only thing we need to know is that we are all souls working together to grow and prosper. Go now to meet your guides, but please treasure what you have learnt today. You are working with all of us as part of an immense group, for peace, love, harmony, and expansion. You are never alone; you are part of the whole."

I thank him from the bottom of my heart. Then, the beautiful being vanishes into thin air as swiftly as he appeared, leaving me uplifted by his enlightening message.

I admit to having forgotten, quite frequently, the truth that I am not alone. When the going gets though, when I am flooded with doubts and unanswered questions, when things don't happen as I expect, when I am affected by other people's issues or insecurities, I feel weak, wrong, separate. This being of light reminded me that none of that is real. I am never alone, we are never alone, and it feels wonderful.

The Dance of the Soul

I go upstairs looking forward to meeting my higher self, who is sitting there waiting for me. I give her a big hug as a way of saying, "I am sorry for being filled with doubt, for wanting to control, for always needing to know what is coming next instead of concentrating on what is happening now, for forgetting that each of us has an important role to fulfil, and for disturbing the flow of life with insecurities, worries, fears and lack of trust. Basically, I am sorry for listening to my ego too much."

We understand that you all give in into the hypnotic ways of the ego, some of you more than others. However, you know that soul is getting stronger within you when you become aware of the fact that you are paying attention to your ego more than necessary. We do not say the ego is bad; after all, it exists for a reason. We are saying that many of you have given the ego the freedom to rule you and your life when that is not its reason for being. Many have allowed the ego to overshadow the soul. Unaware, they have turned away from their divine purpose of happiness. Always remember: The ego segregates, the soul integrates. The ego weakens, the soul strengthens. The ego is fearful, the soul is loving. The ego is darkness, the soul is light.

We want you to accept, once and for all, that you are being taken care of even when you don't feel that way; that your life is as it ought to be at that time, for there are no right or wrong turns; that you can choose to walk with purpose, starting at any point in your life, because it is never too late; that you have the knowledge, the skills, and abilities you need to fulfil your mission; and that what you believe you lack, you will learn, have, be, and do when time requires you to do so.

It is not feasible within the confines of your physical world to know, be, and have all you need and want at a given stage of life. Events take place in a chronological succession to make your life easier to handle, even though from our perspective and dimension, everything happens in an instant. Please, do not rush; instead savour every second of your present. Otherwise, you will never be satisfied with your life. You will always be looking for the next step, the next thing, missing out on what is taking place in the present. All your desires will manifest at the appropriate times, not before, not after. You are working in synchronisation with other souls; therefore, all your actions have to flow in accord with theirs, like in a dance. Enjoy the knowledge that you are part of this dance of the souls. All of humanity is, in fact, although some are aware of it. This is what the awakening is all about.

Today you have been awakened to another truth: the power of your thinking not only influences your life, but also connects, works, creates, and collaborates with others at a higher level of consciousness, changing life in this world. It is our expectation that once you become awakened to this truth, you can work without struggle or blockage, you can flow in life without fear, and you can dedicate your power to your life mission with determination and the ability to handle anything that comes your way.

I was moved by this beautiful and powerful message, and I gave thanks to my guides for showing me, once again, how amazing and grand we are. In that state of gratitude, I created the following empowering statement: *"I now accept and embrace my purposeful mission, as I am part of this soul community working together; therefore, I put my energy and focus on having thoughts that empower us and make us all grow. I leave behind any thoughts of fear, doubt, worry, or uncertainty, because I know that I am surrounded, supported, and guided by powerful, wise, divine masters and spirit guides. Any fears I can think of disappear, and have no reason to exist. I am grateful for my life and for being. I love you all."*

CHAPTER 29

Point of Power: Your Vibrations

Everyone is connected through the mesh of vibrational consciousness that is part of the universal intelligence, Source. Whatever you experience through your feelings, whether they were created through action, thought, observation, or imagination, has an impact on your vibrational energy. In the same way, every time you think, your feelings and emotions are affected by that thought. It doesn't matter what triggered your thinking, whether you were imagining what you desire, reminiscing about past experiences, pondering the future, or observing your present reality; you were provoked to think, and your thoughts influence your emotions, which affect your vibrational energy.

It is easy to deduce that when you experience emotions and feelings and your vibrational energy is affected, that effect is transmitted to others through the ethereal layers; in that way, the spiritual consciousness is affected. It is also easy to deduce that your vibrations influence your immediate consciousness. This is how important you are; this is why you are a creator. This explains, for example, why there are developing areas on this planet where poverty, sickness, and hunger are rampant, as well as areas of abundance, riches, and progress. The experience of a group observing what surrounds them is energetically transmitted to those close to them. The essence of what is transmitted could be either good or not so good; nothing is sifted out or excluded from the vibrational network. Then others, who pick up the surrounding vibrations, are influenced by the dominant consciousness of the group; poverty and illness or prosperity and health are reflected in their lives, so they share the fate of the group. By unconsciously hooking into the prevalent vibration, a person accepts the effects of whatever that vibration carries along with it.

The question is simple, then: Are your vibrations an intentional reflection of your heart's desires? Or, are you automatically hooked up to the prevalent vibration? In other words, are you consciously or unconsciously affecting the universal consciousness with your vibrations? Nothing prevents you from experiencing anything in this physical world that can be experienced, regardless of the circumstances or the time. The only key to experiencing something wanted or unwanted is to be aware of which flow of consciousness you are connected to. Your awareness is your point of power.

Change the Frequency

When you are exposed by some means to adverse situations or conditions that you do not wish to experience, and as a result of that contrast, you also know that what you want to experience, the way to move away from where you are towards where you want to be is to change your vibrations. You need to learn to connect to the vibration of what you desire, as well as to tap into your higher layers—the high-level vibrations—that have further reach and are more powerful and clear.

The lower layers are the ones closest to your physical body. They carry the energy of what surrounds you, that is, the predominant vibration of the group. By remaining switched on to these lower layers, you will continue to experience versions of things that are not in harmony with you. However, by raising your awareness to the higher layers, the ones that vibrate within your inner light, you can connect with consciousness more in sync with what you desire. As a result, you will be exposed to what you desire, you will attract what you desire, and you will manifest what you desire in your physical realm. Consequently, you can be an oasis in the middle of the desert, you can have abundance when there is scarcity, you can be healthy when there is disease, and you can feel peaceful when there is despair. There is nothing you cannot be, do, or have if you desire it from your purest point of the self—your soul.

How do you connect to those higher levels of consciousness, those purest layers of energy? By connecting to your inner light, by acknowledging the partnership with your soul, and by being soul in your physical experience of life. How do you achieve all this? Through meditation; through using your soul centre in your solar plexus to connect with your heart's desires; through filling yourself with light; through finding your truth; through being love; through connecting with soul-base emotions; and through seeking happiness and goodness in everything and everyone. If you do not engage in these practices, if you do not choose to connect with this higher level of consciousness, then you are choosing to be controlled by the environment that surrounds you, which is a reflexion of the immediate consciousness.

The truth is that the state of the surrounding consciousness is irrelevant—although it is preferable, from your human perspective, that the energy of your surroundings is positive, abundant, and harmonious. What is actually relevant is how aware you are of your power, how much you utilise it, and how frequently you are *being* by default, led by the outer circumstances. Your manifestations or your point of attraction are the result of your attitude to what you are exposed to, and your reaction to what your senses tell you about your reality. These could be total contrasts to what you really desire. Feelings that you are powerless to change anything, powerless to get different results, are due to the consciousness you are connecting to; that is what you will get in return.

Switch to Your Point of Power

However, if you stood in your position of power, if you trusted and believed in that power, and asked, lived, and acted from that point of power, your manifestations wouldn't be the result of reaction to what your environment tells you; they would be the result of creation from your soul's point of power. Therefore, be blind, deaf, mute, and indifferent to what you do not desire so you will not get sucked into the whirlpool of unwanted "reality." Intend to become a focused and deliberate observer of what you desire in order to bring it into your sphere of possibilities. Focus on your desires and expect them to be part of your life—they will be. They will become your reality regardless of what happens around you and in the world. Understand that you are not controlled; you are in control. Understand that you can become the driver of your life and steer the journey to the path of your purpose. This is the way to live; there is no other way.

CHAPTER 30

The Power of Oneness

We Are Human Seeds

I am in another wonderful meditation. As I close my eyes and clear my mind to connect with my guides, images start to come up. However, the images I see are not of me walking along the beach or in the forest as usual. Instead, all I can see is darkness; all around me it is dark. I am standing still. It feels like I am in a box. This increases my sensation of confinement. I am not moving or intending to move; I am just trying to figure out where I am.

Then, as if it were the most natural thing to do, I snap my fingers and a light turns on. The light is dim, so I can only see my immediate surroundings. I realise that I am not in a box or enclosure as I had thought. I am underground, buried! Although the situation seems awful, the fact is that I feel fine. Realising that I am buried doesn't produce in me any feelings of suffocation, despair, or fear. On the contrary, I feel calm, and more importantly, I can breathe without effort. The whole scene feels natural and normal. Then, again in a natural way, I stretch my arms upwards. Whatever is covering me breaks loose, and I come up easily to the outdoors.

At this moment, I realise I am like a seed. I am a seed that has just broken the soil that was its womb, and has now been born. I realise with wonder and amazement that I am a seed of the human race. I am emerging in the field of wildflowers not far from the temple. I look around and see many other human seeds rising, just as I did a few seconds ago. They are not only emerging from the ground, but from everywhere: the trees, the mountains, the water, the air, flowers, birds, clouds. It is a very strange scene, but at the same time, incredibly beautiful and glorious. I turn around in all directions and I can see life being born everywhere. There are no words that can express in a precise way what I am feeling to be part of this scene, this act of birth. The only word close enough is "love," pure love.

Once I am completely out of my cocoon, I see myself in my human adult form, wearing a simple long dress, my hair swinging freely in the air. The day is beautifully clear and warm, and a melody fills the atmosphere. It is made of birdsong, forest sounds, and dancing water, and it perfectly harmonises with the aromas of the Earth. I stretch up further, extending my arms up as high as I can. Then, feeling settled, I start off for the temple as usual.

I feel deeply touched by this meditation. Never before have I felt so connected and in unison with everything around me. I feel like I am the air, the melodies, the aromas, the forest, the mountains, the birds, and the flowers. I feel like I am not just me; I am *in* everything, and everything is in me.

The Concept of Oneness

I am sure you enjoyed the beginning of this meditation, with all those human seeds being born here and there. That was a very artistic and graphic way of showing you what you are. Everything is made of the same essence: the skies, the stars, the trees, the animals and plants, the rocks, the whole planet for that matter, and of course, you. You are born from the same inner lining, the same fabric of what Mother Earth is made of, and for that reason, when you physically die, your body becomes dust and your soul goes back to the source. Both acts enable you to return to the essence you originated from. The objective of this meditation was to make you experience the concept of oneness, to emphasise the fact that we are all one, part of the same thing, made of the same elements, and sharing the same life energy. We are all one: physical and nonphysical, material and ethereal, form and spirit. This is our way to request that you finally give up the idea that you, that we, are separate from everything else. This is our way to bring to your awareness once again to the impact and consequences of your actions. When you attack species to the point of endangering them, when you abuse the environment, when you pollute the air, when you exhaust natural resources, when you go against nature in pursue of your technological advances, when you mistreat the weak, when you go to war in the name of global peace, when you kill each other to prevent different ideas or points of view from co-existing, when you engage in any activity that goes against love, harmony, peace, compassion, union, freedom, and uniqueness, what you are really doing is destroying yourself—man—because you are everything that you are destroying.

You cannot think of anything as "something else" or "someone else," because everything is made of the same essence. It might look different, it might feel different, it might act and think differently, but it is no more than a different version of you. The truth is that if you see past the illusion of differences, you will find and see yourself. Everything you see on your planet, inside it, and around it, was once a seed planted by a universal powerful intelligence that created all. This universal intelligence created everything from the same essence, only with different shapes, forms, and levels of development. Everything has a purpose for existence; everything has a reason to be. From the beginning of time, humans have been playing the role of that creative energy here on Earth by determining what exists and what doesn't, what can be spared, what is needed, who owns it, who is more worthy of what, and whose ideas should prevail, not realising that with their actions, they have been destroying what the source created: their home and everything that lives in it. They have used the power of their creative energy to build and prosper, but they have also misused it to destroy and to segregate.

But these are new glorious times. The new era has brought light to the spirit of the planet, and men are awakening to the fact that they are not separate entities from the rest. You are not superior to the animals and plants that inhabit your planet; you do not have more right than they do to be here. You are awakening to the light. You are slowly leaving behind a period of darkness that has seen you endanger your planet to a state of emergency, with drastic climate changes and species diminished to the point of extinction. This period of darkness is coming to an end. The Era of Light is near. All of you will finally understand that there is no "me" or "them," only "us," and that we are all working and living together without borders or differences, categories or hierarchies. You will finally learn to live as one, in harmony and peace, breathing the same life force energy from the source, sharing your DNA, your histories, your essence.

The Breath of Life

In the marvel of nature, bees fly from flower to flower to allow the pollination process to occur, thus ensuring the reproduction of those flowers and therefore, the perpetuation of their existence. In the same magnificent way, breathing life energy in and out of your bodies allows communication between everything on this planet and in the universe. This communication is essential to life, evolution and growth on the planet, and in the universe as well. Up until now, it has existed in a "weaken" state, full of noise and interference, due to your feelings of separateness. Humans have interacted with the universe in an unconscious manner, unaware of the real implications of their actions. For the process of communication to be clear and continuous, it must be performed with full awareness of its purpose. The arrival of the Era of Light will bring another advancement to the universal community: you will accept and embrace the concept of oneness.

Oneness implies sharing your essence with the universe by consciously breathing life energy, and by knowing and understanding that breathing is not just the act of filling your lungs with oxygen to continue living. Breathing is much, much more! Breathing enables a continuous stream of life, love and wisdom flow into and through everything and out into the planet. Each time you breathe in, you are inhaling love. You are receiving, channelling, and processing the energy source of life that carries the essence of all that lives, has lived, and will live on the planet and the universe. This life force sustains, cleans, purifies, feeds, heals, and nurtures you. Each time you breathe out, you are returning it to the outside world, changed with the imprint of your experiences. Now that you have been awakened to the meaning of the act of breathing, make your intention to breathe more consciously and become a strong link in the communication process. Throughout your day, take a moment to be present and centred, while inhaling the love that lives in all that surrounds you and exhaling the love that lives in you enveloped with gratitude. When you bring awareness to your breathing, you raise your vibrations, connect with your inner light and embrace your oneness. You are all one, not just because of your essence, but also because of this life force that runs through your bodies and the love that you are. This life force permeates all things, connects all things, and *is* all things. Embrace the concept of oneness and rejoice.

PART VI

What Do I Do Now?

Congratulations, you have come so far! You are almost at the end of the book, and you have remained true to your promise of connecting with your inner voice and re-establishing a relationship with it. You have been rewarded with mind-expanding discoveries, you have learnt a bit more (or a lot more) about yourself and your inner being, you have questioned some outdated beliefs, and hopefully, you have set many new intentions for a fresh new start. The magnitude of the impact of what you have learnt has on you and your life depends on how attentive you were while reading the words in this book, and how conscious and truthful you were in doing the work of the exercises and meditations.

All along, without even knowing it, you have been communicating with your soul. In the process, you have been awakening to a completely new dimension of your being. You now know where your inner voice lives within you, what it feels like, and how it sounds, and you are on your way to establishing a great relationship with it, which has been the end goal all along. By learning to connect with your inner voice, you have been granted the key to the universal knowledge and wisdom. It is available to everyone. In order to open the door to all that knowledge, you have to follow the simple ritual of asking, listening, and being open to following its guidance with trust.

Now is the time to make new choices. You have to choose; you always do. Choose to make great choices, amazing and glorious ones! Do not continue to live your life by default, in autopilot mode. You can do much, much better. You can create your best life and live it by applying the knowledge you have gained from reading this book. This knowledge has been shared with you not just from human to human, but also from soul to soul. The process is simple: focus on an area of your life that you wish to improve, ask for assistance from your soul, then listen for guidance and be willing to follow through. You will be amazed at what turns up in your life. Trust me, I know!

It Is Time to Choose

It is time to choose. Choice is power; it is the power of free will. Be grateful and claim it, but above all, use it wisely to live a purposeful life. I know you can do it and I know you want to do it; therefore, I am going to give you a last little push to help you start moving forward to an amazingly fulfilling life. I know it can be overwhelming to start making changes, especially changes of the essence of your life and of concepts and beliefs you have probably been holding since you were very young. Fear of change and the new can stop you even before you start. This time, however, it will not. You are determined to live from your soul's perspective and I trust you will. For that reason, in the following chapters I have included some starting points to show you simple ways you can start walking the path to becoming a mindful creator of your life. I wish you all the best, from my heart.

CHAPTER 31

Time to Choose Love

If you make only one choice, choose love. If work on only one change, base that change on love. If you give only one thing, wrap that thing in love. If you empower your thinking, make that empowerment come from love. If you scrutinise your body, look at it with eyes of love. If you say only one word, make that word "love." If you enjoy a fulfilling life, live it from the simplicity of the power of love.

The power of love has come upon Earth, and is bathing the planet in a powerful cleansing shower of truth and light. Love is the key to all mysteries. Love sheds light even on the darkest times. Follow love and you will be guided to the right path of wisdom, passion, and glory. Love is freedom, and freedom is the shedding of boundaries that constrain your ability to manifest your desires and accomplish what you came here to achieve.

Love is all there is, and we Spirit Guides, Angels, Beings of Light, and God are always loving and supporting you. You are all very much loved. Always remember this, especially when you are down, upset, lonely, or in any other kind of need. In those challenging moments, just focus on the love we feel for you, and all will be well. We are always connected by the vibrant, strong, pure bonds of love. We are sending our love to you right now. Feel it, enjoy it, appreciate it, and share it.

Choose Love Every Day

If you make one change today, make that change based on love, because love is the essence of everything that exists, has ever existed, or will exist. How do you know whether you are choosing love in your everyday life? Happiness, peace of mind, health, trust, wonder, success, self-drive, fulfilment, appreciation, abundance, beauty, and enthusiasm are all synonyms of love. When you find them constantly present in your life, this is an indication that you are choosing love in your daily endeavours, and that life is reflecting love back to you with overflowing abundance. When any of these expressions of love are scarce or missing from your life, you need to assess what areas of your life need more loving attention. Then bring conscious intention to those areas to overflow them with love and see them thrive. The intention to experience love is all you need to do to start bringing love into your life.

If there is a challenging area in your life where you find it difficult to show and appreciate love, remember that the love you put in is not primarily directed at the specific life situation, but at yourself. It is the effect of loving yourself that has an impact on your life situation. When you see life from this perspective, no matter what troubles you are experiencing, if you are willing to give love to yourself by respecting, honouring, caring, appreciating, acknowledging, valuing, and trusting yourself, that love will be transferred to every area of your life.

When you find yourself caught up in an unloving experience involving only yourself or involving others, too, ask yourself what is most important—to always be right, to prove or justify yourself, to satisfy a need for approval, to be accepted and accepting, to please, to fit in, to be superior, to follow someone else's standards; or to be in control of the emotions you feel and choose the ones that make you feel good? I hope you will agree with me that it is the latter. Therefore, the next time you find yourself caught up in an unloving experience, reach for the love within yourself to find the best feeling you can have in that moment. Then expand that feeling to the present situation. In that way, you are changing the dynamics of the situation by changing the energy to one of love. As soon as you bring your awareness to what really matters, to your purpose—happiness—everything else falls into perspective. Then you can consciously act from your point of power: love. (Review what you learnt in Chapter 13: The Power of Love.) When you choose love, you are choosing to live life from your inner light instead of from darkness.

Exercise: Choosing Love

Love is the most rewarding of choices because it makes you feel great and it makes your life work. This exercise is very simple: for every experience you encounter and every person you interact with, be aware of how you are feeling. If you notice that you are feeling anything like joy, peace, enthusiasm, motivation, tranquillity, excitement, compassion, connection, empowerment, certainty, well-being, or adoration, then you are experiencing love in its various shades, and everyone and everything involved in the experience has a core intention of love. In this instance, continue doing what you are doing: giving and receiving love.

On the other hand, if you become aware that whatever you are experiencing doesn't produce loving feelings in you, then by choosing love at that moment, you can put yourself into a loving state. You can do this very simply and without worsening the way you feel by either removing yourself from the situation as soon as possible, or, if that is not a viable option, by learning to connect with the vibration of love within you, and disconnecting from the lower level of vibration presented by your surroundings (remember Chapter 29: Point of Power: Your Vibrations). Note that by leaving the situation or disconnecting from it, you are not closing yourself off to what is happening around you; on the contrary, you are choosing to open up to a clearer and better channel for connecting with your essence and whatever you desire to take place.

The Way Love Feels

An easy way to become familiar with how love feels within you, which is, by the way, different from person to person, is to take a few minutes going through your life experiences and recalling the ones in which you felt true, strong, wonderful feelings of love—for example: the feeling of safety provided by the warm hug of your parents, loud laughter and the mischief of hours of play with your siblings and friends, the delicious smell of freshly baked cookies at your grandma's kitchen, the taste of your first kiss, your pride and sense of accomplishment when you graduated, the excitement of your wedding day, the sight of your newborn baby, the face of the person you are madly in love with, the understanding words of a friend, the fragrance of the flowers in your garden. In summary, recall any experience when you were appreciated, respected, rewarded, pampered, loved, cared for, helped, healed, hugged, kissed, or welcomed. Also, remember to include moments when you felt the same for others, as love is always a two-way road. List in your journal all of these experiences when you felt love. The more you can recall, the better. If you want to write a short paragraph about each one, go for it and have fun. I am sure that by now, you are feeling uplifted. Perhaps you even have some tears of happiness in your eyes. If you are presently going through a rough time, if love has been scarce lately, do not use this exercise to feel unhappier about what you are missing. Use it to give yourself a boost. If you have experienced love in any form, you can experience it again. The fact that you are doing the exercise shows that you are already in the process of experiencing it again, and abundantly.

Now that you have gotten in touch with the vibration of love within you, you need to attach it to a cue so it will be easy to retrieve the feeling when you need it. This works much like to the shortcut links on the desktop of your computer, or the speed dial buttons on your phone; they take you to what you wish to access very quickly. Relate your vibration of love to a smell, a taste, a place, a song, a food, a colour, a flower, a particular object, or a person, so when you recall the object or person, you will also bring forth your feeling of the vibration of love. Once you make your pick, go through the experiences you wrote down in your journal and link each one of them to your cue. In the following days, practice thinking about your cue and feeling the vibration of love. Also, whenever you find yourself experiencing loving feelings in life, attach the feelings to your cue.

Now returning to the beginning of the exercise, if you find yourself in any situation where you need to disconnect from the low-level vibrations around you, bring your love cue to your awareness. Remember one of the many experiences when you felt great, and change your current feeling to an uplifting one. With a bit of practice, you will find that soon be able to create in yourself a state of peace and love, no matter what is happening around you, by connecting with the vibration of love. You might be surprised to discover that your life has more moments of loving experiences in it than not. What more could you ask for? Now smile: you have done it.

CHAPTER 32

Time to Choose Light

I am ready for another magnificent meditation. I close my eyes, relax, and drift into the quiet of my mind. Images start to appear and I see myself once more walking along the beach, enjoying the wonderful, peaceful scenery.

After a while, I head for the water and go in, immersing myself in the depths of the ocean. I have never done this before in this meditation. I swim and swim without stopping, and the light from the surface slowly disappears. I enter the darkness of the submerged world. The deeper I go, the heavier I become. I am surrounded by darkness. The intense silence of the depths is broken only by my loud heartbeats. I can breathe with ease, and I am neither cold nor upset by the pressure of the water—yet I am scared of this place, of the complete darkness and of not knowing of what is out there, or where I am going. I don't like the way I feel, but I keep on swimming, deeper and deeper with every stroke, as if something is pulling me towards the bottom of the ocean.

Then I stop swimming and linger on the spot. There is nothing around me but darkness and solitude. As I wait for something to happen, a feeling of uneasiness grows in the middle of my body, in my solar plexus. I don't like this place, and I don't like the way I feel, even though I am fine and there is no threat. In order to shake these unhappy feelings, I think about the beautiful beach I was walking along at the beginning of my meditation, and of the meeting with my spirit guides.

At that moment, I feel a gentle tugging, a pulling at my solar plexus, like an invisible cord drawing me upwards. I let myself be lifted, my arms and legs extended, my body fully stretched out and relaxed. My eyes close in trust. I find myself enjoying the ride enormously. I am floating and swinging in the water; the higher I go, the lighter I feel.

Suddenly, I am back at the surface, floating on the water. The sun shines full on my entire body, slowly drying the drops of water on my skin. I breathe in deeply a few times to fill my lungs with air and fill my body with life energy. I stay there, drifting carelessly on the water, my eyes still closed, a big smile on my face. I feel so good now; it's much more beautiful up here with the sun, the sky, the songs of the forest, the trees, the sound of running water, the peacefulness. It is definitely much more beautiful up here than down there, in the depths of the ocean. The darkness made me feel empty, lost, lonely, and restricted, even though I was swimming freely and there was no threat, at least no apparent one. In contrast, up here where the light shines, I feel awesome, safe, and at peace.

When I finally open my eyes, I am standing, completely dry and refreshed, at the entrance of the temple. As usual, I go upstairs to meet my higher self, who is waiting for me to share another piece of wisdom.

Light vs. Darkness: Our Choice

Hello my dear, had a nice walk?

Let me guess, this meditation was to show that light is the way to go.

Exactly! You have experienced yourself in both states: the light of the outdoors and the darkness of the depths, and now you are free to choose whichever one you prefer. You can be either way, but being in the light makes you feel much better, doesn't it? You can be in the darkness and choose to stay there until you are ready to come out to the light. It doesn't matter how far down you are; you will always be able to reach the light. There is always help, too; you don't have to do it alone. Once you get to the surface, everything is wonderful, clear, and peaceful. The cord that lifted you up represents your inner power, your soul, the inner guidance that shows you the way to the light. The cord appeared when you started reaching for pleasant emotions, when you started disconnecting from the fear and uneasiness of what surrounded you.

Fear, stagnation, negativity, lack of forgiveness, control, overbearing nature, resentment, judgement, and criticism, in other words, ego-based emotions, are the ones that keep you submerged in the depths of darkness. When you start acknowledging them and become more aware of the emotions you frequently experience, when you decide they no longer serve you and start replacing them with soul-based emotions, it is then that you begin your ascension to the surface. It is then that you begin your journey to the light.

This is another metaphor, another visual representation of what it means to be in the light. Metaphors resonate differently with each person. Each person takes and uses the examples that affect them the most to gain the understanding that will allow them to make the decision to shift from darkness to light. Moreover, even though a person may understand the concepts, he will make the shift only when he is ready to do so. Often, although people know they live in darkness, they are not ready to embark on their journey to the light, to get rid of all the baggage that sinks them into the depths. They choose to swim on the spot and experience feelings that aren't pleasant but are familiar, instead of choosing another way of feeling, and by extension, another way of being.

Eventually, everyone will make the shift because the light is their destination, but they can only do so when the time is right for them—that could very well be a different physical life. The journey from darkness to light can take many lives to complete. Since you are reading these pages now, your times of darkness have shifted in previous lives; you are now ready to start or continue on your journey to the light. Enjoy the ride.

Exercises: Choosing Light

Any of the exercises in this book are a great way to get you in the direction of ascension to the light. Every time you choose consciousness over unconsciousness, mindfulness over autopilot-mode, feel-good emotions and thoughts over draining, negative ones, being connected over feeling isolated, seeing the glass half-full over seeing it half-empty, wanting to expand over staying within your comfort zone, reaching out over being constricted, laughing over feeling gloomy, health over disease, honesty over lies, self-love over criticism, forgiveness over resentment, or love over fear, you are choosing light over darkness.

Every time you use your inner powers, you are choosing light. Every time you ask, listen, and act upon the guidance of your soul, you are choosing light. Every time you connect to your intuition, you are choosing light. Every time you acknowledge God or the source of all creation and are grateful for your life, you are choosing light. As you can see, it is not so difficult to choose light. Small changes to what you choose to be, feel, do, or even have can make a huge difference, not only to your life, but also to the lives of others, and to the planet as a whole. It is time to choose light.

CHAPTER 33

Time to Choose Dreams

Daydreaming is a kind of visualization, and it is part of the process of manifestation, the process of creation. Moreover, it is the way your soul expresses its desires to your physical being by means of your mind. The greatest minds of the past knew about the power of daydreaming. They applied it by spending time in contemplation, allowing action to subside for a time, and letting the mind run free to entertain amazing, even crazy ideas. Many of these ideas would later become inventions, literary masterpieces, works of art, and great discoveries in every field of life. Take the word of Victor Hugo, who said, *"There is nothing like a dream to create the future."*

What Type of Dreamer Are You?

How much time do you spend daydreaming? Are you someone who does not daydream because you see it as a waste of time? If so, your life is probably busy, hectic, and cluttered, so there is little or no time for this kind of activity. You do not realise that a little time spent in quiet daydreaming, would provide you not only with a healthy break from the rush of the day, but also with direction and clarity about how you could be living your life. Are you, instead, someone who have forgotten about your innate ability to pleasurably dream? Dreaming makes you feel good. You submerge yourself in a make-believe place where all your desires can come true. Remember that you are allowed to dream and to have incredible dreams and desires, just as you did when you were a child, and to turn your life into a happy adventure full of possibility. If on the other hand, you overdo it by spending excessive time immersed in your daydreams, you need to become aware of this and determine the reason for your behaviour. Are your daydreams leading you in a direction you desire? Or are you using them as a way to switch off from a reality that is so different from what you desire that you feel powerless to change it?

You Are Allowed to Dream

The key to daydreaming is to find a happy and healthy balance of time and motivation, as well as to understand the importance of engaging in the activity. Set a time each day to be connected and in touch with your desires.

Do not feel bad or guilty about spending time in contemplation of your desires. Rather, feel pleased by the experience of living in the world of your dreams, for this gives you the drive to work on other things in your present life. This way, you have the best of both worlds of spirit and mind. Those who are in touch with their dreams understand that the soul uses them to communicate through the doors of the imagination.

When you daydream, you go into an altered state where all that you experience is real and possible. You connect at a vibrational level with everything included in the dream: people, places, things, circumstances, even the environment. An interchange of energy takes place, and your conscious mind is imprinted with the effects of that interaction, which in turn affects the way you feel about yourself and about your life. The more you daydream and the more you connect with the various components of your dreams in that altered state, the stronger the imprint becomes, and the more empowered and driven you are to make those dreams a reality. The power of daydreaming doesn't lie in whether or not your dreams become reality exactly the way you imagine they will. The power lies in the effects the daydreams have on your vibrational state. When you spend time seeing, feeling, enjoying, and entertaining your dreams as possible, you elevate the rate at which you vibrate. In turn, this enhanced vibration gives you a more positive outlook on life by making you happier, more optimistic, and healthier in mind, body, and spirit. Moreover, your vibrations resonate more with the things that you dream about, drawing them closer to your sphere of possibilities.

Daydreaming is not reserved for the young and those with great lives ahead of them. It is for everyone, regardless of age or life situation. When your life is good and seems to be working, it is easy and natural to engage in daydreams about greater abundance—you will do it almost unconsciously. However, when the times are tough and challenging, you tend to stay immersed in your issues rather than spending time dreaming. But it is in times like these that the power of dreams will serve you the most. If necessary, you will need to call upon your strength and determination to disconnect yourself temporarily from whatever circumstance is adversely affecting your life. Dream about solutions, positive outcomes, resolutions. See yourself in a better situation. In this case, daydreaming acts like a rope lifting your spirits and feelings upwards, towards peace and well-being. It also puts you in a more positive mindset to work towards resolution of this particular stage in your life. It is, as many say, "the light at the end of the tunnel."

On some level, all dreams are real; they exist in another dimension or a different version of your life. When you daydream, you connect to the feeling of having that dream life and bring it into your physical life. The key is not only to stay with the dreams, but also to focus on and take action towards them. Otherwise, they will always stay as dreams. Go for it!

How to Act On Your Dreams

- *Clarify your true desires.* The first thing is start looking after yourself better. This means spending time every day, even for a few minutes, to enjoy the feeling of having what you desire. When you connect with your dreams, you are connecting with your soul. What do you see in that dream life? Are you healthy, beautifully dressed, wealthy, in command of your life, free of worry, engaged in an interesting project, enjoying a fulfilling relationship, nurturing children, buying a new home, travelling, being assertive, studying, starting your own business, working for a cause that you feel strongly about, helping others, or just doing stuff that you love? Spend time finding out what you desire, because your true desires directly align with your purpose.

- *Connect with the feeling of having what you desire.* Then start aiming for what you dream of. Step by step, make your dreams your goal. Detach yourself from any expectations or time frames; it is not your job to think about how, when, or who. Your only concern is to spend time connecting to your dream feelings—the fuel that keeps your drive alive—and acting upon them. Keep your focus on all the things you desire.

- *Surrender to the present time.* This is one of the key elements of working with your dreams: accept what is *now* in your life. Understand that your present life situation does not always reflect what your life might be later. Do not feel discouraged or let down if your dreams seem too big or unattainable compared to your present situation. Look around and you will find plenty of evidence of people who transformed their lives completely because they believed in what they saw in their minds and in their dreams. Learn to work with life; do not fight it, do not curse it, do not blame it. Every experience is a stepping-stone on your journey of life. Look at your life now and see how you can steer it, how you can turn it in the direction you wish to go—then do it.

- *Make the decision to follow your desires.* When opportunity arises, work on anything related to your dreams, no matter how small or insignificant that action might seem. You will notice that as you take action, the world around you will start to change; you will start attracting other things that will push you forward. Don't wait for something else to happen, don't make any more excuses, don't blame anyone or anything for your inability to follow your dreams. You can start right now to do something, anything, to make your dreams real.

- *Trust in yourself.* You can achieve anything you set your mind to as long as you believe it. Surround yourself with people who support you in your endeavours and encourage you to think outside the current box of your life. However, do not feel dependant on anyone, do not fully rely on people whose qualities you feel you lack. It is often true that what you seek in others is what you yourself need in order to move forward. Look for people who show qualities that you admire, and be attentive to the qualities in others that attracted you; these are the qualities that you need yourself. Those qualities are in you, you need to bring them to the surface. Trust in yourself!

- *Enjoy the ride.* As always, enjoy the process. Following your dreams is not a race against time or another person. Following your dreams is a pursuit unique to the individual. It can take you your whole life, even several lifetimes, to achieve your goal. Therefore, do not worry about how many mistakes you make before you get something right. With practice and trust in your inner powers, you will get more right than wrong. Enjoy the feeling of liveliness that following your dreams gives your spirit. When you lose your ability to dream, you become like a wilted flower: your spirit shrinks, your life becomes empty, and you feel like some part of you is dead. That is not how you are supposed to feel. Love your dreams and be grateful for them in your life.

Exercise: Act on Your Dreams

This exercise applies the steps presented above.

- *Be clear about what you desire.* You might want a great many things, but you know it is a waste of energy to want them all at once. After all, you have your whole life to attain them. Instead, concentrate your attention and energy on the desires that you believe are most important at this stage of your life, and leave the rest aside. You are not forgetting about them, nor are you letting them go; you are just setting them aside for a later time. Make a list of what you want on nice paper with bold colours—be excited about it! Take time to refine your list. It can change and it will—trust me on that. It doesn't matter what your desires are, whether they are about money, health, relationships, inner growth, or anything else—if that is what you truly desire, then go for it. Do not compare yourself to others.
- *Feel excited.* If you are happy with what you desire, you won't have any problems with feeling good, excited, and enthusiastic about your life, or with believing you can have it. Spend a few minutes every day daydreaming about what you want. You could create a scrapbook with pictures representing your dreams, and browse through it during your daydreaming time, or as often as you can.
- *Accept your present.* Be grateful for your life and know that everything that has ever happened to you was preparing you for your life journey. Even though you cannot see it now, everything will come clear at the end. So bless your life, and life will bless you.

- *Act upon your dreams.* Keep your desires ever-present in your mind and intend to engage in activities that will move you towards them as much as you can. Do not give in to the worrying and wandering of the mind, nor waste energy on things that aren't aligned with your goals. Before you engage in any type of activity, ask yourself whether it will help you move closer to achieving your goals. If it will, work on it knowing that you are flowing with life. If it won't, determine whether you really have to do it. Assess whether it really needs your attention or can be delegated, set aside for later, not done at all. This may seem ruthless, but sometimes fear of acting upon your dreams makes you disperse your focus and energy on irrelevant endeavours. If the task has to be done, work on it gracefully, engaging your soul in the process; you will finish it faster and feel good about it, as well. Seek every opportunity you can to work towards your dreams.

- *Trust in yourself* and in your power to achieve what you desire. Seek help, be creative, learn new skills, spend time with uplifting and encouraging people, try new pathways, and be prepared to fail as part of the process. Do not give up on your dreams, do not give in to procrastination, do not delay any longer the changes that you know you must undertake. Any excuse you can come up with will only undermine your self-confidence and slowly create a state of stagnation in your energy levels. Then you will be moving away from what you truly desire. Nothing can be done as to how you dealt with your dreams in past, but you know what you can do from now on. Start trusting in yourself and focusing on what really matters.

- *Enjoy the feeling* of acknowledging what you'd like to become, and the thrill of discovering where your dreams will take you, perhaps someplace you never thought about before. Be happy with yourself for taking the time to discover the inner desires that resonate in your heart, then taking the steps to follow them. Rejoice for being in harmony with your divine nature, which is always guiding, supporting, and inspiring you to follow the path that you came here to walk. Be proud of detaching yourself from expectations, barriers, and limitations by assuming a can-do mindset. Finally, be grateful for your dreams, because they enhance your life and make you blossom.

CHAPTER 34

Time to Choose New Beliefs

Our beliefs direct our lives every single moment of every single day, without the need for our conscious input. Most of us are completely unaware of this programming. Fortunately, many are waking up to this fact, and are working to reprogram their beliefs in order to take charge of their lives. Our beliefs are the blueprint for how we act, feel, and respond—in other words, for how we function in everyday life. They are imprinted on us from the day we are born. Some beliefs originate from a time before our births, and they continue to be reshaped as we progress on our journey through life.

We rarely question our beliefs until something dramatic takes place that affects our lives directly or indirectly. This drama opens a temporary window to our awareness, offering a clearer view of what is happening in and around us, and sometimes providing a more objective and detached picture of what is really happening. This opportunity for clarity allows us to become awakened to the fact that we can make different choices, we can have different points of view, we can consider different ways of thinking, and at the same time, we can allow others to do the same. During these critical times, some will embrace their newfound clarity and change their beliefs, aiming to overcome the particular issue at hand. However, others will choose to remain in the comfort of what they already know, following the same patterns of behaviour even though those patterns do not serve their lives in general. They are unaware that they continue to perpetuate what it is already present in their lives.

Renewing Your Beliefs

As part of the process of discovering your inner voice, you will be inspired to re-evaluate all the beliefs that are shaping your life. This is a natural thing to do as your partnership with your soul becomes more established; through the strengthening of the connection with your inner being, you will become less fearful of change and more trusting of your power. For the first time, you are no longer afraid of getting in touch with your inner beliefs.

The re-assessment of your present beliefs is a huge undertaking on your part; it takes time, courage, inner strength, and most importantly, honesty. If the re-assessment is conducted with integrity and the intention to bring light into your life, it will allow you to determine with clarity which of your beliefs align with who you really are and who you want to become. You will discover that many of the beliefs you currently hold belong to the ego, or to someone else, or were imposed on you by your surrounding world. In any case, they do not belong to you. This dysfunction in your belief system has been causing your inner conflict, confusion, distress, discontent, and even illness. The process doesn't stop at the evaluation stage; it is not enough to highlight and distinguish the beliefs that support you on your life journey from the ones that do not. Further work is required. After the re-evaluation of your beliefs is complete, you are in position to take action, to take charge of the boundaries of your life and expand them so you can grow in the process. Through review of your belief system, you will be in a position to choose which beliefs you want to keep, which need to be changed, and which must be discarded because they no longer serve you.

Bear in mind that the process of coming face to face with your beliefs can be intimidating and scary, like entering a dark tunnel and not knowing where it will lead you. The ego will fight with all its might, making fears and unknowns seem larger and more threatening than they really are in order to dissuade you from changing. Do not give in. Listen to your inner guidance, and keep on going.

If you have reached this moment in your life of being offered the opportunity to become conscious about how you live your life, how you behave, and how you think, grab it with both hands. Do you want to live your whole life on autopilot? Or would you prefer to live consciously? There is a reason why you have reached this fork in your path, and it might well be that you are ready to jump to the next stage on your journey of life. Which way will you choose: the same old way that is familiar and safe, or the new, exciting, and empowering way? Remember also that any change you decide to undertake doesn't have to be huge or even noticeable on the outside. Profound, life-defining change always begins from inside, from the depths of your being, when you allow yourself to be you, when you let your soul be free.

Exercise: Renewing My Beliefs

You have probably come across exercises for identifying, changing, and revamping your beliefs. You may have given one a try, although you probably felt disappointed when the activity didn't have the obvious, life-changing outcome you were expecting. If you have never made a conscious effort to get in touch with your beliefs, that is good news, since you do not have any kind of expectations about what the outcome should be. In any case, with this exercise, I am not trying to reinvent the wheel, but aim to make you connect with your inner fabric, that makes you who you truly are, and to acknowledge that you are the one who makes any difference. This exercise could fade into the background and become part of your will-do list, or it could become a powerful tool of change and growth—the choice is yours. The difference this exercise makes in your life depends on your intention to practice it for as long as it takes, how prepared you are to uncover some unpleasant things as well as some magnificent ones, your perseverance, and your willingness to accept change in whatever shape or form it might present itself, before finally being able to turn from a frog into the prince or princess you really are. As the old saying goes, "What you put in is what you get out."

The exercise has a few steps. You can do them all at once or you can take your time to complete each one at your own pace. The more you immerse yourself in unearthing and examining the beliefs that are ruling your life, the better your chances of becoming fully aware of what is taking place in your life, from inside out. Be honest with yourself and allow any feelings of guilt to be washed away by the hands of your soul. No one has to see your list, and no one will be hurt by your claiming the freedom to choose what to believe in. A belief that might have been useful at one time might not serve you anymore; it is valid to deal with such outdated beliefs as is appropriate.

Step 1. Write Down Your Beliefs, Messages, and Thoughts

Take some time to go over your life, not only your present situation but also the various stages as you were growing up. Think of all the beliefs, messages, and ways of seeing life that you have been gathering from various influential sources up until now. Examine the different areas and aspects of your life, such as your talents, your skills, your health, your finances, your career, your sexuality, your relationships, your family and friends, your personal development, your dreams, your hobbies, your religion and spirituality, your life purpose, and any other area that has significance in your life.

All this input amounts to the rules you live by today; they define how you behave, think, communicate, interact, dream, and cope with everyday situations; your expectations, limitations, abilities, and restrictions. Now you are ready to acknowledge these rules, make them visible, and give them a name. On the left hand side of a sheet of paper, write down all of these rules in the form of a list. If you can, group them by areas of your life. Use multiple sheets, if you need to. Write everything down, both the positive and the negative beliefs.

Step 2. Sort Out Your Beliefs

In this step, you will be separating the good and positive beliefs from the disempowering, useless ones. Basically, you are decluttering your beliefs system.

Before you embark on the big clean-up it would be helpful for you to have a clear idea of who you are or want to be. What are the traits you want? How would you like to behave and live? What do you want to do in life? What is the state of your health or your relationships? Think of the people you usually look up to: What do you admire about them? Remember that what you really admire in others is what you have to develop in yourself. Do not think about what others want you to be, or what you have been told you should be. Unplug yourself from the well-intended advice of family members, friends, co-workers, media, and society. Do not look for outside reference to tell you about yourself. Look for the answers inside. You know all you need to know about yourself and about what you want to become.

On a separate sheet of paper, write a point-form list of key elements of the person that you dream of becoming, the person you can see in your mind and feel in your heart. Now you are ready to begin the sorting process. Go over each of the entries you wrote on step one and do the following:

- If a belief supports your ideal self and empowers you to move forward to achieve your goals, then it is a good belief to hold, a belief worth keeping. Highlight it with green or any other colour of your choice that screams, *yes, go, great,* or *awesome.*
- If a belief doesn't serve you or support you in your endeavours, cross it out and write a comment next to it like, "Send to the recycling bin."
- If you are unsure whether a beliefs is supportive or not, mark it with a coloured asterisk (*).

Step 3. Revamp Your Beliefs

Now your beliefs are sorted into three groups:

- *Supportive Beliefs.* These are the entries highlighted in green or in your favourite colour. In order to acknowledge these beliefs and make them vibrate strongly within you, write them all out again on a separate sheet of paper and hang the list somewhere you can see them often. You can make them into a piece of art and frame it as a sign of the pride and empowerment you feel for holding them. You can also write these supportive beliefs in your journal so you can refer to them any time you need to. Even better, you can scan the list and make that into the screen-saver on your computer. Feel happy for holding such an array of empowering beliefs!

- *Unsupportive Beliefs.* These are the ones that you sent to the recycling bin. You can easily identify these beliefs because they keep you stuck in your ways and don't allow you to change or to try alternatives. They set restrictions on you, and that is the reason they are also called "limiting beliefs." You want to go one way, but these unsupportive beliefs set you in the opposite direction, or they don't allow you to move at all. In fact, they hold you back. When you recognise that you hold a limiting belief, you are claiming your power back because you are in a position to do something about it. You can decide that you will no longer hold that belief, or you can replace it with a more positive one. Either way, you are taking its power away and regaining control of your life.

Read all these beliefs, one by one, and as you do so, make a mental picture of yourself picking each one up and placing it in a rubbish bin. Feel the relief of getting rid of what you do not need, of freeing your system of a cluttered way of thinking. Feel yourself get lighter as you dispose of each unsupportive belief. Once you have gone through all the crossed-out entries and the mental rubbish bin is full, imagine yourself lighting a match and throwing it in the bin. You are symbolically burning those disempowering beliefs to set the intention that you do not want them in your life any longer. You can try a literal version of this exercise by writing the unsupportive beliefs on a piece of paper, which you put in the bin and set on fire. Always keep safety in mind when performing the real deal.

Now that you have detoxed yourself, breathe in deeply and enjoy the feeling of your refreshed energy running freely through your body, mind, and spirit.

- *Undefined Beliefs.* These are the ones that you marked with an asterisk. The way to deal with these beliefs is to inspect them very closely. Recall situations when you used each of these beliefs or rules. In the majority of cases, did it make you feel empowered, supported, strong, in control, happy? Or did it make you feel the opposite? Now you can decide whether to get rid of it or change into something more positive. Say, for example, you hold this belief: "I am of service when needed." Although this is a very noble belief, you recall that in many instances you didn't feel so good acting on it because you were busy or tired or had other plans. You can see now that, in those instances, you were putting other people's demands before your own needs. This contradicts your new view of yourself. However, you also recall some other instances when you felt great helping and assisting others, and for that reason, you do not wish to let go of this belief. Therefore, to turn this undefined belief into a supportive one, you can change it in the following way: "I am of service when needed; I am allowed to say no but still feel good about it." Now you are allowing yourself the option to decline a request for assistance when you don't feel like fulfilling it. Modifying old beliefs will help you to redirect your priorities and look after yourself with a process in line with your new vision of yourself. As you go through the undefined beliefs list, add the new, updated beliefs to your list of supportive beliefs to remind you of the new *you* that is resurfacing.

Step 4. Take Action: Supportive vs. Unsupportive Beliefs

After all the effort and time you have put into reviewing and possibly discovering your belief system, you have now a clearer picture of why your life is the way it is, why you behave and act in certain ways, and why you feel and think the way you do. You know now where you stand

and where you want to go. The only way to move forward is by taking conscious action. It is time to take responsibility for your life; living by default or going through life on automatic pilot are no longer appealing options. The next step is an obvious one, although it is not always the easiest: elect to keep all your supporting beliefs present in your life, and decide to discontinue the ones that steer you away from the path you want to walk. To embrace this kind of change, you need to firmly set the intention to get rid of the negative beliefs that are restricting your life. "I let go easily of the beliefs that hold me back" is a great empowering thought. It will help you get through the process. Say it every day. Place it somewhere you can see it often to be reminded of your intentions. Be firm and determined to accomplish your task, but also be understanding when you slip. Allow yourself time and do not try to change many beliefs all at once; choose only a few to work on at one time. Appreciate that some of those beliefs have been with you for a long while, and are rooted in your mind and habits through your memories and experiences. Therefore, they will not be easy to dig up. Another obstacle you will have to deal with is the reaction of the people in your life who may not want you to change. They might not understand or agree with your new way of thinking.

How to Change

Use empowering thoughts, affirmations, and visualizations to help you shift those negative beliefs into more positive ways of being. Try different approaches to life situations. By being more present, you have the chance to observe what is happening. Notice how you feel and then respond from a more inspired position. For example, if you have always felt the need to be right, choose now not to engage in an argument just to prove your point, as you understand that there are many valid points of view. Another example might be to allow yourself to enjoy the pleasure of something that you like from time to time without being overcome by feelings of guilt for the indulgence. You now understand that you deserve to be pampered and cared for.

A great way to discontinue negative beliefs with ease is to direct your focus towards creating or identifying situations where your positive beliefs are evident. Learn to nurture and appreciate these beliefs because they are the ones that bring happiness, healing, drive, and excitement into your life and help you on the path to accomplishing whatever you decide to achieve. By nurturing your positive beliefs, you shift your focus to what you desire, and become more aware of greatness and blessings in your life. This shift in you brings the light into whatever empowers your life, and sweeps away what you no longer want into the background.

Reviewing and updating our beliefs is a lifelong process. We are always changing, constantly evolving and growing; so is our perception of life and all that we believe. Do not be afraid to changing your views on something that you thought you were completely certain about up until now. Being able to change the way you think and to accept different points of view is a sign of an open mind and a willing heart. The intention of this exercise is not to find fault or blame in yourself or in others, but to bring clarity to your life by making you more aware of which beliefs are ruling you and the world around you.

This exercise highlights the barriers you have erected that are stopping you from being fulfilled, happy, healed, and empowered. With clarity, you can make better choices. This exercise can help you regain the power to make positive changes in your life by taking action to discard or modify unsupportive beliefs while acknowledging and rejoicing in the goodness that is already supporting you and your life. Be blessed.

AFTERWORD

Opening the Doors to Your Soul: The Beginning of a New Journey

Let's celebrate! We've made it to the end of this amazing experience, the co-creation of this book. It has been an incredible endeavour that would never have been possible had I not listened to and trusted the calling of my inner voice, and had we—you and I—not been willing to ask for information, insights, truths, love, and light. As I told you at the beginning, this is a communication from soul to soul, a subconscious dialogue between spirit that has enriched us at many levels and has changed us forever in so many ways. I hope that you enjoyed reading this book. I am sure that you will come back to it over and over again, each time surprised by the discovery of a new idea, a new thought, or a new tool to assist you and enhance the journey of your life.

For now, it is my wish for you to regain zest and enthusiasm for your life ahead and for the power you possess to create it the way you dream it. It is my wish for you to be overflowing with empowering questions and a thirst to seek answers; both will push you forward onto new pathways. It is my wish for you to feel thrilled by your newborn desires, knowing that you have a purpose and a destination that you are determined to discover and follow; and by the beautiful and precious sensation of feeling alive and harmonious within yourself and within the whole. If you haven't yet realised it, something magical has taken place over the reading of these pages: *you have changed!* You are not the same person who started at the beginning—can't you feel that inside? You have opened doors within your subconscious mind that awakened your conscious mind to new levels of knowledge and understanding. It doesn't matter know much or little you have taken in; it is enough for you, at this stage of your journey, to redirect your path in the direction of the light. My last wish is to have provided you with enough material to inspire you to revise your beliefs, to refresh the way you see life, to reawaken long-forgotten dreams, and to create new ones, and to take any opportunity you are presented with to steer your life onto new ground.

It doesn't matter where you are in life, whether you are at the top of the mountain enjoying spectacular views and believing you have it all, at the bottom feeling overwhelmed or discouraged, or somewhere in the middle struggling to reach the top. The message of this book is clear and firm: no matter who you are, what you do, where you are, or what your life situation is; you have the power to turn any challenge into an amazing journey of transformation.

You can open the doors to your soul, and by setting it free, you will shift the understanding of yourself from that of a physical being to that of a spiritual one. This shift in consciousness, this awakening of the self, will see you becoming who you really are, who you were meant to be. Once you reach this place, everything is possible. Celebrate the beginning of this new journey, a journey of growth, happiness, harmony, love, and healing. Let your intentions be your guide. Focus on every single step of your path, allowing the full picture to develop and evolve before you at its own pace and rhythm. Find purpose in the way you feel inside. Walk the paths to your destination using the directions of your inner guidance.

Become friends with the voice within you, learn to trust it, savour the way it feels and sounds, and with time, you will discover that the voice and you have become one. This is when your life will take on a new meaning and dimension and you will live your life for what it truly is, a journey to happiness. Rejoice in your divine nature and do not be afraid to call yourself what you really are: a beautiful and eternal soul evolving through this human experience of life.

The Essence of You

I'd like to conclude the writing of this book with another of my meditations. Each one of them has brought me great knowledge, new perspectives, reassurance, healing, inspiration, peace, and love. I hope that through the meditations, you have not only sensed those experiences too, but have also discovered your own inspirations, answers, and quietness within. The intention of this meditation is to offer you one last way to show who you are and what your essence is. Enjoy.

As usual, I am walking along the beach, when suddenly, I am transported to a strange place full of crimson-red curtains coming down from high above. I go through one set of curtains, and then another one appears. They are made of a heavy, rich material that feels soft to the touch, like velvet. I take this as a game, and I walk amongst the beautiful curtains feeling both curious and happy, as if seeking my way out of a maze.

After a while, I reach a place full of yellow cushions. They are arranged in a circular pattern surrounded by the red curtains. Bouncing, I take myself through to the centre of the circle, and in a childlike manner, I throw myself backwards to rest on the soft cushions. I am feeling exited, happy, and relaxed. Now as I look up from this position, I can see a clear sky greeting me through the curtains, which do not look like curtains any more. I sit up and blink a few times to take in my surroundings. The curtains now resemble huge rose petals, and the cushions, the centre of the rose.

I realise with amazement that I am sitting inside a crimson rose. I am inside a rose! As this realisation takes hold of me, I am engulfed by the incredible fragrance of the rose. The perfume is mesmerising and the sensation inexplicable. I give in to the experience. As I lay down again with my eyes closed, I stretch my arms and legs and surrender to the essence of the rose. I am blending with it; the rose and I are becoming one. I rest there for a while, rejoicing in the experience, breathing in the perfume that is pure happiness to my senses.

I feel good all over, and calm; this peace is healing my whole being. I am inside a rose in a huge rose garden, the garden beside the temple.

I am the size of a bee resting inside a beautiful rose. Now my higher self cuts the rose from the rose bush and lays it on the bench in the garden. When I open my eyes, I am normal-sized again, sitting on the bench with the rose resting on my lap. I pick it up very gently and smell it. It is beautiful. My higher self is sitting by my side, smiling. I thank her for this amazing experience, although I do not need words to show her my appreciation and love.

"I wanted to show you one more time that you are part of the rose essence too. Never forget what you really are. You are part of everything, and everything is part of you. I love you," she said.

The Essence of the Whispers of Wisdom from Your Soul

1. You are a divine, eternal being, a powerful, loving soul living in a perfect physical vessel.
2. The purpose of this physical life is to be happy and to enjoy the abundance that surrounds you. To that end, you exercise your free will; it is always within your own power to choose where you are going and who you are being.
3. Love is not inside or outside or all around—in fact, you are love. Moreover, you are part of everything, and everything is part of you.
4. Accept that you are a physical and nonphysical being—mind, body, and light. Accept your divinity and become whole, and holy.
5. You are as divine and powerful as the essence that created all. You are God in the flesh. Do not feel bad or uneasy about accepting this truth.
6. Become consciously aware of who you are, and hold that awareness in your mind as you flow with life. Find your inner light and start acting upon your power.
7. You each have an equally important place, purpose, and reason to exist.

8. Love holds everything together; by embedding love into everything you think, do, and are, you can live with purpose.

9. Become a "human being" more than a "human doing" by being more in touch with our inner light.

10. The partnership with your soul is the most important of all the relationships in your physical life.

11. Stop resisting life and instead, embrace it from the heart. Sit still, listen to your soul and trust in its guidance, your intuition. Enjoy the ride, wherever it takes you.

12. Acknowledge your inner powers, accept and welcome them as a gift from God to you, and integrate them gratefully into your life.

13. There is nothing that cannot be accomplished, nothing that is impossible when you summon your power within.

14. The recipe to a fulfilling life is simple and gratifying: reconnect with the light within, unmute your soul, and restore its voice.

15. Life is a present for you. Appreciate and acknowledge it by being present in life.

16. The new way of living life simply asks you to experience life from a different perspective, a different point of power, and with a new attitude. This new way of living is really a new way of being.

17. The power of your thinking not only influences your life, but also connects, works, creates, and collaborates with others at a higher level of consciousness, changing life in this world.

18. We are all one: physical and nonphysical, material and ethereal, form and spirit. Embrace the concept of oneness and finally give up the idea that you, that we, are separate from everything else.

19. You are working in synchronisation with other souls; therefore, all your actions have to flow in accord with theirs, like in a dance. Enjoy the knowledge that Spirit is always

walking by your side, reminding you that everyone and everything is an active participant of the creation process through the dance of the soul.

20. Always remember: The ego segregates, the soul integrates. The ego weakens, the soul strengthens. The ego is fearful, the soul is loving. The ego is darkness, the soul is light.

ACKNOWLEDGEMENTS

I would like to thank my husband, Alex, who always supports me in my projects and passions. You are always there when I need an encouraging word, a willing listener, or just a hug. Thank you for your love, understanding, and trust.

I thank my beautiful daughters, Jessica and Isabella, whom I love so much, for gracefully listening to my ideas and believing in me. You give me joy and bring meaning and purpose to my life.

I am grateful to my family, who accept me as I am, even when I seem to be the odd one out. I am blessed with your love, warmth, and support. To my dear friends, thank you for sharing your gifts and uniqueness with me and for being part of my journey. You bring laughter, joy, and colour to my life. I love you all.

Thank you to all the angels in disguise whose support, encouragement, positive vibes, and faith made an amazing difference in turning my dream to write a book into a reality.

Thank you to the staff of Balboa Press for their guidance and support in the publishing of my first book.

I also would like to thank my clients, who trust me to guide them through their own healing and inner growth. Listening to your stories and experiences has made me more appreciative of the many blessings in my life. Thank you for giving me the great opportunity to bring some light into your life.

Most of all, I want to thank God, my higher self, my spirit guides, and my spirit teachers for blessing me with all your wisdom, patience, and unconditional love. Thank you for allowing me to share these messages with the world. Without you, this book would not have been born.

Thank you.
I love you all. Be blessed.

Liliana

ABOUT THE AUTHOR

Liliana C. Vanasco attended the University of Buenos Aires, where she graduated with a bachelor's degree in computer science. For over twenty years, Liliana enjoyed a successful career as a software engineer and information systems analyst for large international corporations in the banking, mining, and information technology industries. Over the last twelve years, Liliana has trained in and been practicing *reiki* healing, meditation, crystal healing, and life coaching, that she complements with her studies of counselling, and transactional analysis. She has also trained in the philosophies of Louise L. Hay and leads *Heal Your Life* workshops and groups.

The shift in her interests and her career began in the late 1990s with the onset of her own personal journey to find balance and remain happy in a demanding and stressful life. Her search for harmony and meaning led her to discover meditation. This practice guided her to focus more deeply on her spiritual growth and discover the purpose of her life. During this time of change, new doors opened for her to explore her creative nature and discover more about herself. She began reading extensively, studying, and attending seminars and workshops within the mind-body-spirit field.

All these studies gave Liliana the tools to design, write, and lead her own workshops and provide individual life coaching. For the last seven years, Liliana has been sharing her knowledge on meditation, the use of positive thinking, the power of the law of attraction, the natural way to heal the self, the connection with the inner self, and the importance of living a life in a purposeful way. However, it was not until Liliana realised she had a greater message to share and a bigger role to play that she finally opened her channels to spirit. This culminated in the writing of her book, *Freedom of the Soul: Whispers of Wisdom from Your Inner Being to Live a Life of Purpose.*

Liliana is an enthusiastic, creative, practical, focused, and inquisitive individual, and she uses these qualities to motivate and inspire everyone she gets in contact with. Liliana's mission is to continue spreading and sharing the spiritual truths and principles contained in her book with the intention of awakening those who listen, especially those who are going through life unconsciously, disconnected from their souls and lacking purpose. Her desire is to reach as many people as possible so she can empower them with her message to live life from the soul's perspective and thereby raise their awareness, inspire them to consciously choose how to live life, and enable them to discover their uniqueness and gifts.

Liliana lives in Perth, Australia, with her husband and two daughters, where she devotes her time to raising her family, writing, coaching, practicing reiki, teaching, and enjoying the magic of life.

APPENDIX

Connecting with Your Infinite Wisdom through Meditation

Meditation is the process I use to cross the bridge from my conscious, physical awareness to my source of infinite wisdom: my inner voice. At the time that I wrote this section, I was reading the book *Think and Grow Rich* by Napoleon Hill. I was pleased to discover that in Chapter 11 of his book, Hill discusses this process of reaching a state of total silence that enables you to perceive your inner voice. He calls it "creative imagination:" "The faculty of creative imagination is the direct link between the finite mind of man and Infinite Intelligence," Hill explains. In brief, the procedure he presents is to first stimulate your mind so that it vibrates on a high level, and then hold in your mind whatever it is that you seek answers to. Then relax and clear your mind of all thought and wait until your subconscious mind takes over and delivers guidance. He provides a list of men of outstanding achievement who have supposedly applied this method, including William Shakespeare, Ralph W. Emerson, and Thomas Edison.

I used creative imagination to write this book. I stimulated my mind through self-guided meditation to raise the level of my vibrations so I could perceive with clarity the messages delivered by my inner voice and my other spirit guides. As you may know, although there is only one source of energy and wisdom, that source has infinite aspects, some of which come to us as the various tones or voices that we perceive when we meditate. During my meditations, I mainly connected to my inner voice, or higher self, the larger, nonphysical extension of me, but I was also fortunate enough to connect to other beings of the light, who provided me with guidance and wisdom, and showed me kindness, patience, and their infinite love for us. I have been exposed to amazing experiences during these meditative states, and I have shared many of them with you in this book.

I hope you enjoy the journey you are about to take by following this meditation. Use it to discover the path to your own sanctuary, your own "infinite intelligence." Use it to connect to your inner voice or voices. Be open to their wisdom. You will know they are the ones talking to you because their messages are always kind, warm, loving, encouraging, and enlightening. They will never make you feel bad, never discourage you, never put you down. They want you to thrive, to live your life with purpose, and to be happy. They want you to find the way to becoming who you really are, to awaken to truth, and to journey to the light.

Before You Begin

Your Spiritual Guides

This meditation will take you through the process of meeting your higher self and other spiritual guides. The key to success is not to set any expectations about the characteristics of your guide, such as how it will look ("it" meaning he, she, it, or they) and whether it will be a person or an animal, female or male, young or old, etc. Your guide will present itself to you in a way that is easy for you to connect with it. My own higher self and spirit guides appear to me in medieval costume, like wizards and princesses. I guess that this is due to my interest in stories about those times and my love of magic, sorcery, and mystery. When I see them, I easily connect with their power and wisdom through the way they look and talk. You might not even see your guide at all, but only hear it and have conversations with it. Or, instead of just one guide, you might have a group of guides of collective energy. As you can see, there are no right or wrong ways to communicate with your spiritual guides. We all have unique ways of connecting with our inner wisdom. Trust that regardless of how that connection happens, it is the best way to have a rewarding and fulfilling experience.

The Meditation Process

Do not worry if you cannot see or hear anything at the beginning of the meditation. Trust your feeling that you have made a connection, and go to each meditation with the knowledge that your guide will be there waiting for you. Remember that worry, expectation, and impatience act as barriers to your intention to raise your vibrations and make connection.

The process is simple and requires very little of you. Sit in a comfortable position and bring yourself into a relaxed state of mind, similar to your state of mind when you are drifting off to sleep. Set your intention to be at peace and in a state of total allowance, with expectations about your willingness to be there in silence, but not about what must happen and how. There is no right or wrong way of doing it. Whatever unfolds while you are in this state of communion between you and *you* (the nonphysical side of you) will be amazing and beautiful, no matter what form it takes. You might meet your guides or receive insights. Your requests for healing might be answered, or you could just get a breather from the challenges of everyday life—but these are not the most important outcomes. It is most important for you to become quiet, calm, and at peace. These are all states of being that contribute to your well-being.

Once you meet your guide, you will probably spend your first meditations trying to feel comfortable connecting with it and getting to know about it. Once this stage is over and you have asked as many questions as you desire, go to meditation with a specific issue or query in mind, and set the intention to receive answers. Once you get used to the process, you will find yourself looking forward to meeting with your guide, not only for the insights you receive, but also for the wonderful feeling the experience gives you. You will also be blessed by other guides and spiritual beings visiting you from time to time, to aid you with their wisdom on specific matters.

The Place Where You Meditate

The place where you perform your meditation is important; try to make it a special place. It has to be quiet, without disturbing noises. You can add your own touches to turn it into a sanctuary, a beautiful place just for you and your spirit guides. For example, you could use soft cushions to support you if you meditate sitting or lying down on the floor, or you could cover your comfortable meditation chair with silky, colourful fabrics. Burn some candles or incense to enhance your sensations. Put some fresh flowers in a small vase to connect with nature. Decorate with crystals or any other elements and trinkets that are meaningful to you. Play soft music to create a relaxing atmosphere. Make use of anything that can help you create a peaceful place that induces in you an instant feeling of well-being.

The place where you meditate can be a corner in a quiet room of your home, or it could be outdoors, underneath a tree, or on a bench in a garden or park. As you can see, the actual location is irrelevant. What is important is your state of mind when you go to meditate. Not much is required besides your sincere intention to be with *you*.

The Place Where You Meet Your Guides: The Sanctuary

The place where I meet my guides in meditation is a very old temple. This Temple is my sanctuary, a place where I feel safe, loved, happy, and calm. It is stunningly beautiful too. To reach this amazing place, I go through delightful scenery: a peaceful white beach, an exuberant forest crossed by a narrow river, and an open field of wildflowers. I greatly enjoy visiting these places, discovering new features, new smells, and new signs, but most of all, meeting my guides in the temple.

Spend some time imagining what your sanctuary looks like, feels like, and smells like. It doesn't have to be a temple; it can be any kind of place as long as it is one that is right for you. Your sanctuary could be a bench in a beautiful garden, a temple, a church, a cave, or any other place that feels familiar to you. Where is your sanctuary located? What surrounds it? Is it in the mountains or in an open field? Is it on a beach or underwater? Is it in the sky, out in space, or even on another planet? Let your imagination play; let it show you your sanctuary. You'll know you have found it when you can identify yourself with it, and you feel safe, happy, and peaceful each time you visit it.

As you continue to make trips to your sanctuary, the experience will become more real; details that you didn't notice on earlier visits will show up here and there. I can assure you that all of these details, even the smallest ones, have a meaning and purpose for your journey. Just as in our dreams, our unconscious minds talk to us through symbols, in our meditations, our inner wisdom talks to us through signs. The signs are present not only to bring clarity to the answers that you are seeking, but also to fill you with wonder and awe.

In the following meditation, I use a temple as the place where you meet your guides. However, you can adapt the meditation to include your own sanctuary.

Meditation to Connect to Your Higher Self and Other Beings of Light

Close your eyes and sit down comfortably and calmly in your special place. Take a few deep breaths.

As you breathe in and breathe out, feel any tension dissipate as you become more and more relaxed. Your whole body feels relaxed. Your head, shoulders, arms, and hands, your legs, thighs, and feet feel heavy and relaxed. If any thoughts come into your mind, just let them go. Acknowledge them, but don't follow them. Let them go.

Imagine a bright golden light from above your head. If you look closely, you can make out sparkles of purple light embedded in the beautiful golden light. This warm gold and purple light shines down over your head and slowly makes its way down your arms and body, your legs and feet, and then into the ground. The continuous stream of light embraces you all over with a wonderful, warm feeling. You feel happy. You feel relaxed and at peace. You feel loved. Engulfed in these feelings, you are becoming the light yourself.

The light has formed a gold and purple cocoon around you. In this place, your mind is free to be silent so you can perceive the messages of your inner wisdom. In this cocoon, you can imagine anything, see and hear anything. In this cocoon, you are safe.

Now imagine yourself walking along a beach. The day is clear and bright. The water is calm and your feet enjoy its warmth as you walk carelessly along the edge of the water on this tranquil beach. You are dressed in light clothes and your hair is free and flowing in the light breeze coming off the ocean. You can see dolphins playing joyfully, and maybe saying hello.

Ahead in the distance, you see the shore turning into the ocean. The scenery is full of hills covered in shades of green, yellow, and brown. They seem to extend forever. What else can you see? What is this place showing you? What does it want you to discover? Now you look to your left and see an enticing, beautiful forest. You can continue walking along the beach, or choose to explore the forest. Either direction will take you to the place where you will meet your guide.

So, imagine yourself walking in the forest. Tall, majestic trees rise into the sky. Ferns, shrubs, and vegetation of untold beauty fill every space of this magnificent forest. Use all your senses to enjoy the experience. Feel the ground under your feet, smell the scents in the air, hear the sounds of the forest. What can you see? What can you touch? Multicoloured butterflies fly freely from flower to flower. As you look up at the sky, you can see the sunlight fighting its way down through the entangled foliage, creating amazing shades of earthy colours. You have never been in a place like this before—but you are here now, feeling, touching, hearing, seeing, and being one with the forest.

You hear water running in the distance and walk towards the sound. As you get closer, you see a narrow river running through the forest and a wooden bridge over the river. You cross the bridge—you might stay a few minutes on the bridge to take in anything this place might be offering you—and then continue walking to the other side of the river. As you do, breathe in the moisture that permeates the air. Enjoy the feeling of being cleansed and refreshed.

You continue walking in the forest, admiring your surroundings and immersing yourself completely in the experience. Feel yourself going deeper and deeper into silence.

Now you come along to an open field covered in purple wildflowers. You continue walking in this field covered with small purple flowers. In the distance to your right is the beach where you were walking before. Take in the beauty of this magnificent place. What else you can see? Turn around in the field of flowers. Behind you, the forest is becoming smaller and smaller as you walk away; to your right, the beach remains peaceful and glowing; to your left is an unending purple carpet of flowers; in front of you, in the distance, you see a temple.

You walk towards this temple, and as you get closer, you notice its details. Now you are standing in front of the temple; walk slowly up to its huge entrance and let yourself in. What can you see? Take time to observe where you are; absorb its energy, enjoy it. Are there windows letting in natural light, or is the space illuminated by candlelight? Do you notice any doors or stairways leading to other rooms? Are there pictures hanging on the walls? Are there statues? What else is there?

Now you notice your spirit guide is standing at the front of the room waiting for you. Look at your guide. What does it look like? How old is it? Is there more than one? If you cannot see it, what do the presence and energy of your guide feel like? There are two comfortable armchairs; your guide invites you to sit, and it sits down in the other chair. Greet your guide and ask for its name, if you need one. You may not feel the need to address your guide by name. If you have any questions, ask them now. Relax and be assured that you can ask about anything. Be open and allow the experience to flow. Listen for answers; they could come as words, images, sounds, symbols, or feelings. Let your imagination interpret what you are receiving. Pay attention, but at the same time, feel tranquil and enjoy the experience.

Stay in this receptive mode for as long as you desire and feel comfortable. If you are experienced, you will easily be able to establish a conversation with your guide. If you are meeting your guide for the first time, take your time to get to know it before starting to ask for guidance. At this point, if you wish, you can start writing down the messages you are receiving in your journal. Once you've finished, give thanks to your guide for having come to meet you. Express your gratitude until the next time you meet with a smile, a hug, or whatever way feels best for you.

Slowly start feeling your body again. Feel your feet touching the ground. Feel a beautiful earthly energy pulling your feet downwards, bringing you back into your present. Become aware of your surroundings and how you feel. Once you are ready, open your eyes.

———————————————

Give yourself a few minutes to absorb the experience. Think about what happened and what you have learnt about your guide. It is good practice to write down some notes about the messages you receive. You can do it either during the meditation, which is called "automatic writing," or immediately after it, when the ideas are still fresh in your mind. It is amazing how much more you discover about your insights when you reread them later. Get your journal and take a few minutes to write anything that you feel like writing: notes, comments, sensations, even drawings. Why not try to draw a picture of your guide?

I made a picture of my personal spirit guide when I first met him—at least, I tried. Many, many years later, out of the blue, I found a poster with an image of a wizard who looks exactly like him. As you can imagine, I bought it and framed it, and since then, it has been hanging in my meditation place. His image is a magnificent reminder that he is in my life, guiding me along the way.

Meeting your guide is a very rewarding experience. Rest assured, they are always with you, and they enjoy direct encounters as much as you do. You can meet different guides in this way; each one will provide specific advice about your endeavours, answering questions and guiding you on the many stages of your life. These guides come to share with you and assist you with anything you need. They would like you to understand that you are never alone; you needn't ever feel that you are. If you have the intention to walk with your guides, to ask for and be open to their help, then an answer will always be at your heart's reach. Be blessed.

REFERENCES

Hill, Napoleon. *Think and Grow Rich*. Cronulla, NSW: Stuart Zadel, 2005.

Kingston, Karen. *Clear Your Clutter with Feng Shui*. London: Judy Piatkus, 1998.